SOUTH HOLLAND PUBLIC LIBRARY

DISC   DD

3 1350 00384 3

DI034013

SOUTH HOLLAND PUBLIC LIBRARY
708/527-3150
M-TH. 10-9, FRI. 10-6, SAT. 10-5
www.shlibrary.org

DISCARD

CHRISTMAS FOOD AND FEASTING

The Meals Series

Series Editor

Ken Albala, University of the Pacific, kalbala@pacific.edu

The Meals Series examines our daily meals—breakfast, lunch, dinner, tea—as well as special meals such as the picnic and barbeque, both as historical construct and global phenomena. We take these meals for granted, but the series volumes provide surprising information that will change the way you think about eating. A single meal in each volume is anatomized, its social and cultural meaning brought into sharp focus, and the customs and manners of various peoples are explained in context. Each volume also looks closely at the foods we commonly include and why.

Books in the Series

Picnic: A History, by Walter Levy
Breakfast: A History, by Heather Arndt Anderson
Barbecue: A History, by Tim Miller
Afternoon Tea: A History, by Julia Skinner
Christmas Food and Feasting: A History, by Madeline Shanahan

CHRISTMAS FOOD AND FEASTING

A HISTORY

Madeline Shanahan

ROWMAN & LITTLEFIELD
Lanham • Boulder • New York • London

Published by Rowman & Littlefield
An imprint of The Rowman & Littlefield Publishing Group, Inc.
4501 Forbes Boulevard, Suite 200, Lanham, Maryland 20706
www.rowman.com

6 Tinworth Street, London SE11 5AL, United Kingdom

Copyright © 2019 by The Rowman & Littlefield Publishing Group, Inc.

All rights reserved. No part of this book may be reproduced in any form or by any
electronic or mechanical means, including information storage and retrieval systems,
without written permission from the publisher, except by a reviewer who may quote
passages in a review.

British Library Cataloguing in Publication Information Available

Library of Congress Cataloging-in-Publication Data

Names: Shanahan, Madeline, author.
Title: Christmas food and feasting : a history / Madeline Shanahan.
Description: Lanham : Rowman & Littlefield, [2019] | Series: The meals series
  | Includes bibliographical references and index.
Identifiers: LCCN 2018042843 (print) | LCCN 2018043466 (ebook) | ISBN
  9781442276987 (electronic) | ISBN 9781442276970 (cloth : alk. paper)
Subjects: LCSH: Christmas cooking. | Comfort food. | LCGFT: Cookbooks.
Classification: LCC TX739.2.C45 (ebook) | LCC TX739.2.C45 S52 2019 (print) |
  DDC 641.5/686—dc23
LC record available at https://lccn.loc.gov/2018042843

∞™ The paper used in this publication meets the minimum requirements
of American National Standard for Information Sciences—Permanence of
Paper for Printed Library Materials, ANSI/NISO Z39.48-1992.

Printed in the United States of America

3 1350 00384 3929

For Mum
Thank you for always "keeping Christmas."

CONTENTS

LIST OF ILLUSTRATIONS   ix

SERIES FOREWORD, BY KEN ALBALA   xi

INTRODUCTION   1

CHAPTER 1: A SHORT HISTORY OF CHRISTMAS   9

CHAPTER 2: MEATS AND MAINS   35

CHAPTER 3: PUDDINGS AND DESSERTS   67

CHAPTER 4: FESTIVE CAKES   95

CHAPTER 5: SWEET TREATS   119

CHAPTER 6: DRINK   143

CONCLUSION   169

NOTES   177

BIBLIOGRAPHY   205

INDEX   219

ABOUT THE AUTHOR   229

ILLUSTRATIONS

"Scrooge's Third Visitor" 28

"The Compliments of the Season" 43

"Bringing in the Boar's Head" 55

"Christmas at Windsor Castle: Roasting the Baron of Beef for the
Christmas Banquet" 58

"Her Majesty the Queen's Sideboard at Christmas Time" 59

Christmas Day with the RAF in Tripolitania, Libya, 28 December
1942: Cooks serving Christmas pudding and mince pies for the
airmen 74

"Stirring the 'Xmas Pudding" 76

James Gillray. "The plumb-pudding in danger; or, State epicures
taking un petit souper" 79

"Newsletter of Australasia. A Narrative to Send to Friends. Christmas in Australia. A Happy New Year to Friends Far, Far Away" 86

"The Queen's Twelfth Cake" 104

"Park's New Twelfth Night Characters" 108

"Dishes of minced pies for all manner of Flesh or Fowl, according
to these Forms" 123

"Forms of minced Pyes" 124

Reproduced nineteenth-century cookie 130

"The Wassail Bowl at Christmas" 150

"Scrooge and Bob Cratchit" 155

SERIES FOREWORD

Custom becomes second nature, and this is especially true of meals. We expect to eat them at a certain time and place, and we have a set of scripted foods considered appropriate for each. Bacon, eggs, and toast are breakfast; sandwiches are lunch; meat, potatoes, and vegetables are dinner, followed by dessert. Breakfast for dinner is so much fun precisely because it is out of the ordinary and transgressive. But meal patterns were not always this way. In the Middle Ages people ate two meals, the larger in the morning. Today the idea of a heavy meal with meat and wine at 11:00 a.m. strikes us as strange and decidedly unpleasant. Likewise when abroad, the food that people eat, at what seems to us the wrong time of day, can be shocking. Again, our customs have become so ingrained that we assume they are natural, correct, and biologically sound.

The Meals series will demonstrate exactly the opposite. Not only have meal times changed but the menu has as well, both through history and around the globe. Only a simple bowl of soup with a crust of bread for supper? That's where the name comes from. Our dinner, coming from *disner* in Old French, *disjejeunare* in Latin, actually means to break fast and was eaten in the morning. Each meal also has its own unique characteristics that evolve over time. We will see the invention of the picnic and barbecue, the gradual adoption of lunch as a new midday meal, and even certain meals practiced as hallowed institutions in some places but scarcely at all elsewhere, such as tea—the meal, not the drink. Often food items suddenly appear in a meal as quintessential, such as cold breakfast cereal, the invention of men like

Kellogg and Post. Or they disappear, like oysters for breakfast. Sometimes an entire meal springs from nowhere under unique social conditions, like brunch.

Of course, the decay of the family meal is a topic that deeply concerns us, as people catch a quick bite at their desk or on the go, or eat with their eyes glued to the television set. If eating is one of the greatest pleasures in life, one has to wonder what it says about us when we wolf down a meal in a few minutes flat or when no one talks at the dinner table. Still, mealtime traditions persist for special occasions. They are the time we remind ourselves of who we are and where we come from, when grandma's special lasagna comes to the table for a Sunday dinner, or a Passover Seder is set exactly the same way it has been for thousands of years. We treasure these food rituals precisely because they keep us rooted in a rapidly changing world.

The Meals series examines the meal as both a historical construct and a global phenomenon. Each volume anatomizes a single meal, bringing its social and cultural meaning into sharp focus and explaining the customs and manners of various people in context. Each volume also looks closely at the foods we commonly include and why. In the end I hope you will never take your mealtime customs for granted again.

Ken Albala
University of the Pacific

INTRODUCTION

There is a moment that comes to so many of us in the late afternoon on Christmas Day, when we look at the postmeal dining table festooned with scrunched paper crowns, splattered with cranberry sauce and gravy, and graced with a half-eaten hacked-up plum pudding, and we are torn between cracking on with the inevitable tidy-up and retreating to the sofa for a double Baileys and a snooze. In this moment we vow that we "will never eat again," and our resolve lasts for an hour or so, until a box of Cadbury Roses chocolates is passed around and we somehow find room. If excitement and anticipation are the feelings almost universally shared by children at 5:00 a.m. on Christmas morning, being stuffed and exhausted are the ones that unite their parents come 5:00 p.m.

This postmeal fatigue is brought about by the enormous quantity of food consumed, but also by the sheer amount of work involved in preparing the festive feast. A recent estimate suggested that, on average, twenty-seven hours go into making Christmas dinner,[1] most of which is still done by women. And this is on top of the additional workload of the season: shopping, wrapping, writing cards, making costumes for Nativity plays, putting up lights, decorating trees, assembling toys, and posing as a benevolent supernatural being. The workload (not to mention expense) involved in the lead-up to 25 December, and the pressure to enjoy the day, have made more than one domestic cook crack in the early afternoon when the turkey is still not done. And yet, year after year, we still faithfully "keep Christmas." While some opt to avoid the work altogether and dine out, most families still gather for a home-cooked meal annually. Journalist Hattie Garlick asks the question:

> Is it still Christmas if you eat the festive meal in a restaurant? Does it still count if you haven't risen at 5am to discover your turkey doesn't fit in the oven? Is something sacrosanct lost if you haven't muttered your intentions to murder Aunty Mira for her crime of catatonically slow potato peeling?[2]

For many of us, the answer appears to be very clear: Eating out and convenience foods simply will not do; Christmas is not just about eating but also about preparing the food. Cooking a set of dishes gifted to us by our ancestors over time and using recipes often handed through families is an integral part of the feast. This idea may seem romantic and nostalgic, but then so is Christmas.

If we look to the history of Christmas food and feasting, we see that this compulsion to overdo things, to revel in both nostalgia and excess, and to end the day full, drunk, and merry is nothing new. Today we may have taken the sheer abundance of food to levels that our ancestors could not possibly have imagined, but the need to drink and feast together at this time of year is truly ancient, predating Christianity itself. In the twenty-first-century Western world, there are precious few great communal festivals steeped in such rich meaning and tradition. Our calendar has been pared back, and for many people Christmas is the one time set aside in their year for magic, fun, feasting, and family.

Before embarking on our exploration of festive food, it is necessary to provide some definitions and limitations for this book. First, although it may seem obvious to many readers, it is important to clarify both what Christmas is and which aspects of this complex, textured festival this work will tackle. Throughout the Christian world, Christmas marks the Feast of the Nativity. The biblical story tells of how the Virgin Mary gave birth to Jesus, the Son of God and Savior of mankind, in a stable in Bethlehem. Angels announced his birth, and, upon seeing a bright star in the sky, shepherds came to adore him. Twelve days later, on the Feast of the Epiphany (6 January), three Wise Men from the East came to give gifts of gold, frankincense, and myrrh to the infant king in his manger. As the following chapter will explain, the Bible contains only limited evidence indicating the actual date of Christ's birth. Different options had been proposed by early theologians, but, in the fourth century AD, 25 December was chosen to mark the Feast of the Nativity, and it remains one of the most significant days in the liturgical calendar, holding profound spiritual significance for Christians globally. As chapter 1 will also discuss in detail, though, the feast drew strength from, incorporated, and adapted elements of the pagan winter festivals of Europe, so it inherited a wealth of tradition. Many of these customs continue in some form today, such as bringing greenery into the house, gift giving, and (as this book will explore) certain food and feasting rituals. Today, these rituals—and the many others that have been stitched in or reworked over the millennia—are deeply culturally embedded, and so they may relate to, but also sit outside of, the religious holiday itself. In short, Christmas is a complex, multifaceted festival, steeped in millennia of cultural traditions and inheritances. The sacred and the profane sides of Christmas have come into tension with each other over the centuries, but both have shaped the festival and its food as we know it today.

The other definition, or limitation, that requires some explanation is the cultural focus adopted here. This is not a book about Christmas food globally. Rather, it is the story of how the British Christmas (or perhaps, more precisely, the English Christmas) meal evolved, both on its native shores and beyond. This book takes a detailed look at the origins, form, and structure of the codified modern British Christmas dinner, as well as its most iconic festive foods and drinks. However, it is also the story of what happened to that meal as it was disseminated throughout the Empire, becoming entrenched in places most strongly associated with the British diaspora, now broadly termed either the "English-speaking world" or, more precisely (if politically loaded), the "Anglosphere." In these places, spread across the globe, keeping not just Christmas but a very precise model of Christmas became a key marker of cultural identity. This version of Christmas did not remain static, though; it changed and adapted to different climes, blending with the Christmas celebrations of other cultural groups to create new traditions and aesthetics. Looking beyond Britain, to places strongly associated with its diaspora (such as the United States of America, Canada, Australia, and New Zealand), helps us to understand the cultural significance and meaning of this feast with more complexity: Which parts of the meal were mandatory and kept against all odds? Which were disposable? Which elements changed and adapted to context? Christmas in America is of particular interest. There we see the way in which the British celebration fused with the traditions of different European groups to create a unique festival, complete with its own culinary inheritances from multiple sources. While a British framework for Christmas may have been introduced to the United States, a reflexive relationship of exchange ultimately developed in the modern period, so that, today, the British Christmas has in turn been culturally, aesthetically, and (most important for the purposes of this book) gastronomically influenced by American traditions. This relationship between two of the great powerhouses of Christmas cultural production—responsible for plum pudding, mince pies, and crackers on one side of the Atlantic, and eggnog, candy canes, and Santa on the other—is fascinating to explore.

Focusing on the British Christmas and its descendants is an acknowledged limitation of this book, but it is one that is in place for good reasons. First, Christmas was extraordinarily important to the British, and to the English in particular. The festival as they conceptualized and experienced it needs close attention, both because it was culturally unique, as we shall see, but also because it came to have such a huge impact on how Christmas is celebrated in so many parts of the world today. Christmas appears to have been a central way of keeping the Empire community connected, and food played a critical role in that. Australian historian Ken Inglis notes that "wherever they went in the world, the English took their Christmas with them."[3] Mark Connelly, whose *Christmas: A History* (2012) has examined the role that Christmas played throughout the Empire, also argues that "Christmas and Englishness were felt to be indistinguishable and the values of one were those of the other."[4] And, as we will discover in this book, festive food played a central role in this process, with dishes such as plum pudding becoming indispensable markers of cultural identity.

Another reason for the cultural focus of this book is that there is something remarkable about the British Christmas meal. Historian Clement A. Miles, who wrote one of the first scholarly works addressing the history of Christmas, *Christmas Customs and Traditions: Their History and Significance* (1912), argued that "in the mind of the average sensual Englishman perhaps the most vivid images called up by the word Christmas are those connected with eating and drinking."[5] All countries and cultures place food at the center of the festival, and most have particular Christmas culinary traditions and specialties. What is remarkable about the British Christmas dinner, though, is how extraordinarily codified it is, with its set menu of turkey, ham, and plum pudding. This dinner is prepared annually in kitchens around the United Kingdom, with the same trimmings and mealtime rituals appearing on tables throughout the land. The fact that this same meal (give or take a few tweaks) has been successfully transplanted to many places around the world, from Ireland to the furthest reaches of the Empire, is even more remarkable. It tells us that this is a meal that means something, and that it has a story which needs to be looked at in depth.

The need for depth, and a close investigation of the origins of culinary traditions and individual dishes, is the final reason for this limited cultural focus. As this book will show, not only is there a vast range of dishes associated with Christmas in the Anglosphere, but each of these has a truly fascinating story to tell. Many of these stories stretch back to the medieval world, if not earlier, with some clearly having pre-Christian origins. The aim of this book is to trace the origins of each dish in detail, and then to place it in its broader cultural and historical context. In order to pursue this level of detail and close analysis, a cultural focus needed to be adopted. If this book demonstrates anything, ideally it is that the Christmas menu of just this one cultural block is vast and its stories endless, so there would be enormous value in pursuing such an approach in looking at the festive food traditions of other nations, cultures, and peoples in the future.

In order to understand the development of Christmas food over the centuries, we need to start with the evolution of the festival itself. Chapter 1 will outline the history of Christmas, from its connections to its pagan predecessors (the midwinter festivals of Europe) to the present. This chapter will identify the key developments in Christmas over time and consider the changing meaning of the festival in each period. This history will identify the elements that have remained relatively constant over time, those that likely preserve remnants of deeply embedded folk culture, but it will also explore how Christmas has been used as a forum or cipher for social, cultural, religious, and political debate. And so the initial chapter will aim to provide not just the much-needed context in which to situate the story of food in the following chapters but also an explanation for how and why Christmas has come to hold such cultural relevance.

Moving on to the food-focused discussion, chapter 2 will consider the dishes that make up the main course of Christmas dinner. It will explain the historical significance of the meat-heavy feast and trace the origins and meaning of eating large roast poultry and ham at this time of year. This chapter will also consider the role that other meats played in the past, which are no longer designated as Christmas foods, such as beef. Fish and seafood, which have not retained their festive status in Britain but are central to expressions of cultural and national identity in certain New World contexts, will also be discussed.

Chapter 3 will be devoted to the history of the Christmas dessert course and the sweet dishes that follow the meat-heavy main meal. This chapter will tackle the story of the plum pudding, or Christmas pudding—that most iconic and indispensable of British festive dishes. It will also explore the history of recipes such as the sherry trifle and Antipodean pavlova. These may play second fiddle to Christmas pudding, but they each have their own story to tell (and a cherished place in the traditions of many families).

Chapter 4 will explore the history of festive cakes. The story of the fascinating Twelfth cake, once one of the most celebrated parts of the festival, and its successor, the more sedate Christmas cake, will be explored at length. The story of these cakes and their changing of the guard is not just a culinary tale but also one that bears witness to the changing role of Twelfth Night in the modern period. This discussion will be followed by an outline of some of the most popular Continental European cakes that have penetrated Christmas tables in the English-speaking world in recent decades, showing the festival's ability to adapt and change.

Adding to the surfeit of sweetness, chapter 5 will look in detail at the sugary treats and totally unnecessary extras available over Christmas, which make it a truly indulgent extended holiday. From medieval mince pies and Victorian chocolate boxes to much-loved iced American cookies and striped candy canes, this chapter will delve into the role of sugar in the festival as both foodstuff and decoration.

Chapter 6 will then discuss the history of alcohol consumption over Christmas and the central role that drinking has played from the pre-Christian past to the present. It will explore the history of wassailing at length, as well as some of Christmas's most iconic drinks, such as lambswool, mulled wine, punch, eggnog, and regional specialties such as sloe gin and atholl brose. Rituals associated with alcohol consumption at Christmas are some of the most ancient parts of the festival, which tell us about the need to celebrate together and wish for a prosperous New Year.

This exploration of Christmas fare will ultimately demonstrate just how central food and drink have been to the festival over the millennia, and it will consider the meaning and significance of our most cherished recipes, menus, and culinary traditions. These highly nostalgic dishes and rituals may be the inheritances of Christmas past, but their future is secured by the feast's ability to change and adapt, absorbing new influences and reflecting new meanings gastronomically.

1

A SHORT HISTORY
OF CHRISTMAS

Heaped up upon the floor, to form a kind of throne, were turkeys, geese, game, poultry, brawn, great joints of meat, suckling pigs, long wreaths of sausages, mince-pies, plum-puddings, barrels of oysters, red-hot chestnuts, cherry-cheeked apples, juicy oranges, luscious pears, immense twelfth-cakes, and seething bowls of punch, that made the chamber dim with their delicious steam.

—Charles Dickens, *A Christmas Carol* (1843)

Before we begin on the story of Christmas food and feasting, we need to start with the story of Christmas itself. In this case, not the biblical story so much, but rather the story of how the feast has evolved and been observed over time; from its pre-Christian roots, to its undeniably commercialized present. This context is critical to understanding the development of festive fare. As Christmas, and our relationship with it, has changed, so, too, have the rituals and the food used to celebrate it. The structure of the feast, the experience of the meal, and the dishes themselves, have all evolved in response to the changing festival, which has shown itself to be extraordinarily resilient and adaptable over the millennia.

PAGAN WINTER FESTIVALS AND THE EARLY CHURCH

Long before there was any notion of Christmas, Europeans marked winter with a series of festivals. This was a time of great abundance of food and drink, when the work had been finished and the short, cold days meant that there was little to do but enjoy the seasonal fare on offer. Food was plentiful, as the late autumn harvest and the seasonal slaughtering of beasts had been completed, and hunting season was at its peak. The new stock of alcohol was ready to be enjoyed after its period of postharvest fermentation. These festivals highlighted the abundance of nature, but critically, they also marked the fading of the sun and included a series of rituals to ensure that its light would return and that the New Year would be fertile and prosperous. Within these European festivals lay the cultural foundation stones of the later Christian festival, and even today many of our Christmas traditions have a direct connection to these ancient rites. No singular one of these festivals, which stretched from November through to January, is the direct ancestor of Christmas. Rather, the significance of each of them paved the way and created a cultural framework for the later adoption of the Christian festival in their region. Importantly, though, each left their mark on the rituals and traditions of Christmas as we know it today.

The Roman Saturnalia is the pre-Christian festival that survives most in contemporary popular imagination as the precursor to Christmas. Held to honor the agricultural deity Saturn, it was originally marked on 17 December in the Julian calendar, but by the late republic had been extended to 23 December; running for almost a week.[1] The revelries of Saturnalia were closely followed by *Dies Natalis Solis Invicti*, or "The Birthday of the Unconquerable Sun," on 25 December, honoring the sun god, Sol Invictus. This was followed by the Kalends of January, which marked the New Year. So, in short, the Romans more or less feasted from the start of Saturnalia on 17 December to 1 January, and multiple rituals took place over this period, intended to ensure that the sun would return and the New Year would be fertile and prosperous.[2]

The mythology surrounding Saturn shaped the nature of the festival in his honor hugely, and the modern Christmas retains elements of this. Saturn was believed to have been an ancient king who once ruled over the world during a golden age in which people enjoyed the beauties of nature and its bounty in a state of innocence.[3] Thus, the festival was a time of generosity, peace, and goodwill, when classes mingled in a shared state of communal nostalgia for more innocent times.[4] Saturnalia involved a sacrifice at the Temple of Saturn in the Roman Forum, a public feast, and gift giving. This was followed by a riotous party in which drinking and gambling were encouraged and the social order was upended, as slaves were served by masters.[5] A "king," or *Saturnalicius princeps*, was elected for the night to rule over the festivities.[6] Kalends was also marked by drinking, feasting, and gift giving. Over this New Year, festival houses were decorated with evergreens—symbols of fertility and regeneration.[7] Although aspects of Kalends and Saturnalia would feel completely foreign, other elements, such as the public feasting and the exchange of gifts, are central parts of Christmas as we know it today. The topsy-turvy nature of Saturnalian revels, in which the social order was inverted and a king reigned over the chaos, also shows a clear continuity with the medieval Twelfth Night's Lord of Misrule, which will be discussed in more detail below. There is also something of the essence of Saturnalia that continues in Christmas to this day. This harkening back to a golden age in a ritualized form of nostalgia is undoubtedly a part of our Christmas. The emphasis on generosity, social leveling, and peace between all mankind is a theme that remains central to our modern festival.

Saturnalia, described by Catullus as "the best of days,"[8] remained popular until the fourth century AD. It never disappeared entirely, though; as the Roman Empire was Christianized, this earlier festival appears to have been incorporated into Christmas celebrations.[9] After considerable debate among early church scholars, in the fourth century, 25 December was selected as the date on which the Feast of the Nativity would be observed. Despite the actual date of Christ's birth being fiercely disputed,[10] this day may have been chosen because it allowed the church to draw on the cultural embeddedness of both Saturnalia and the Sol Invictus festival.[11] Symbolically, the selection of this date saw the birthday of the Savior, the "son" and light for all mankind, replace the birthday of the pagan sun[12]—although such contentions are, unsurprisingly, the subject of great debate among biblical scholars, early church historians, and theologians.[13] In any case, the observation of the feast on this day soon spread to the Eastern church as well. By 380, Christians in Constantinople also celebrated the Nativity on this day, whereas previously they had marked it on 6 January.[14] In his book *The Battle for Christmas*, Stephen Nissenbaum argues that the selection of this date, despite the limited evidence in its favor, was the moment at which the tension between the biblical and cultural, the sacred and the profane, elements of Christmas began. In Nissenbaum's words:

> In return for ensuring massive observance of the anniversary of the Saviour's birth by assigning it to this resonant date, the Church for its part tacitly agreed to allow the holiday to be celebrated more or less the way it had always been. From the beginning, the Church's hold over Christmas was (and remains still) rather tenuous. There were always people for whom Christmas was a time of pious devotion rather than carnival, but such people were always in the minority. It may not be going too far to say that Christmas has always been an extremely difficult holiday to Christianize.[15]

But Saturnalia was not the only pagan festival to influence Christmas. As Europe was Christianized, the church allowed earlier regional deities and traditions to be incorporated in to the new religion. Gods and goddesses became saints and pagan festivals became Christian feast days. As sources are scarce, relatively little is known about earlier British festivals, but it seems likely that a complex series of feasts were observed throughout winter, beginning in November. These festivals were then converted into a series of Christian feast days, which is when they come into sharper historical focus. These began with Halloween on 31 October, All Saints' or All Hallows' Day on 1 November, and All Souls' Day on 2 November. Next was St. Martin's Day on 11 November, a hugely important folk feast, which appears to have had a significant impact on the modern Christmas. This was the day when livestock were traditionally slaughtered and goose was consumed at a great feast. Clement Miles argues that Pope Martin I made Martinmas a festival in the fifth century in an attempt to Christianize the day that marked the start of the Germanic New Year and had profound cultural and ritual significance.[16] Martinmas was then followed by St. Clement's Day (23 November), St. Catherine's Day (25 November), St. Andrew's Day (30 November), St. Nicholas's Day (6 December), St. Lucia's Day (13 December), and St. Thomas the Apostle's Day (21 December), when the poor traditionally begged for corn. All of these may have been based on earlier pre-Christian traditions, and were celebrated through present giving, fortune-telling, singing, and ceremonial feasting.[17] Then, finally, we arrive at the Twelve Days of Christmas, beginning on the night of Christmas Eve (24 December) and ending with the Feast of the Epiphany (6 January). Over time, in the postmedieval period, many of these feast days ceased to be marked, and Christmas absorbed aspects of their most cherished traditions. So, we see a sort of cultural funneling effect, in which Christmas inherited the weight of ritual originally spread throughout a season and developed over millennia.

Before moving on, more must be said about the Germanic New Year and the festival of Yule. Frustratingly little is known about a feast that was clearly extremely significant for pre-Christian Germanic peoples and has undoubtedly left its mark on Christmas as we know it today. Although it was once believed to have marked the winter solstice, it seems likely that the season of Yule actually lasted from the Germanic New Year of mid-November through to January.[18] As we have seen with other festivals at this time of year, eating and drinking were central, and chapter 2 will look more closely at the sacrificial elements of the Yule feast as they relate to meat consumption. Some sources suggest that during Yule, the Norse god Odin may have led a ghostly "wild hunt" through the skies, houses may have been decorated with greenery, and Yule logs and other fires lit as part of the feast, but very little is known with any certainty. We do know that by 960 King Haakon of Norway had Christianized the Yule festival, decreeing that it would be marked on 25 December, to coincide with Christmas.[19] Yule is now remembered annually through our Christmas vocabulary. Around 730, the Venerable Bede stated that the Britons referred to the months of December and January as "Giuli," or "Yule," but it appears to have quickly become synonymous with "Christmas" in English, describing the extended period of feasting and festivity.[20]

CHRISTMAS IN THE MEDIEVAL WORLD

In 567, the Second Council of Tour officially marked the twelve days between Christmas and the Epiphany as an extended feast. After the long fast of Advent in the lead-up to Christmas, the twelve days began at sunset on Christmas Eve (24 December). Then came Christmas Day (25 December), marking the birth of Christ, followed by St. Stephen's Day (26 December), when alms were given to the poor. This charitable association is the origin of the later name "Boxing Day," which may refer to the tradition of contributing money or gifts to the Christmas boxes of servants or staff in thanks for their service. It may also refer to the tradition of collecting money for the poor in alms boxes. St. John's Day was marked on 27 December, when various wine-drinking rituals were customary. Holy Innocents' Day, or Childermas, was 28 December,[21] and the Feast of the Holy Family was on 31 December. The first day of January marked the Feast of the Circumcision of Christ, the Solemnity of Mary, and New Year's Day, although the date at which this was marked changed multiple times over the centuries. The twelve days ended in the Feast of the Epiphany, marked on 6 January in Britain. Twelfth Night was the high point of the twelve days, and it was an evening of great revelry, as will be discussed later. Epiphany celebrates the arrival of the three Wise Men and the revelation of Christ's divinity.[22]

In the millennia that followed the church's decision to celebrate the Feast of the Nativity on 25 December, Christmas spread alongside the new religion, so that by the thirteenth century nearly all of Europe marked the occasion. As Christmas spread, it appropriated and merged with the pagan festivals that it encountered. In the process, it became a remarkably layered and textured feast, steeped in ritual and tradition. By the end of the sixth century, the feast had reached England, where it became enmeshed with midwinter Anglo-Saxon and Celtic pagan festivals.[23] In 877, Alfred the Great enshrined the Twelve Days of Christmas into law, making it a holiday during which even servants should be relieved of work.[24] By the late tenth century, laws passed by King Ethelred ordained that Christmas must be a time of peace.[25] Sometime in the mid-eleventh century, the word *Christes maesse* entered Old English, translating literally as "Christ's mass."[26]

Social anthropologist Kaori O'Connor describes this mixing of the old and new that we see in the medieval Christmas, and which continues to characterize the festival as we know it today:

> The Medieval Christmas was the high point of the sacred and secular year, retaining many of the associations of pre-Christian midwinter festivals, onto which it had been grafted. A transition between the old year and the new, it took place in a period of sacred time, when normal activities were suspended. They were replaced by rituals and practices that aimed to consolidate community, and emphasised continuity by commemorating the past while looking ahead to the future.[27]

The marking of the medieval Christmas required a significant investment by elite households, who were required to show open-house hospitality over the course of twelve days. After the fast of Advent, and before the Lenten fast would begin, this was a time for indulgence, when music, dancing, games, food, and drink were plentiful. In the words of one fifteenth-century commentator, "In Cristenmasse wyke . . . then is no tyme to faste."[28] Another fifteenth-century observer bemoaned the fact that Christmas was supposed to be a holy day but had become hedonistic, with "gloteny by surfet of diverse metys and drynkes."[29] Entertainment was also crucial, and carol singing and other performances became important parts of the festivities.

Occasions for communal feasting like this, and lavish displays of hospitality, were critical to the functioning of feudal society, and no lord could neglect his duty in this respect. As Bridget Ann Henisch observes, the hero of the late fourteenth-century romance *Sir Cleges* almost ruins himself with lavish spending on Christmas feasts.[30] In 1250, Henry III disgraced himself with inadequate feasts and the following year went begging from house to house looking for hospitality.[31] Such behavior was not befitting of a medieval king at the best of times, but at Christmas, a time to display one's wealth, power, generosity, and benevolence, this was simply unforgivable. Christmas, like other feasts, was intended to cement bonds of kinship and responsibility and to reinforce the social order of the medieval world. It was also a time to release the tensions and pressures of the feudal system and to enjoy a temporary respite from want and work—a lord who neglected his responsibilities in this respect did so at his own peril.

TUDOR AND EARLY STUART CHRISTMAS

From the sixteenth century on, Christmas comes into sharper focus and sources tell us of the Tudors' great love affair with the festival. The court took the delights of the twelve-day feast to new levels and reveled in the temporary period of chaos and excess. A Lord of Misrule, or "Master of Merry Disports," was appointed to preside over the revelry.[32] On Twelfth Night, a bean king was also chosen to reign over the chaos of what had become possibly the most celebrated night in the festival. Traditions associated with the selection of this individual will be discussed in more detail in chapter 4. Boy bishops were another tradition. Henry VIII appointed a boy to take the place of his senior chaplain during Christmas.[33] All of these temporary appointees inverted the social order; as servants were waited on by masters, peasants governed and children assumed power. The connections between these rituals and Saturnalian festivities are clear.

In addition to sumptuous feasts, the Tudors celebrated with elaborate costumes, masques, mummeries, and pageants. Henry VIII loved to don disguises and famously participated in a masque on Twelfth Night.[34] The food itself was also brought in with great ceremony and pageantry. Particular dishes were accompanied into the hall with chants, cheers, dedicated carols, and performers. More will be said about some of these dishes and the rituals associated with their presentation in the following chapter.[35] We also know that the Tudors placed great emphasis on decoration for the feast. Rich drapery, carpets, and trestle tables dressed with fine linens and table carpets helped to create an air of opulence and luxury for the occasion.[36] The palace and humbler homes alike were also decorated with holly, ivy, and bay, possibly reflecting earlier pre-Christian traditions.[37]

Open-house hospitality and the communal experience continued to be central to the social function of the celebration. The English poet Thomas Tusser, writing in 1557, described the spirit of hospitality expected at Christmas: "At Christmas we banquet, the rich with the poor / Who then, but the miser, but openeth his door?"[38] Here we see the temporary leveling between classes, open-house hospitality, and an emphasis on abundant food and drink. Keeping Christmas was not entirely the lord's responsibility, though; all classes contributed. Tenants in the medieval and Tudor period bought produce, traditionally poultry, as part of their rents, and courtiers and servants gifted food to their lords and masters.[39] Most important, Christmas remained a shared communal experience and was very much a public event throughout the Tudor period. There was no understanding that it should be spent privately at home in the company of one's nearest and dearest—that came later.

As we saw in the medieval period, keeping Christmas in this fashion was a central duty of a lord, and failure to meet this expectation was judged harshly. An early seventeenth-century poem, "The Old and the New Courtier," discusses the perceived decline in hospitality after the reign of Elizabeth I, as lords increasingly left the country in favor of London:

With an old fashion, when Christmas was come,
To call in all his neighbours with a bagpipe and drum,

And good cheer enough to furnish out every old room,
And beer and ale would make a cat speak, and a wise man dumb.
Like an old Courtier of the Queen's
And the Queen's old Courtier
With a new fashion when Christmas was drawing on.
Upon a new journey they must all to London be gone,
And leave none to keep house in the country but their new man John,
Who relieves all his neighbours with a great thump on the back with a
cold stone.
Like a new Courtier of the King's
And the King's new Courtier.[40]

Here we see a longing for Christmas past beginning to creep in. Even in the seventeenth century there was a burgeoning nostalgia for the merry medieval Christmas, when true hospitality was practiced. These are themes that we will see repeated on multiple occasions over the centuries. The ideal Christmas was one that was communal and generous, but as the early modern period progressed, people became increasingly worried that it was a thing of the past, whose glory could never quite be matched in the present.

THE PURITANS

In the midst of all this early modern revelry there were those who were disgusted by the excess, and as the seventeenth century progressed, their influence mounted. The Puritans took a harsh stance on Christmas, which they saw as an idolatrous pagan festival with no theological basis, as the Bible makes no mention of the date of Christ's birth. The connection between Christmas and Saturnalia had not escaped their notice, either. In 1656, Hezekiah Woodward described 25 December as "the old Heathens feasting Day, in honour to Saturn their Idol-God."[41] Just as bad as the pagan origins and lack of biblical evidence in support of the feast was the fact that it encouraged excess, drunkenness, and gluttony. In Philip Stubbes's *Anatomie of Abuses*, published in 1583, the author summarized the Puritans' view of Christmas as follows:

> More mischief is then committed than in all the year besides, what masking and mumming, whereby robbery, whoredom, murder and what not is committed?

What dicing and carding, what eating and drinking, what banqueting and feasting is then used, more than in all the year besides to the great dishonour of God and impoverishing of the realm?[42]

In England, this tension came to a head when Christmas was banned during the Civil War and under Cromwell's Commonwealth. After a series of measures intended to restrict how the day was marked, in 1647 Parliament formally abolished Christmas, Easter, Whitsun, and other holy days.[43] Such a ban had already been enforced in Scotland since the late sixteenth century, where Puritans had wielded power for some time. This ban meant that all religious and secular Christmas traditions were forbidden. Churches could not hold special services, businesses needed to remain open, and celebratory traditions and foods such as mince pies and plum porridge, seen as both idolatrous and indulgent, were condemned. While some reformers could be pragmatic in their broader agenda for calendar reform, they were united in their hatred of Christmas and frustrated by their failures to eradicate a festival that was so culturally rooted.[44] Bernard Capp argues that the reformers' attack on Christmas may have had the unintended consequence of making it a more secular festival. He suggests that while they were successful in restricting the activities of churches, often forcing them to close altogether on Christmas, they could not prevent the celebration by laypeople, who continued to enjoy their mince pies and make merry. And so their campaign may have had the effect not of eradicating Christmas but of making it considerably more secular and focused on the profane.[45]

These Puritanical views certainly had a strong hand in shaping the history of Christmas in America. In areas settled by Puritans, there were repeated attempts to repress the holiday. The Puritans of New England were particularly anxious about Christmas, and from 1659 to 1681 it was illegal to celebrate the festival in Massachusetts.[46] Minister Cotton Mather, best known for his role in the Salem witch trials, railed against Christmas, asking, "Can you in your consciences think that our Holy Saviour is honoured by mirth, by long eating, by hard drinking?"[47] Like their counterparts in Britain, they objected to the excess, intemperance, debauchery, promiscuity, laziness, and gluttony displayed over the twelve days and cited the lack of biblical evidence for the holiday. They also objected to the rowdy public eating and drinking, the inversion of the social order, and the disdain for authority that it encouraged, as well as the imposition that demands for hospitality and charity placed on wealthy homes.[48] To quote Stephen Nissenbaum, their view was "that Christmas was nothing but a pagan festival covered with a Christian veneer."[49]

Attitudes to Christmas marked a sharp divide between colonies in the New World, and between communities within them. Restad explains that

> as the first settlements grew into more established communities, patterns of Christmas celebration peculiar to the colonies began to appear. Geographic separation from European homelands, the proximity of disparate religious and ethnic groups to each other, and the hardship of new beginnings disrupted old habits and holidays. . . . Numerous Christmases abounded, persisting as an expression of individual heritages.[50]

Restad argues that while it may have been widely celebrated, because of this diversity in the New World, where multiple attitudes to and experiences of Christmas abounded, it did not retain the importance to society that it did in medieval and early modern Europe, where it fulfilled a very clear collective and public social function. Rather, ways of marking Christmas varied hugely across the different colonies, depending on the ethnic mix of the region.[51] So, while Puritans in New England banned the festival and Calvinists, Presbyterians, and Quakers recoiled from its excesses, southerners reveled in it. To them, Christmas represented a nostalgic and idealized version of the English feudal system, where lords practiced open house from their stately homes and inferiors gathered to show their deference and enjoy the hospitality of their master. Sources from the seventeenth century on highlight the importance of Christmas in the South, and the hospitality one could expect to be greeted with.[52] Southern society was ultimately dominated by Anglicans, who brought both the culture of the English gentry and an idealized view of a traditional Christmas with them. And, of course, other European groups who came to and founded settlements across America also brought their own festive traditions with them. As the following section will discuss in more detail, the traditions of initially Dutch and later German communities in particular helped shape America's unique iteration of the festival profoundly, and they have left a significant imprint on the modern Christmas globally.

THE RESTORATION AND GEORGIAN PERIOD

Despite the best efforts of the Puritans, Christmas survived the Commonwealth and was formally and victoriously resurrected during the Restoration, but it was not unscathed.[53] The festival had taken some heavy blows, which had rubbed off some of its sheen.[54] Gone were the days when noble Tudor families held rowdy public feasts open to all. The Christmas that returned was a more pared-back affair, and while some traditions ceased altogether, others survived and adapted to the modern world. In the words of Claire Hopley, "Christmas after the Restoration became a patchwork cut from both old and new cloth."[55]

And so while it may have come back in a somewhat reduced form, Christmas continued to be kept from the Restoration and throughout the Georgian period. This was not an era in which the main novels and carols associated with Christmas today were generated, and so it is not an age that we immediately imagine when we think of the festival, but it was always kept. The popular assertion that it was invented by the Victorians is simply not true, although more will be said about their role in shaping the modern Christmas in the following section. The cultural significance of Christmas in the early Georgian world is demonstrated by the following words of French traveler Cesar de Saussure, writing in the 1720s:

> Christmas day is the great festival of all Christian nations but on that day the English have many customs we do not know of. They wish each other a Merry Christmas and A Happy new Year; presents are given and no man may dispense with this custom. On this festival day churches, the entrances of houses, rooms, kitchens and halls are decked with laurels, rosemary and other greenery.[56]

As chapter 3 will discuss, Saussure also had much to say on the food enjoyed by the English at Christmas. And, as the following five chapters will likewise show, the eighteenth and early nineteenth centuries were a particularly important period in the development of Christmas cookery.

While the ban on Christmas may not have been highly effective in England, where its cultural roots ran deep, the Puritans were far more successful preventing it from taking hold in the areas of America under their control. Of course, there were always those who kept Christmas quietly and privately, but there was no shared public experience of the festival there for some time.[57] Nissenbaum argues that long after the official ban on Christmas had been lifted, it was still viewed with caution and suspicion. In fact, Christmas did not gain legal recognition as a holiday in New England until the mid-nineteenth century.[58] All this time, though, Christmas had been kept with great gusto in the South, and slave-owning states were among the first to legalize the holiday.[59] Shauna Bigham and Robert E. May argue that by the antebellum period Christmas had become deeply embedded within southern culture and had an important function within the system of slavery. It was a time at which the pressure valve of slavery was temporarily released; slaves were able to drink, feast, and dance, and the burden of their workload was lifted.[60] The continuity with Saturnalia and the medieval world is striking here.

By the mid-eighteenth century, tales of merry southern Christmases began to filter back to England and became part of the mythology of the South. These stories of great mirth and open-house hospitality triggered a deep nostalgia in the English, who saw the South as upholding elements of their own cultural golden age now lost. In 1746, the *London Magazine* wrote that all over the South "an universal hospitality reigns; full Tables and open Doors, the kind salute, the generous Detention, speak somewhat like the old Roast-beef Ages of our Fore-fathers."[61] This is an important moment when the American Christmas enters a form of discourse with the British festival for the first time. Whereas previously the creative input had flowed one way—from the Old World to the New—over the next two centuries a more reflexive relationship developed. Americans took the customs handed to them but created an aesthetic and momentum that in turn went on to shape Christmas in Britain and the world over the following centuries.

Of all the Americans to influence the nineteenth-century evolution of Christmas on both sides of the Atlantic, no one did so more than Washington Irving, a writer from Manhattan. In 1820, Irving published a book of short stories, *The Sketch Book*, which was a huge success. In addition to classics such as "The Legend of Sleepy Hollow" and "Rip Van Winkle," it included five Christmas tales set in a fictional British stately home, Bracebridge Hall. The setting was likely based upon Aston Hall in Birmingham, where Irving spent considerable time in the early nineteenth century. While there, he became fascinated by the English Christmas and feared for its decline. His stories depict the festive season as hosted by Squire Bracebridge, where hospitality is extended to all and traditional customs such as the wassail bowl and Lord of Misrule are kept faithfully.[62] The narrator of the story gives voice to Irving's sentiments about Christmas:

> Of all the old festivals, however, that of Christmas awakens the strongest and most heartfelt associations. There is a tone of solemn and sacred feeling that blends with our conviviality and lifts the spirit to a state of hallowed and elevated enjoyment. . . . The English, from the great prevalence of rural habit throughout every class of society, have always been fond of those festivals and holidays, which agreeably interrupt the stillness of country life, and they were, in former days, particularly observant of the religious and social rites of Christmas. It is inspiring to read even the dry details which some antiquaries have given of the quaint humors, the burlesque pageants, the complete abandonment to mirth and good-fellowship with which this festival was celebrated. It seemed to throw open every door and unlock every heart. It brought the peasant and the peer together, and blended all ranks in one warm, generous flow of joy and kindness. The old halls of castles and manor-houses resounded with the harp and the Christmas carol, and their ample boards groaned under the weight of hospitality. Even the poorest cottage welcomed the festive season with green decorations of bay and holly—the cheerful fire glanced its rays through the lattice, inviting the passengers to raise the latch and join the gossip knot huddled round the hearth beguiling the long evening with legendary jokes and oft-told Christmas tales.[63]

As we see in this quote, the Bracebridge Hall stories exhibit a deep-seated nostalgia for Christmas past and an anxiety over the supposed decline of these traditions. These are themes that Victorian writers continued to explore during the following decades, and Irving was a direct influence on the leaders of the Christmas revival, such as Charles Dickens, who was his close friend. Through the New-York Historical Society, Irving was also part of a network of well-to-do New Yorkers of Dutch origins, known as Knickerbockers, including John Pintard and Clement Clarke Moore. Pintard, the founder of the Historical Society, took an active interest in Christmas from the 1820s on, and he appears to have suffered from a serious case of nostalgia for "old customs" and "ancient usages."[64] Pintard had become concerned by the rowdy public nature of Christmas in early nineteenth-century New York. Callithumpian bands paraded the streets, and mobs of drunk young men became increasingly intimidating and antisocial.[65] This concern, and a belief that traditions and ceremonies held real value for society, spurred this group of Knickerbockers into action. Through their writing they helped to reinvent a more wholesome family Christmas, a pattern that only gained momentum in the Victorian period, as we will see.

These men were also responsible for the development of the modern Santa Claus, who took on a starring role in this new family-focused event. It is not true to say that they "invented" Santa; his origins can be traced back to St. Nicholas, a Turkish saint who saved three sisters from prostitution when he threw each of them a bag of gold through a window. There were also well-established traditions of St. Nicholas visiting houses and leaving money, fruit, and nuts for children on 6 December. This ritual, and St. Nicholas's legacy, was consciously reworked by these Knickerbockers in the first decades of the nineteenth century, though. Pintard was passionate about St. Nicholas and tried to establish him as the patron saint of New York City, promoting the idea that his visit was part of an established ancient custom of New Amsterdam. Irving also popularized the image of St. Nicholas in his *Knickerbocker's History* (1809). It was undoubtedly their peer Clement Clarke Moore, though, who made the most significant contribution to the development of the modern Santa Claus. Written for his children in 1822, and published the following year, his poem "A Visit from St. Nicholas" transformed him from being a dignified bishop into a "jolly old elf" flying in a sleigh pulled by eight tiny reindeer. He leaves toys for the children and then, after tapping the side of his nose with his finger, vanishes up the chimney. While elements of the story were drawn from elsewhere, and were not the imaginings of Moore alone, this poem brought Santa as we know him today to life.[66] Soon Santa was visiting children in America annually, and he had been adopted in Britain by the 1840s, where he merged with the earlier folk figure of Father Christmas.

The 1820s was a revolutionary decade for the American Christmas in many ways, being not just when Santa as we know him came into existence but also when Christmas trees took root in the country. The history of Christmas trees can be traced back to pre-Christian fertility rituals where evergreens were bought into the house over winter. In the Christian era, the ritual continued, and popular myths developed around the trees in an attempt to find a nonpagan origin for the practice. One of the most famous of these is the tale in which Martin Luther, feeling inspired by God's work on a Christmas Eve walk, returned home with an evergreen that he decked with candles to represent the stars in the heavens. The first records of decorated trees in post-Reformation Europe are from early seventeenth-century Germany, and they had spread throughout most of the Continent by the early to mid-nineteenth century. They may have been in England by the late eighteenth century but were certainly not widespread among the general populace at this stage. Their widespread popularity in Britain is thought to have developed after Prince Albert presented his young wife Queen Victoria with one in 1840.[67] In America, the Pennsylvania Dutch are credited with having introduced the Christmas tree in the early nineteenth century, as a festive connection to their homeland. The earliest references to decorated trees in America all date to the early 1820s, but the practice seems to have become more widespread in the 1830s and 1840s.[68] Nissenbaum argues, though, that while there is some truth to the idea that the Christmas tree was brought by the Pennsylvania Dutch, in reality its adoption predates any significant German settlement in the United States. He argues that it was spread not by immigrants but by commercial literature and marketing.[69] He writes:

> The Christmas tree entered American society through the avenues of commercial culture, but it did so in the name of pre-commercial folk culture. This is exactly what happened with the figure of Santa Claus. We might go so far as to say that both rituals were part of an early "folk revival" of sorts, a revival that emerged close behind the full blown emergence of commercial culture itself.[70]

The relationship between revived folk rituals that provided an air of authenticity and commercialization is a persistent theme from these first decades of the nineteenth century on, gathering momentum in the Victorian period, as we will see below.

THE VICTORIANS

No one did Christmas quite like the Victorians. The romantic, nostalgic aesthetic of the age saw the festival elevated to new heights. It is not true to say that they invented Christmas, though, as many popular commentators frequently claim.[71] As this book will show, almost all of the festive foods we love most predate the nineteenth century in one form or another. The same can be said for most of our other cherished Christmas traditions. As we saw with Christmas trees and Santa Claus, they both have an earlier genesis, and so were not invented, but they were certainly reinvigorated and remodeled in the nineteenth century. New traditions were introduced as well, such as Christmas cards and crackers, and in the process the Victorians left their stamp on Christmas forever.

The Victorians were nothing if not nostalgic. They looked to Britain's medieval and Tudor past as a golden age, and the genesis of their nation and ultimately Empire. Britain's ascendancy to the role of global super-power left them searching for origin myths, and so they looked to the past for stories, traditions, cultural rootedness, and a moral compass. The social, demographic, economic, and environmental changes brought about by the Industrial Revolution, coupled with its unprecedented levels of urbaniza-tion, prompted a romantic, idealized longing for simpler times and an agrarian idyll. And it is in this context that we need to see their relationship with Christmas. As with all forms of nostalgia, there is an anxiety in their fascination with the Christmas of their ancestors. It reveals a need to cre-ate a tangible connection to a past that was seen as better, more pure, and that was in danger of slipping away. The Victorians had a deep-seated fear that Christmas was disappearing and that it urgently needed resurrection.[72] Looking to history became a way of coping with the changes of the nine-teenth century. It connected people to the past, to stability, and to reliable patterns of English life.[73]

The Victorians traced the English tradition of Christmas back to the halls of the Anglo-Saxons and Normans.[74] Christmas, then, became a national fes-tival, combining the culture and customs of the Anglo-Saxons, with whom Victorians felt connected, with the civilizing influence of the Normans. Ac-cording to William Francis Dawson, writing in 1902:

> The Anglo-Saxon excesses are referred to by some of the old chroniclers, intemperance being a very prevalent vice at the Christmas festival. Ale and mead were their favourite drinks; wines were used as occasional luxuries. . . . And while it is quite true that the refined manners and chivalrous spirit of the Normans exercised a powerful influence on the Anglo-Saxons, it is equally true that the conquerors, on mingling with the English people adopted many

of these ancient customs to which they tenaciously clung, and these included the customs of Christmastide.[75]

Looking to the Anglo-Saxons fed their yearning for a stronger sense of English identity and cultural rootedness, but it was the Tudor period that the Victorians saw as their "golden age." The Elizabethan Christmas in particular came to be seen as a representation of "Merrie England" at its peak. The concept of traditional open-house hospitality appealed to the Victorians at a time when the classes were being restructured and the social responsibilities of the new capitalist elite and the urban workforce were less clear.[76] According to Mark Connelly, Victorian commentators focused on how the rich and poor came together in the Tudor Christmas. They saw the decline of the festival as evidence that England had become less cohesive, more stratified, and that the divide between classes was no longer being bridged by mutual social obligation. The heart of England was believed to be in its countryside, and Christmas feasts of the feudal past depicted a gentry and aristocratic class who invested in their social responsibility through hospitality.[77]

While they may have idealized the medieval and Tudor world, they did not endorse all of its excesses. Rather than reinvigorating the wild public festival, Christmas was remodeled as a domestic occasion, focused on children and close family.[78] Stephen Nissenbaum has observed that placing children at the center of the festival was another way of inverting the social order, akin to Saturnalia, with age replacing class as the basis for gift giving.[79] He also argues that the purpose of the temporary chaos created during Christmas had been to create a sort of safety valve to release the tensions of class inequality, but as the labor relationship changed, the paternalistic bond between the upper and lower social orders no longer served a purpose. This meant that the unruly behavior of the proletariat became increasingly threatening to elites, who were no longer willing facilitators of the disorder and instead opted to close their doors and retreat to the domestic sphere.[80]

The retreat from chaos, and the bringing of orderliness to the festival, may have been one factor in the decline of Twelfth Night celebrations from the mid-nineteenth century on. In this new model of a family- and child-centered Christmas, the riotous merriment of Twelfth Night ceased to have a place. By the twentieth century, only Christmas Day, Boxing Day (26

December), and New Year's Day were especially marked, with the emphasis being placed on 25 December. In Dickens's great work *A Christmas Carol*, to be discussed in more detail below, Bob Cratchit is grudgingly given just one day off. Whereas once Epiphany had been the highlight, and each day of the feast had its own rituals, during the Victorian period Christmas Day increasingly absorbed all of the attention. Bridget Ann Henisch describes Christmas Day as being like a cuckoo, robbing the rituals of the twelve-day festival. Henisch states that "Christmas Day was transformed from the first scene into the grand climax of the drama."[81] It absorbed the rituals, energy, and essence of the whole season.[82] By the end of the nineteenth century, Twelfth Night had almost entirely ceased to exist.[83]

If Washington Irving began the great Christmas revival in the 1820s, his friend Charles Dickens took that baton and ran with it over the following decades. No single person has shaped the modern Christmas more than Dickens. Kaori O'Connor argues that "Dickens did not consciously re-invent Christmas, but he re-imagined it, catching the mood of the early Victorian era, when the nation was seeking the lost ideals of its past in order to unite a society undergoing potentially divisive change and to inspire a new golden age of imperial expansion."[84]

Dickens wrote about Christmas prolifically, but his best-loved festive work, and the one that shaped popular imagination the most, is undoubtedly *A Christmas Carol* (1843). This is the story of the miserly curmudgeon Scrooge, who is visited by the Ghosts of Christmas Past, Present, and Future one Christmas Eve. Confronted with the truth of his behavior, and seeing the bleak forecast for his future if he continues in his selfish, greedy ways, Scrooge awakens on Christmas morning a changed man. His first act before going to spend Christmas with his good and dutiful nephew is to send his hardworking employee Bob Cratchit an enormous turkey to feed his struggling family and a promise that he will strive to fulfill his duty as an employer in the future. This is the ultimate Christmas morality tale, but it is not a religious story. As O'Connor observes, "The de-sacralized spirituality of the tale perfectly conveys the increasing secularization of Christmas."[85]

As in all eras, food played a central role in the Victorian celebration, and Dickens continually highlights the centrality of festive food in his writing. Traditional Christmas fare was used to highlight Englishness and stability in the face of rapid social and economic change.[86] The shared Christmas

"Scrooge's Third Visitor."
Illustrated by John Leech. In Charles Dickens, *A Christmas Carol* (1843). iStock/duncan1890.

dinner, eaten in the early afternoon, became the pinnacle of the day. In the mid-nineteenth century, the classic menu that we know today of roast goose or turkey as the centerpiece, followed by plum pudding, was both codified and popularized. This codification will be discussed at length in the chapters that follow; for now, though, it is important to recognize that the festive meal itself was a central part of the Victorians' reimagining of Christmas. It celebrated traditional English fare, but also the shared experience of coming together as a family in the home. It became a sort of ritualized performance of the Victorian ideologies of both nationalism and domesticity. In short, the consumption of the Christmas meal came to be seen as so central to British national identity that charitable organizations raised funds to help the poor participate in the ritual.[87] More will be said about such charities and organizations like "goose clubs" in the following chapter.

Tara Moore has commented on just how central food is in Victorian literary depictions of Christmas, and how excess is juxtaposed with descriptions of hunger and starvation. This motif became a powerful and culturally topical way of commenting on social and economic injustice, which resonated deeply with the Victorians, who had romanticized and nationalistic notions of Christmas. Moore emphasizes the role that food plays in Scrooge's "conversion narrative." Not only does he finally understand the importance of charity and goodwill in gifting Bob a turkey on Christmas morning, but he himself has at last come to understand the importance of Christmas indulgence and traditions:

> The food in *A Christmas Carol* contributes to Scrooge's alteration. . . . It is noteworthy that Scrooge indicates his conversion in his relinquishment of the incorrect Christmas food, such as his pre-visitation gruel, for the proper food markers of a Christmas Englishness, represented by his gift turkey and the Christmas bowl of smoking bishop he shares with Bob Cratchit on Boxing Day.[88]

Given that Christmas became such an important motif of Britishness in the mid-nineteenth century, it is unsurprising that it became central to identity debates throughout the Empire. According to the *Illustrated London News*, "The Britisher, whether at home or in a distant colony, clings to Christmastide."[89] Mark Connelly argues that the shared experience of Christmas unified the Empire.[90] Even in the midsummer sun of the Southern Hemisphere,

Christmas was faithfully kept despite the hot weather and distance. The press reveled in the problem posed by the weather in countries such as Australia, New Zealand, and South Africa, and in highlighting it repeatedly they drew attention to the size and supremacy of the Empire. Canadian newspapers made much of the fact that they were the only major British colony to enjoy the Christmas season covered in snow as it should be.[91]

Regardless of where one was in the world, though, food played a central role in keeping Christmas, with roast turkey and plum pudding being mandatory festive fare throughout the Empire. However, the development of more seasonally appropriate alternatives became a part of Christmas in the colonies as their sense of independence and identity developed. Mark Connelly cites commentary in the *New Zealand Herald* from 1872, promoting the beautiful summer produce available and defending the experience and value of the Antipodean Christmas:

> Talk about Christmas in the old country! Can the shops there show such a heap of beautiful red luscious strawberries? Where are their white and black-hearted cherries? Where their Summer pears and apples, their yellow and ripe gooseberries, their peas, their cauliflowers and asparagus, their new potatoes, their tomatoes, their delicate French beans, their materials for salads? Why the sights of fruit windows such as were to be seen yesterday is a set-off against anything the finest shops in London at this period could produce.[92]

Despite the willingness to embrace the season and culinary innovations in these more distant climes, the traditional British favorites were never done away with entirely. Swimming, outdoor sports, and picnics became typical of the Antipodean Christmas, but the pudding always came along for these outings. Similarly, tales of Christmas in camp in India depicted elaborate, luxurious feasts of goose and turkey being eaten under the trees.[93] Chapters 2 and 3 will look at the development of Australia's Christmas meal specifically, but similar debates about domestically appropriate festive food were had throughout the Empire.

THE TWENTIETH CENTURY TO THE PRESENT

By the start of the twentieth century, Christmas was, in all critical aspects, the festival we know today. The twelve days had been whittled down, and all the main traditions now familiar to us had evolved: Santa Claus, Christmas trees, decorations, greeting cards, crackers, pantomimes, carols, and, as the following chapters will explore in detail, the codified meal of roast poultry, ham, and Christmas pudding.

Keeping Christmas was critical to keeping spirits up during the two world wars, both at home and for those serving in distant lands. The cultural significance of Christmas and the yearning to mark it against all odds is demonstrated by the astonishing Christmas Truce of 1914, when British and German forces on the Western Front celebrated the day together, emerging peacefully from the trenches and exchanging small gifts of cigarettes and buttons, playing football, and singing carols. Soldiers wrote home to their loved ones in Britain marveling at what had come to pass, and the press reported extensively on the event, which symbolized the hope for peace and goodwill among men in a time of darkness. Those on the home front in both wars also had their own set of challenges during Christmas. With so many of their loved ones away and food shortages starting to bite, putting on a merry Christmas was no easy task. The rationing of World War II in particular created great challenges for the Christmas cook, and the Ministry of Food did its best to help ensure that the holiday could still be appropriately celebrated. An extra ration of sugar and fat was given out before Christmas, and the stores of tinned and dried fruit were distributed to assist with preparations. People coped by planning well in advance—hoarding small amounts of flour, butter, and sugar throughout the year for their Christmas cooking. Ration cookbooks and the Ministry of Food suggested alternatives and substitutes for festive recipes.[94] Chapter 3 will discuss some wartime versions of that most critical of all Christmas foods, the pudding. Families also joined pig clubs, and other collectives, to ensure that they would have meat on the table, as chapter 2 will discuss in more detail.

In the postwar years, as disposable household incomes rose rapidly, Christmas became increasingly egalitarian, as more and more families could afford to participate in the full gamut of fun to be had, but it also became increasingly commercialized. The process of commercialization began in the Victorian period, but it grew exponentially throughout the twentieth century. Christmas spending went through the roof. The traditional charity of Boxing Day was replaced by the almost ritualized shopping frenzy of the annual Boxing Day sales in the United Kingdom and many Commonwealth countries. This is akin to Black Friday in the United States: the official start to the Christmas shopping season, which begins the day after Thanksgiving. What was once a small stocking of fruit, nuts, and trinkets became a sack full of toys for children. This pattern shows no signs of slowing down. Spending remains astronomical, and each year the shops seem to start their Christmas campaigns earlier and earlier. Many contemporary commentators rue the direction that Christmas is headed in, wringing their hands over the commercialization of the season. A look at the history of Christmas shows us that these concerns have always been there, though. The Puritans' disdain for the season of excess and drunkenness, and their anxiety that the festival had only a tenuous religious basis, is similar to the anxiety about the commercialization of the festival felt today. Shoppers, revelers, and gluttons butt heads with the moral condemnation of those reminding them that "Jesus is the reason for the season." This tension between the secular, hedonistic elements of the festival and the religious aspect is as old as Christmas itself.

The commercialization of the festival has also led to new rituals emerging. Parents now annually take their children to visit Santa in department stores and shopping centers. Most families will have a photograph of at least one child screaming on Santa's lap somewhere in their archive. The character of Rudolph the Red-Nosed Reindeer was also born out of commercial interests, when Montgomery Ward, a Chicago retailer, commissioned Robert L. May to create the story in 1939 as a Christmas promotion. Rudolph went on to be popularized in multiple animation specials and the famous song written by May's brother-in-law, Johnny Marks. Christmas films and television specials have also become a sort of modern-day ritual, akin to the traditional pantomime. Films such *It's a Wonderful Life* (1946), *Miracle on 34th Street* (1947), *White Christmas* (1954), *Babes in Toyland* (1961), *National Lampoon's Christmas Vacation* (1989), *Home Alone* (1990), *The Muppet Christmas Carol* (1992), *The Nightmare before Christmas* (1993), *Bridget Jones's Diary* (2001), *Love Actually* (2003), and *Elf* (2003) have become much-loved favorites. These films, and many more, are watched annually and have left their own marks on the festival. Most of them faithfully promote the Victorian message that Christmas is a time to be with family and those you love most. As with cinema and television, the twentieth century also saw the release of some of our best-loved Christmas pop music. Traditional hymns and carols are still cherished, but it is the crooning of Bing

Crosby, Eartha Kitt, Wham!, Mariah Carey, the Pogues, and Michael Bublé that have become the secular soundtrack of the season that surrounds us in every shopping center from at least October until the end of the year.

The role of Hollywood, television, and record companies meant that, over the course of the twentieth century, America began to have an even greater influence over Christmas. This was a process that began in the early nineteenth century, as Irving's works proved so popular and the Knickerbockers' Santa Claus became a global phenomenon, and it has gained momentum ever since. While the fundamentals of Christmas in the English-speaking world remain British, the modern Christmas has become increasingly shaped by American art and aesthetics.

If this short history of Christmas has shown us anything, it is that Christmas survives against all odds. In the words of Claire Hopley:

> If the history of Christmas in Britain were represented as a line on a graph, it would peak in the early sixteenth century, before the Reformation tamed its Saturnalian and medieval frolics; descend inexorably into the slough of 1647, when Christmas celebrations were banned; trace gently up to the post-Reformation plateau where it rested until the early nineteenth century, and then soar unwaveringly to today's heady peaks.[95]

Christmas has had to adapt over the millennia, and has been met with hurdles along the way, but in the face of extraordinary cultural change it is still here, and it shows no signs of fading.

2

MEATS AND MAINS

There never was such a goose. Bob said he didn't believe there ever was such a goose cooked. Its tenderness and flavour, size and cheapness, were the themes of universal admiration. Eked out by apple-sauce and mashed potatoes, it was a sufficient dinner for the whole family; indeed, as Mrs Cratchit said with great delight (surveying one small atom of bone upon the dish), they hadn't ate it all at last! Yet everyone had had enough, and the youngest Cratchits in particular were steeped in sage and onion to the eyebrows!

—Charles Dickens, *A Christmas Carol* (1843)

Once Santa has visited, and the presents have been ripped open with frenzied excitement, the focal point of Christmas Day undoubtedly becomes the main meal. The scene of a family gathered around a table groaning with food, and the man of the house proudly carving a golden roast turkey, has been captured countless times: being celebrated on idealized Victorian Christmas greeting cards, in novels, and in numerous Christmas movies. Sending out for a turkey is the first thing Scrooge does on Christmas morning having awakened a changed man, as we shall discuss in more detail below. Just under a century and a half later, Chevy Chase memorably cut into a bird so overcooked that its interior had more or less vaporized in the 1980s Christmas classic *National Lampoon's Christmas Vacation*. As the previous chapter explained, during the nineteenth century Christmas became a family-centered, domestic festival, and the significance placed on the main celebratory meal, to be enjoyed with one's nearest and dearest, must be read in that context. While it is not extraordinary that a celebratory meal like this would be important in a festival of this nature—indeed, meat-oriented feasting has occurred at ritual events and times of significance throughout human history—the development of the strictly codified menu adhered to during Christmas in the English-speaking world is noteworthy. Whereas many cultures mark Christmas Day with a special meal, the nature of the specific set menu still followed by so many families in the Anglophone world is remarkable. Its evolution is a fascinating story, which will be the focus of this chapter.

Christmas dinner is and always has been marked by excess, and, like so many celebratory feasts, this means meat, meat, and more meat. In the words of Ferdinand the duck in the movie *Babe* (1995), "Christmas? Christmas means dinner; dinner means death! Death means carnage; Christmas means carnage!" And with ten million turkeys slaughtered annually in the United Kingdom[1] and another twenty-two million in the United States for Christmas tables alone,[2] it is fair to say that Ferdinand the duck had a point. The abundance of meat and multiple species consumed at Christmas dinner highlights the modern festival's connections to its pre-Christian European heritage. As chapter 1 discussed, the modern Christmas contains many remnants of earlier sacramental rituals, such as bringing trees and greenery into the house. Nowhere are sacrificial elements more apparent, though, than on the festive table, which is laden with symbolically charged foods. Celtic, Germanic, and Nordic peoples appear to have held communal feasts in honor of the gods in midwinter. Animals were sacrificed during these festivals as a central component of the fertility rituals necessary to ensure that light and life would return in the New Year.[3] Rituals aside, the midwinter slaughtering of beasts was also connected to the very real-world issue of seasonality. Traditionally, animals had to be slaughtered at their very fattest in late November, as it was impossible to keep them fed over winter.[4] Many species of fowl, such as geese, were at their most succulent in late autumn, hatching in the spring and having had time to reach maturity.[5] Autumn and winter were also the traditional hunting seasons, meaning that game was plentiful at this time of year. In short, this combination of slaughtered, fattened livestock and game meant that fresh meat was at its most plentiful throughout the Christmas season.[6]

Accounts of Christmas feasting during the medieval period consistently highlight the sheer abundance of meat consumed. Although there was no codified Christmas menu at this stage, alcohol, luxury foodstuffs such as spices, and plentiful meat signified the celebratory essence of the feast. The generous bounty of luxury foods available on feast days made a sharp contrast with the regular fasts that dotted the medieval calendar, at which meat was prohibited. Accounts from royal households give us some indication of the sheer quantity of food needed to display adequate hospitality during Christmas. On Christmas Day 1213, guests at King John's feast were treated to twenty-seven hogshead of wine, four hundred head of pork, three thousand fowl, fifteen thousand herring, ten thousand eels, one hundred pounds of almonds, two pounds of spices, and sixty-six pounds of pepper.[7] During Christmas at Westminster Hall in 1399, Richard II is reported to have slaughtered twenty-six oxen, three hundred sheep, and countless fowl for his guests.[8] A passage from the contemporaneous, late fourteenth-century *Sir Gawain and the Green Knight* illustrates what such a Christmas feast would have been like: "For there the feast was held full fifteen days alike with all the meat and the mirth that men could devise."[9]

Early modern descriptions of Christmas feasts continued to highlight the abundance. In 1573, Thomas Tusser described a Christmas celebration as follows:

Good bread and good drink, a good fire in the hall,
Brawn, pudding, and sowse, and good mustard withall.
Beef, mutton and pork, shred pies of the best,
Pig, veal, goose and capon, and turkey well drest,
Cheese, apples and nuts, joly carols to hear
As then in the country, is counted good cheer.[10]

Sources from this period demonstrate that the modern festive favorites of pork, turkey, goose, and "shred pies," or mince pies (see chapter 5), were already a part of the feast, but rather than forming a codified meal, they were just some of the many rich festive dishes on offer. Excess, generosity, and plenty were key, rather than the presentation of a particular set of dishes as we see later.

Documentary sources, such as bills of fare, receipt books, household accounts, and estate records, bear witness to the sheer animal casualties that occurred during Christmas in the sixteenth and seventeenth centuries. Peter Brears notes that the Willoughbys at Wollaton ate sixteen venison pasties on Christmas Day in 1547.[11] This was no small feat, as a venison pasty, which was one of the most popular celebratory dishes in the later medieval and early modern period, contained an entire side of deer and was encased in up to twenty-four pounds of pastry. Robert May's 1660 bill of fare for Christmas, published at the start of the Restoration, highlights the extraordinary number of dishes served over two courses, and the emphasis on poultry. It also shows that despite Cromwell's best efforts, Christmas remained a day for feasting.

A bill of fare for christmas day and how to set the meat in order

Oysters
1. A collar of brawn
2. Stewed Broth of Mutton marrow bones.
3. A grand Sallet
4. A pottage of caponets
5. A breast of veal in stoffado
6. A boil'd partridge.
7. A chine of beef, or sirloin roast
8. Minced pies.
9. A Jegote of mutton with anchove sauce.
10. A made dish of sweet-bread
11. A swan roast.
12. A pasty of venison.
13. A kid with a pudding in his belly.
14. A steak pie.
15. A hanch of venison roasted.
16. A turkey roast and stuck with cloves.
17. A made dish of chickens in puff paste.
18. Two bran geese roasted, one larded
19. Two large capons, one larded.
20. A Custard

The second course for the same mess.

Oranges and Lemons
  1. A young lamb or kid.
  2. Two couple of rabbits, two larded.
  3. A pig souc't with tongues.
  4. Three ducks, one larded.
  5. Three pheasants, 1 larded.
  6. A Swan Pye.
  7. Three brace of partridge, three larded.
  8. Made dish in puff paste.
  9. Bolonia sausages, and anchoves, mushrooms, and Cavieate, and pickled oysters in a dish.
  10. Six teels, three larded.
  11. A Gammon of Westphalia Bacon.
  12. Ten plovers, five larded.
  13. A quince pye, or warden pie
  14. Six woodcocks, 3 larded.
  15. A standing Tart in puff-paste, preserved fruits, Pippins, &c.0
  16. A dish of Larks.
  17. Six dried neats tongues
  18. Sturgeon.
  19. Powdered Geese.
Jellies.[12]

This menu highlights the sheer opulence of the occasion, but there was still no prescriptive set of Christmas dishes that needed to be followed. Like Thomas Tusser's sixteenth-century poem quoted above, dishes associated with the modern Christmas meal were listed—namely, minced pies, turkey, and geese—but they appear alongside a host of other dishes not specifically associated with the festival.

Eighteenth-century bills of fare also indicate that a wide range of meats and dishes were consumed during Christmas, and literary accounts provide colorful descriptions of some of these festive favorites. Jane Austen's novels refer to the gifting of food at Christmas, highlighting game, meat, and pies specifically.[13] In *Persuasion*, Mrs. Musgrove's tressels and trays are described as "bending under the weight of brawn and cold pies" set out for her guests.[14] And, of course, nineteenth-century novels continue to highlight the excess of food. As illustrated in the previous chapter (see page 28), Dickens's Ghost of Christmas Present is found in Scrooge's room surrounded by an abundance of festive fare.[15] Importantly, though, it was around the time that Dickens wrote his Christmas masterpiece that a more codified Christmas meal emerged, with turkey or goose as the centerpiece, supported by traditional sides and ham for the very fortunate. Dickens himself helped to popularize a version of this meal in his detailed rendering of the Cratchit family feast, cited at the start of this chapter. The following section will focus on the main components of this now traditional Christmas meal. It will explore their history in detail, explaining how it was that they came to appear on our plates around the world each 25 December.

POULTRY AND GAME BIRDS

The modern tradition of serving a large roasted fowl as part of the Christmas feast is almost certainly connected to earlier cultural practices. A strong argument can be made that feasting on roasted fowl at this time of year is a tradition inherited from the all but forgotten European goose festivals of autumn and early winter.[16] The Christian feast of Michaelmas (29 September) was especially associated with goose consumption, but this was also a feature of Martinmas (11 November). These are both now largely unmarked feasts, but as they declined, many of their traditions were inherited by Christmas.[17] And so geese, as well as other large domestic and game species, found their way onto the medieval Christmas table. According to food historian C. Anne Wilson, swans and peacocks were the celebratory birds favored by the wealthier classes, while herons, bustards, geese, and chickens graced the tables of those lower down the social order.[18]

These culinary rituals may ultimately connect further back in time again, to the pre-Christian festivals of autumn and winter—namely, the Celtic Samhain (or Hallowe'en, 31 October), the Germanic Yule (the first day of the New Year), and Erntedankfest (Harvest Home). As chapter 1 explained, this appears to have been a time of great ritual significance for pagan peoples across Europe. At a time of year when the trees were bare and the days were getting shorter, the ritual consumption of migratory birds like geese may have helped to ensure regeneration in the spring.[19] Geese appeared and disappeared at key points throughout the year, connecting them both symbolically and in very real terms to the changing seasons. Tamra Andrews has suggested that at such festivals a goose may have been ceremonially sacrificed and its flesh consumed by participants as part of a ritual designed to safeguard the regeneration of the earth.[20] Of course, this was also quite simply the time of year when geese were at their fattest and most succulent.

Turkey Crosses the Atlantic

Being a species native to the Americas, turkey was, of course, unheard of in Europe prior to being brought back by Spanish conquistadores in the early sixteenth century. The origin of the name "turkey" in English is something of a mystery, but it is most likely that the term derived from the perception of them as being exotic.[21] Similarly, other Europeans, including the Spanish, Italians, and French, associated turkeys with India—hence the name *coq d'Inde*, later *dinde/dindon* in French. This French name similarly hints at the foreign and exotic, but it also highlights the connection between the European discovery of turkeys and Columbus's attempt to find a passage the India.[22]

Unlike many other American foodstuffs taken to Europe during the early modern period, turkey appears to have been adopted quite quickly. According to food historian Andrew F. Smith, the first clear reference to the Spanish encountering domesticated turkeys dates to 1518. There are sources that may suggest contact before this time, but they are somewhat ambiguous, making 1518 the first verifiable date.[23] In a very short space of time, though, turkeys had spread far and wide: to the West Indies, Western Europe, the Mediterranean, and Asia.[24] In 1520, Alessandro Geraldini, Bishop of Hispaniola, who supported Columbus on his first voyage, sent a pair of turkeys to Lorenzo Pucci, the Florentine cardinal in Rome.[25] This was the first definitive importation of the species into Europe.[26] They soon became an important foodstuff for the elite and were almost certainly being farmed in Spain in the 1520s, France by 1528, and Germany by 1530.[27] Queen Marguerite of Navarre is recorded as raising turkeys at Alençon in 1534, and Catherine de Medici served seventy "Indian chickens" at a banquet in Paris in 1549.[28]

Turkey was also introduced into England in the sixteenth century. Sir William Strickland is credited with being the first man to have imported them into England. This act may have prompted his adoption of a white turkey-cock as his family crest in 1550.[29] Turkeys were certainly familiar enough by 1541 to warrant mention in English sumptuary laws of that year.[30] Skeletal remains uncovered during archaeological excavations in London also support the finding that turkey was consumed there from the sixteenth century on.[31] The bird was almost immediately adopted by the aristocratic and gentry classes, and soon turkey farms proliferated throughout England. Smith states that by 1577, English farmers kept huge flocks of turkeys, which they drove to market like cattle.[32] As most turkey farms were located in East Anglia, and as wagons would not carry many birds, turkeys needed to be walked to market in London by "turkey merchants." To prevent the birds flying away, one of their wings was cut, and to protect their feet they wore little boots. Hundreds of thousands would be transported to market in this manner during turkey season, in what must have been an astonishing spectacle. Turkeys continued to be driven to market by foot until the mid-nineteenth century, when railroads took over transportation.[33]

Given the established role of large roasted fowl on the English Christmas table, it was only natural that as turkeys rose in popularity, they assumed their place at the feast. In 1573, Thomas Tusser referred to turkey as being a common part of the English Christmas table, so their association with Christmas appears to have been made quite early.[34] Interestingly, a close analysis of court records from early modern London indicates that turkeys were also more likely to be stolen around Christmas than at other times, highlighting their abundance during this season, as well as the fact that they were coveted festive goods.[35] On 23 December 1660, Samuel Pepys noted that he received "a great turkey" from an old friend, Charles Carter, highlighting again that it had become a Christmas staple.[36] In that same year, Robert May published his Christmas menu, included above, in which turkey was served roasted and stuck with cloves.[37] A poem by John Gay, originally published in 1727, highlights that turkey was widespread at Christmas tables by this time:

But man, curs'd man, on Turkeys preys,
And Christmas shortens all our days.
Sometimes with oysters we combine
Sometimes assist with savoury chine;

From low peasant to the lord,
The Turkey Smokes on every board.[38]

By the late eighteenth century, the custom of giving employees turkeys at Christmas was well established,[39] but this tradition may have begun much earlier, and they were clearly common gifts during the festive season. Although turkey was clearly a Christmas favorite, until the nineteenth century it remained just one of many meats and dishes enjoyed as part of the twelve-day feast. For example, on Twelfth Night in 1745, Nicholas Peacock, a farmer from county Limerick in Ireland, was served "a rump of beef pork and petatoes a puding and roast torkey aftr wch we drank sidr and whiskey till late I gott home by night fall."[40] During the Victorian period the turkey became, once and for all, the centerpiece of the Christmas table for comfortable families. Whereas in earlier periods it was one of multiple dishes and meats presented, as illustrated in Robert May's menu, in the nineteenth

"The Compliments of the Season."
Illustrated London News, 16 December 1871. Courtesy of Bridgeman Images.

century it became the iconic focal point of a highly codified meal.[41] In the words of Isabella Beeton, writing in 1861, "A noble dish is a turkey, roast or boiled. A Christmas dinner, with the middle classes of this empire, would scarcely be a Christmas dinner without its turkey."[42] Its official endorsement as the centerpiece of the British Christmas table came in 1851 when the royal family ate their first Christmas turkey, replacing their traditional swan.[43]

The turkey's significance on the Victorian English Christmas table is highlighted in Dickens's *A Christmas Carol*. Upon waking up on Christmas morning full of the true spirit of the season, Scrooge urgently seeks to buy the largest one he can as a last-minute gift for the hardworking Bob Cratchit. This is Scrooge's first act as a reformed man, and the following excerpt illustrates how central food is in Dickens's vision of Christmas:

"What's to-day, my fine fellow?" said Scrooge.

"To-day?" replied the boy. "Why, Christmas Day."

"It's Christmas Day!" said Scrooge to himself. "I haven't missed it. The Spirits have done it all in one night. They can do anything they like. Of course they can. Of course they can. Hallo, my fine fellow!"

"Hallo!" returned the boy.

"Do you know the Poulterer's, in the next street but one, at the corner?" Scrooge inquired.

"I should hope I did," replied the lad.

"An intelligent boy!" said Scrooge. "A remarkable boy! Do you know whether they've sold the prize Turkey that was hanging up there—Not the little prize Turkey: the big one?"

"What, the one as big as me?" returned the boy.

"What a delightful boy!" said Scrooge. "It's a pleasure to talk to him. Yes, my buck."

"It's hanging there now," replied the boy.

"Is it?" said Scrooge. "Go and buy it."

"Walk-er!" exclaimed the boy.

"No, no," said Scrooge, "I am in earnest. Go and buy it, and tell them to bring it here, that I may give them the direction where to take it. Come back with the man, and I'll give you a shilling. Come back with him in less than five minutes and I'll give you half-a-crown."

The boy was off like a shot. He must have had a steady hand at a trigger who could have got a shot off half so fast.

"I'll send it to Bob Cratchit's!" whispered Scrooge, rubbing his hands, and splitting with a laugh. "He shan't know who sends it. It's twice the size of Tiny Tim. Joe Miller never made such a joke as sending it to Bob's will be!"

The hand in which he wrote the address was not a steady one, but write it he did, somehow, and went down-stairs to open the street door, ready for the coming of the poulterer's man. As he stood there, waiting his arrival, the knocker caught his eye.

"I shall love it, as long as I live!" cried Scrooge, patting it with his hand. "I scarcely ever looked at it before. What an honest expression it has in its face. It's a wonderful knocker.—Here's the Turkey. Hallo! Whoop! How are you? Merry Christmas!"

It was a Turkey! He never could have stood upon his legs, that bird. He would have snapped them short off in a minute, like sticks of sealing-wax.

"Why, it's impossible to carry that to Camden Town," said Scrooge. "You must have a cab."

The chuckle with which he said this, and the chuckle with which he paid for the Turkey, and the chuckle with which he paid for the cab, and the chuckle with which he recompensed the boy, were only to be exceeded by the chuckle with which he sat down breathless in his chair again, and chuckled till he cried.[44]

Notwithstanding the triumph of turkey in well-to-do households, its expense meant that goose and even chicken remained the centerpiece of the British Christmas table for many middle- and working-class families until the mid-twentieth century.[45] Even securing one of these less prestigious birds was a challenge for many, and goose clubs became a popular way for poorer families in the Victorian period to do so. By paying a small portion of their wages in weekly installments over the year, even humble households could serve up a roast goose on Christmas Day, as Dickens illustrates in his description of the Cratchit family's meal, quoted at the beginning of this chapter. Over time, though, the turkey came to replace the goose as the preferred Christmas main for most British families.[46] Today, between 76 and 87 percent of families in the United Kingdom celebrate Christmas with a traditional roast turkey.[47] It is also popular in Ireland, as well as many parts of the Commonwealth and the United States, although the festive traditions of these places will be looked at in more detail later in the chapter.

Turkey Cookery

Although today most families simply oven-bake their stuffed birds at Christmas, turkey cooking techniques were considerably more varied in the past. During the sixteenth and seventeenth centuries turkeys were often roasted, sometimes being split down the back to ensure even cooking, as we see in the following late sixteenth-century recipe from *A Book of Cookrye*, which contains the earliest published English recipes for turkey:

> To bake Turky Fowles, Cleve your Turkye foule on the back, and bruse al the bones. Season it with Pepper groce beaten and salt, and put into it good store of Butter, he must have five houres baking.[48]

Parboiling was the most common method of cookery, though.[49] After the meat was parboiled it was baked or roasted briefly, ensuring that the flesh was moist and the skin browned and tasty. Thomas Dawson's recipe of 1587 has detailed directions for boning, parboiling, larding, and baking a turkey:

> To bake a Turkie and take out his bones. Take a fat Turkie, and after you haue scalded him and washed him cleane, lay him upon a faire cloth and alit him through out the backe, and when you haue taken out his garbage, then you must take out his bones so bare as you can, when you haue so done wash him cleane, then trusse him and pricke his backe together, and so haue a faire kettle of séething water and perboyle him a little, then take him vp that the water may runne cleane out from him, and when he is colde, season him with pepper and salt, and then pricke him with a fewe cloues in the brest, and also drawe him with larde if you like of it and when you haue made your coffin and laide your Turkie in it then you must put some butter in it and so close him vp in this sort you may bake a Goose, a Pheasant, or Capon.[50]

In grand Tudor style, after being boned, turkeys were sometimes stuffed with other birds. This technique is known as engastration, and it was associated with feasts such as Christmas because of the sheer opulence involved. The contemporary iteration of this dish is "turducken," where a chicken is stuffed inside a duck, which is stuffed inside a turkey. The turducken is said to have been created by Louisiana chef Paul Prudhomme, but it clearly has medieval and early modern predecessors.[51]

Gervase Markham included a large repertoire of turkey recipes in his collective works dating to the seventeenth century, as well as extensive advice on keeping turkeys. His book *The English Hus-wife* (1615) refers to the turkey's place in "great" and "humble feasts." As Smith has observed, this implies that they were common by 1615 but still considered special fare.[52] Markham includes recipes for cooking birds whole, as well as stews and sauces to accompany them, such as a gravy made with meat juices, onions, white wine, vinegar, breadcrumbs, cinnamon, sugar, and pepper.[53] The famous French chef La Varenne provides a recipe for a sauce to accompany turkey that shows a connection in terms of flavor profile to cranberry sauce, which was not commonly used by the British until relatively recently. La Varenne suggests making a sauce from raspberries, continuing an established European tradition of pairing roast fowl with tart fruit sauces.[54]

A final method of using turkey, which requires some comment because of its close connection to Christmas, is as an ingredient in a standing pie, where it was just one of many species included in a truly excessive spectacle. These large pies developed in the medieval period, and they were made with stiff, strong, hand-raised pastry that would hold its shape upon baking. Judith Flanders refers to one such Christmas pie made for the Salters' Company of the City of London in 1394. The pie reportedly contained pheasant, hare, capon, partridge, pigeon, rabbit, livers, hearts, kidneys, and meatballs, flavored with a rich mix of spices and mushrooms. This was encased in pastry shaped into a huge bird that was then baked and decorated with feathers.[55] Such pies were hugely popular throughout the medieval and early modern period, adored as much for the spectacle as for their rich and luxurious filling. Hannah Glasse includes a recipe for "A Yorkshire Christmas-Pye," which contains a boned turkey, goose, fowl, partridge, and pigeon, in her famous book *The Art of Cookery Made Plain and Easy*, first published in 1747:

To make a Yorkshire Christmas pie.

First make a good standing crust, let the wall and bottom be very thick; bone a turkey, a goose, a fowl, a partridge, and a pigeon. Season them all very well, take half an ounce of mace, half an ounce of nutmegs, a quarter of an ounce of cloves, and half an ounce of black pepper, all beat fine together, two large spoonfuls of salt, and then mix them together. Open the fowls all down the back, and bone them; first the pigeon, then the partridge, cover them; then the fowl, then the goose, and then the turkey, which must be large; season them all well first and lay them in the crust, so as it will look only like a whole turkey; then have a hare already eased (skinned), and wipe with a clean cloth. Cut it to pieces; that is, joint it; season it, and lay is as close as you can on one side; on the other side woodcocks, moor game and what sort of wild fowl you can get. Season them well, and lay them close; put at least four pounds of butter into the pie, then lay on your lid, which must be a very thick one and let it be well baked. It must have a very hot oven, and will take at least four hours.

This crust will take a bushel of flour. In this chapter you will see how to make it. These pies are often sent to London in a box as presents; therefore the walls must be well-built.[56]

It is also important to remember that until the twentieth century many families of more modest means, especially in urban areas, would not have had the facilities to cook these large birds at home. Birds and other joints of meat would often have been cooked in the local baker's oven. The scene of collecting the freshly baked goose on Christmas Day and the excitement for the Cratchit family is recalled by Dickens:

And now two smaller Cratchits, boy and girl, came tearing in, screaming that outside the baker's they had smelt the goose, and known it for their own; and basking in luxurious thoughts of sage-and-onion, these young Cratchits danced about the table, and exalted Master Peter Cratchit to the skies, while he (not proud, although his collars near choked him) blew the fire, until the slow potatoes bubbling up, knocked loudly at the saucepan-lid to be let out and peeled. . . . Master Peter and the two ubiquitous young Cratchits went to fetch the goose, with which they soon returned in high procession.[57]

Serving the Bird

Much ceremony has always been accorded to the carving of the Christmas turkey. Whereas many meats ceased to be carved at the table over the course of the postmedieval period, the ritual of carving the turkey was maintained, and this was an honor normally reserved for the man of the house. Mrs. Beeton wrote with respect to the Christmas turkey, "We can hardly imagine an object of greater envy than is presented by a respected portly pater-familias carving, at the season devoted to good cheer and general charity, his own fat turkey, and carving it well."[58] As carving such an enormous bird is no easy feat, many historical recipe books include advice on the best methods for doing so. Robert May's *The Accomplisht Cook; or, The Art and Mystery of Cookery* (1660) provides extensive directions for the carving of fowl, including turkey and goose. His directions are as follows:

To cut up a Turkey or Bustard.

Raise up the leg very fair, and open the joynt with the point of your knife, but take not off the leg; then lace down the breast with your knife on both sides, & open the breast pinion with the knife, but take not the pinion off; then raise up the merry-thought betwixt the breast bone, and the top of the merry-thought, lace down the flesh on both sides of the breast-bone, and raise up the flesh called the brawn, turn it outward upon both sides, but break it not, nor cut it not off; then cut off the wing pinion at the joynt next to the body, and stick on each side the pinion in the place where ye turned out the brawn, but cut off the sharp end of the Pinion, take the middle piece, and that will just fit the place.

You may cut up a capon or pheasant the same way, but of your capon cut not off the pinion, but in the place where you put the pinion of the turkey, you must put the gizard of your capon on each side half.[59]

A scene from Anthony Trollope's *Orley Farm* (1862) depicts the character Moulder ceremoniously carving the twenty-four-pound turkey. After it was carved, the meat was cut off and soaked in gravy before it was served to the awaiting guests.[60] Dickens also describes the moment the much-anticipated Christmas goose is carved at the Cratchits' table, in this instance by Mrs. Cratchit:

At last the dishes were set on, and grace was said. It was succeeded by a breathless pause, as Mrs. Cratchit, looking slowly all along the carving-knife, prepared to plunge it in the breast; but when she did, and when the long-expected gush of stuffing issued forth, one murmur of delight arose all round the board, and even Tiny Tim, excited by the two young Cratchits, beat on the table with the handle of his knife, and feebly cried Hurrah![61]

Once carved, the Cratchits' goose was served with mashed potatoes, apple sauce, gravy, and sage and onion stuffing. Today, regardless of the species of bird served, no Christmas meal would be complete without potatoes, commonly served mashed and roasted. The other sides mentioned by Dickens also remain common, with every family having their own secret stuffing recipes, which often use sausage meat to moisten and flavor the bird. Brussels sprouts, not mentioned by Dickens, are relative newcomers to the meal, but they are now an indispensable part of Christmas dinner, at least in Britain and Ireland. Although they are loathed by many, from the nineteenth century on they took their place as a traditional side dish, and Christmas would now not be Christmas without them for many families. These small cabbages likely ended up as a Christmas dish simply because they are in season at this time of year and actually improve in flavor after frost.[62] Relatively little is known about the history of brussels sprouts. While they may have been grown in Belgium in the medieval period, it is likely that they were not cultivated in England until the late eighteenth century. In 1845, Eliza Acton published the first printed recipe for brussels sprouts.[63] Today they are often served with butter, chestnuts, or bacon.

Turkey on the American Christmas Table

Perhaps unsurprisingly, given the native origins of the animal, and the influence of English cookery on early colonial food practices, turkey also dominated American Christmas tables until relatively recently. European colonists brought both the tradition of enjoying large roast fowl at Christmas and their domesticated turkey stock with them to North America.[64] As wild turkey populations had been all but destroyed in the early colonial period, the turkey stock that became a mainstay of the American diet were actually descended from imported European stock, and the breed had changed considerably since its first Atlantic crossing. These imported European domesticated birds then bred with wild birds in America to produce new varieties, including the broad-breasted bronze.[65]

In 1847, Eliza Leslie published *The Lady's Receipt-Book: A Useful Companion for Large and Small Families*, which included a series of prescriptive set Christmas menus for American households. Leslie suggested a "plain Christmas dinner" for those of more humble means, as well as more elaborate menus. The "plain dinner" consisted of a roast turkey, cranberry sauce, boiled ham, turnips, beets, winter squash, and mince pies.[66] Here we see a Christmas dinner that is remarkably close to that consumed in

Britain at the time, albeit with some American twists in terms of the side dishes. The more elaborate Christmas dinner suggested by Leslie also included turkey, but it was accompanied by a range of elaborate dishes such as mock turtle soup, stewed rockfish, roasted venison with currant jelly, roast geese with applesauce, French oyster pie, fricasseed chickens, potato snow, parsnips, beer, winter squash, cold slaw, plum pudding, mince pies, orange tarts, cream coconut pudding, Spanish blancmange, apple jelly, and vanilla ice cream.[67]

The tradition of the Christmas turkey developed its own set of rituals in America. Among these was the turkey shoot, which became particularly important in the nineteenth century. Smith explains that turkeys would be tied to targets, tethered to logs, partially buried in snow, or secured in a sort of ministocks, with their head trapped through a hole in a plank of wood. Shooters would then try to hit the head or the exposed flesh in order to win the bird. The Christmas turkey shoot became so culturally iconic that multiple mid-nineteenth-century artists depicted the scene. After the Civil War, animal rights advocates became increasingly critical of turkey shoots, and the tradition declined. According to Smith, it covertly continues today, although it is no longer directly connected with Christmas. Turkey raffles and other contests were also popular traditions in America at Christmas, especially for poorer communities.[68] Like the British goose clubs, these events provided a way for struggling families to secure a Christmas bird.

Despite this early use of turkey on the American Christmas table, over time it became a more discretionary element of the meal there, in a way that it never has in Britain. Cathy Kaufman argues that in the aftermath of the Civil War, and as immigration increased during the second half of the nineteenth century, the turkey-centered Christmas meal became a unifying experience, but not one that was ever entirely embraced. Kaufman has suggested that the consumption of turkey at Christmas came to be influenced by class. Whereas the lower socioeconomic orders maintained the more traditional consumption of turkey, elites began to opt for game and other more prestigious delicacies.[69] Alternatively, Smith argues that the decline of the Christmas turkey in America was primarily due to the increasing prominence of Thanksgiving. With the national "Turkey Day" being celebrated just weeks before Christmas, many families opt for alternatives, and the bird's association with the festival is somewhat diminished.[70] Christmas turkey is still a popular choice for many Stateside, but it is not nearly as dominant as it is in Britain.

WILD BOAR AND PORK

After turkey, pork is undoubtedly the meat most commonly associated with Christmas in the English-speaking world. For many families, the Christmas ham is as important as the turkey, and the consumption of pork at this time of year has a long and fascinating history. The slaughter of pigs traditionally took place in winter. Not only were they at their fattest at this time, but the colder weather also meant that the flesh would not spoil as it was processed and cured.[71] Like fowl, though, the traditional consumption of pigs—or rather boar—in winter may also have had a sacrificial function, originating in pre-Christian fertility rituals.[72] According to folklorists, boar played a special role in the midwinter feast for Germanic peoples, and for the Norse specifically.[73] Freyr and his twin sister Freyja were the Norse god and goddess of fertility. Each twin famously rode a beloved boar; Freyja commanded her great battle swine, Hildisvíni, while Freyr rode his prized golden boar, Gullinbursti. Because of Freyr's particular association with these animals, and as god of fertility and the sun, a boar may have been sacrificed to him during the winter solstice festival, in the hope that he would bless the New Year. Although most sources relating to such rituals are Norse, it is possible that the Anglo-Saxons had similar traditions given their shared Germanic heritage.[74] The Norse and Anglo-Saxons also believed that the boar's head had protective powers. This is evidenced by weaponry and armor with boar-head emblems, such as a helmet with a war crest found at Sutton Hoo, and by descriptions of these objects in epic poetry such as *Beowulf*.[75]

The cultural significance of the animal, and its relationship with fertility, explains the origins of one of British history's most iconic Christmas dishes: the boar's head. References to this dish first appear in medieval England, but it is likely that the boar's head ritual began during the Anglo-Saxon period.[76] Despite these early, likely pre-Christian origins, popular folklore in Britain has it that the boar's head festival originated at Queen's College, Oxford. The legend is that when a scholar was confronted by an angry wild boar on his way to midnight mass on Christmas Eve, he shoved his volume on

Aristotle down the throat of the animal, choking and killing it, intelligence and wisdom triumphing over brute strength. That night the boar's head was decorated and paraded into the hall for all to see.[77] The procession still takes place in Queen's College to this day, as well as in other institutions, where the boar's head, music, and pageantry continue this ancient tradition.

In terms of the actual dish, although it was made to look like a roasted boar's head, the preparation was significantly more complicated. To make a boar's head, the flesh and skin needed to be removed. This meat was then cured and combined with other cuts and pieces of pork. The resulting mixture was bound into the shape of the boar's head and simmered. After being cooked, it was blackened so that it resembled a wild boar's head as closely as possible. The dish was then decorated with sprigs of rosemary and bay leaves, but sometimes adorned further with gold leaf and colorful paper.[78] The use of rosemary in the decoration is symbolic. The herb held special religious significance, as its aroma is said to have come when from baby Jesus's swaddling clothes were hung on a bush to dry and its purple flowers first bloomed when touched by Mary's veil.[79]

The shoulder meat of the boar was also commonly served at Christmas as a dish called brawn, which was particularly popular during the Elizabethan period. The flesh was boiled until it was soft, and it was then placed in barrels full of pickling liquid. This was left until Christmas, when it was ready to be sliced and served. Like the more impressive boar's head, dishes of brawn were often elaborately decorated with sprigs of yew, gorse, bay leaves, and rosemary. These were sometimes frosted or gilded with gold or silver leaf, and intricate designs were achieved with jelly, carved citrus fruits, and barberries.[80]

When the time came to serve the boar's head, it was carried into the hall with much pomp and ceremony. A description of the Christmas feast of Henry II's court, in 1170, states that the boar's head arrived into the hall accompanied by the sound of trumpets.[81] Indeed, it had its own carol that was sung by diners to mark the occasion. "The Boar's Head Carol" was probably written before the sixteenth century[82] but was first printed in 1521, in Wynkyn de Worde's *Christmasse Carolles.*[83] There are multiple versions of the song, but the original published one is as follows:

The bore's head in hande bring I
With garlandes gay and rosemary.

I pray you all sing merely
Qui estis in convivio
The bore's head, I understande,
Is chefe servyce in this lande.
Loke wherever it be fande
Servite cum Cantinco
Be gladde, lords, both more and lasse,
For this hatth ordeyned our stewarde,
To chere you all this Christmasse,
The bores head with mustards![84]

The modern version of the carol is still sung at Queen's College during the annual procession. Like other versions written over the centuries, the college's lyrics differ slightly, but all iterations of the carol focus on the procession and presentation of the decorated boar's head with its garlands of herbs. After the ceremonial entry, the boar's head was carved and served in slices, with mustard as a common accompaniment.

Poems, carols, and culinary sources indicate that the boar's head was still popular in the eighteenth and nineteenth centuries. William King's 1709 poem *The Art of Cookery* describes the entrance of the decorated boar's head, or "brawner's head":

At Christmas time, be careful of your fame,
See the old tenants' table be the same;
Then if you would send up the brawner's head,
Sweet rosemary and bays around it spread.
His foaming tusks let some large pippins grace,
Or 'midst these thun'dring spears an orange place,
Sauce, like himself, offensive to its foes.
The roguish mustard, dangerous to the nose
Sack and well-spic'd Hippocras the wine
Wassail the Bowl with ancient Ribbands fine,
Porridge with Plumbs and Turkeys with Chine.[85]

Isabella Beeton also described the bringing in of the boar's head at Christmas in her famous nineteenth-century work, noting the mandatory use of a

"Bringing in the Boar's Head."
Illustrated by Henry Stacey Marks, 1871. Courtesy of Bridgeman Images.

silver platter for serving and the ongoing association of the ritual with institutions such as colleges and inns of court.[86]

Even when the boar's head started to wane, elite Victorians found creative ways to continue the spectacle with the novelty "boar's head cake." Made famous by Queen Victoria's chef, Charles Elmé Francatelli, preparing the novelty cake was a considerable undertaking and would not have been possible in the average domestic kitchen. Francatelli included the directions for making the boar's head cake in *The Royal English and Foreign Confectioner* (1862), along with a detailed chromolithograph of the beast. After preparing the layers of savoy cake, sticking them together with apricot jam, and allowing them to set, Francatelli instructed the reader to take a sharp knife and carve the block into the shape of a wild boar's head. Confectioner's paste and gum paste were then used to shape the ears and tusks, respectively. The mouth was hollowed out and colored with scarlet royal icing, and two nostrils were scooped out of the snout. The cake was then given a thin coat of red currant jelly and covered entirely with chocolate icing. The eyes were formed with white gum paste and subsequently painted and coated in boiled sugar to add shine. When almost finished, the boar's head was placed on an ornamental stand that had also been covered in confectioner's paste, and then further decorated with confectionary fruits, truffles, and cocks' combs. Finally, just before service, the throat end of the head was to be stuffed with pink and white ice cream made to resemble layers of flesh and fat.[87]

Today, the boar's head festival is still marked in certain colleges and institutions, but the dish itself no longer features on your average Christmas table. Still, we find traces of the ritual in other ways throughout the twentieth century and to the present. A Yule boar, made from bread or a cookie, stands on Danish and Swedish tables throughout the Christmas period today, and while this is outside the geographical and cultural focus of this book, it demonstrates the ancient connection between British and Scandinavian Christmas rituals relating to boars.[88] In the southern US states, a New Year's Day good luck ritual involves a slice of hog jowl being served with black-eyed peas.[89] Peas and beans also have a long history of being associated with good luck rituals at this time of year, as chapter 4 will discuss in more detail. Most important, each Christmas, many families enjoy a glazed Christmas ham alongside the turkey as part of their main meal. This tradition is popular in Britain, Ireland, and the Commonwealth, as well as in Scandinavia, where, again, we see a shared culinary inheritance in this particular area. As discussed briefly in chapter 1, during World War II people formed pig clubs, where multiple families would contribute scraps of food throughout the year in order to receive a share of the meat at Christmas. These clubs reportedly produced an extra four million pounds of pork.[90] This highlights the significance of this particular part of the festival, which people would try to preserve in times of hardship wherever possible.[91] In Australia, where the heat of the season lends itself more to cold cuts of meat, the ham, traditionally bedecked with rings of tinned pineapple and glacé cherries, reigns supreme as one of the most important elements of the Christmas table. During the nineteenth century, grocers advertised their imported hams to colonials homesick for Britain and the wintery Christmas of their childhood.[92] Mary Thomas, an early settler in Adelaide, recalled the first Christmas celebrated in the settlement. She explained that they did their best to mark the occasion with Christmas food, including Christmas pudding and a ham. This was complemented by a parrot pie, presumably a take on the traditional Christmas pies discussed above.[93]

BEEF

Given the cultural significance of roast beef in Britain, and the meat-heavy nature of the medieval and Tudor Christmas feast, it is unsurprising that beef has always had a central place on the Christmas table. Countless sources from the medieval period to the present demonstrate that it has consistently featured in Christmas feasts, even if it does not garner the same attention as the centerpiece turkey and next-in-line ham. Medieval household accounts bear witness to an extraordinary of number of bovine casualties in preparation for Christmas. As we have seen, in 1399 Richard II reportedly slaughtered a mere twenty-six oxen for his guests.[94]

Nothing typified a traditional display of British hospitality more than a succulent roast sirloin. Robert May's 1660 Christmas bill of fare, detailed earlier in this chapter, included several beef dishes, such as the much celebrated "chine of beef, or sirloin roast."[95] The pride of place given to the sirloin roast continued over the following centuries. Ivan Day describes the roasting of a full baron of beef—that is, the entire hind part of an oxen—in the Windsor Castle kitchen during Victoria's reign. This enormous cut of roasted beef was displayed on the dining room sideboard, along with a large game pie, a boar's head, a shield of brawn, and a woodcock pie.[96] Traditionally, plum pudding was served as an accompaniment to roast beef, so that it could soak up the rich meat juices. This combination of roast beef and plum pudding became favored celebratory fare throughout the Empire. As the following chapter will show in more detail, no two dishes represented British identity more succinctly than these did. Of course, dishes such as plum pudding and mince pies were also originally beef based, as chapters 3 and 5 will discuss in more detail. Even when turkey had well and truly established its place at the table, beef continued to feature alongside the bird. In 1862,

"Christmas at Windsor Castle: Roasting the Baron of Beef for the Christmas Banquet."
Illustrated Times, 3 January 1857. Courtesy of Bridgeman Images.

when Anthony Trollope published *Orley Farm*, he described both an enormous turkey and a "mountain of beef" at Christmas.[97] Despite the increasing status of turkey as a festive food, prior to its widespread availability in the mid-twentieth century, roast beef was the favored Christmas main for most households that could afford it.

For many British families today, roast beef remains a firm favorite at Christmas, but it is clear that during the course of the twentieth century it lost precedence to the turkey. This is a shift that is difficult to chart or quantify over time, but it is clear that, despite its persistent presence over the centuries, beef did not become an indispensable part of the modern set Christmas meal in the nineteenth century in the way that turkey and ham did. It is unclear why this is the case, but it may be that roast beef holds such broad cultural significance in Britain as an iconic national dish that it could

"Her Majesty the Queen's Sideboard at Christmas Time."
Graphic, 28 December 1889, 784.

not be a designated Christmas food in the way that turkey could. Its sheer importance meant that it could never be tied to Christmas alone.

Over the Irish Sea the story is different, though, where a dish called spiced beef is a delicacy and designated specialty of Christmas. Primarily associated with Cork, spiced beef is a variety of corned or salted beef. A cut such as silverside or flank is rubbed with salt, saltpeter, brown sugar, juniper berries, and a mix of spices. These commonly include black pepper, cinnamon, cloves, ginger, mace, nutmeg, and pimenton. Once the salting process is completed, the beef is boiled for several hours. Flavorings such as celery, carrots, bay leaves, and Guinness can be added to the cooking liquid. The beef may be eaten hot, but it can also be pressed and eaten cold.

Spiced, salted beefs like this were not unknown in Britain as well in the past. Elizabeth David refers to a similar recipe called hunting beef that has existed in England for at least three hundred years.[98] Other later English recipe books, such as Isabella Beeton's famous work first published in 1861, include variations of the recipe. Beeton's is significantly different, though, advising that the meat be baked rather than boiled.[99]

Despite this shared tradition, a unique set of conditions, related to Ireland's status as a colony in the early modern period and its place in the Empire in the eighteenth and nineteenth centuries, led to the development of this specialty dish. The introduction of the Cattle Acts in 1663 and 1667, which prevented the live export of cattle from Ireland, coupled with the development of the sugar plantations in the West Indies and their need for a steady supply of food, led to the establishment of a commercial corned beef industry in Ireland. Cork City became the major center for this development. As the Empire expanded further over the eighteenth and nineteenth centuries, Irish corned beef provisioned the British navy and helped it to establish colonies across the globe.[100] Today, spiced beef remains strongly associated with Cork City and Christmas Eve. Máirtín Mac Con Iomaire and Pádraic Óg Gallagher discuss annual spiced beef sales in the famous central market in Cork City, the English Market. They refer to one butcher named Murphy who reported that while he sells only small amounts of spiced beef weekly throughout the year, during a ten-day period at Christmas he sells two thousand pounds.[101]

Spiced beef was served for dinner on Nollaig na mBan (Little Women's Christmas) in James Joyce's "The Dead." Nollaig na mBan was held on Twelfth Day (6 January), or the Feast of the Epiphany, and was traditionally a day when women would rest following the hectic work of Christmas. Joyce refers to the round of spiced beef sitting alongside the goose and ham:

A fat brown goose lay at one end of the table, and at the other end, on a bed of creased paper strewn with sprigs of parsley, lay a great ham, stripped of its outer skin and peppered over with crust crumbs, a neat paper frill round its shin, and beside this was a round of spiced beef.[102]

FISH AND SEAFOOD

While fish and seafood have an important place in the Christmas rituals of many countries, they assume only a supporting role in the modern British Christmas. In many parts of Continental Europe, but primarily Catholic countries, Christmas Eve is celebrated with various fish dishes, as it is the last day of the Advent fast. In modern Britain, though, the culinary emphasis is placed largely on the meat-oriented feast of Christmas Day itself, with Christmas Eve having few culinary rituals or associations of note.

This was not always the case in Britain, though. Prior to the Reformation, fish was prominent on Christmas Eve, being the end of Advent.[103] The late fourteenth-century chivalric romance *Sir Gawain and the Green Knight* refers to fish being served in Bertilak's castle on Christmas Eve. It states that there were "many kinds of fish, some baked in bread, some broiled on the coals, some boiled, some in sauces savoured with spices."[104] Lamprey eels were a particular species associated with the medieval English Christmas. The City of Gloucester traditionally sent the monarch a lamprey pie each year. When the city failed to deliver the dish to King John (1167–1216), he fined it the sum of 40 marks. The tradition of sending the monarch a lamprey pie each Christmas was maintained until 1836, when the cost of sourcing the increasingly rare lamprey became too prohibitive. Hannah Woolley included the following recipe for a lamprey pie in *The Queen-like Closet*:

> Take your Lamprey and gut him, and take away the black string in the back, wash him very well, and dry him, and season him with Nutmeg, Pepper and Salt, then lay him into your Pie in pieces with Butter in the bottom, and some Shelots and Bay Leaves and more Butter, so close it and bake it, and fill it up with melted Butter, and keep it cold, and serve it in with some Mustard and Sugar.[105]

As a delicacy, the lamprey's place on the Christmas table was maintained until the early nineteenth century. Mrs. Delany, a member of the Protestant Ascendancy in late eighteenth-century Ireland, gave friends and relations potted lampreys for Christmas.[106]

Another British Christmas fish pie that requires some comment is Cornwall's stargazy pie. The pie and its festival are most strongly associated with the village of Mousehole, Cornwall, where they are said to have originated. The pie is traditionally made for a festival held on 23 December, known as Tom Bawcock's Eve. This commemorates the night when a fisherman by the name of Tom Bawcock braved a fearsome storm and returned with a huge haul of fish, saving the village from near-certain starvation. Popular folklore has it that the entire catch was then baked into a huge stargazy pie, containing seven types of fish. Today, stargazy pie consists of a pastry base filled with whole pilchards or other oily fish such as herring and mackerel.

The critical feature of the pie is that the intact heads of the fish poke up through the pastry, appearing to stare at the heavens. This is said to be the origins of the name "stargazy." On 23 December every year, a huge stargazy pie is paraded through the village, accompanied by a procession of hand-made lanterns.[107]

After the Reformation, fish remained a common part of British Christmas Eve and Christmas Day bills of fare, despite its ritual function having diminished. In addition to lampreys, oysters were traditional Christmas foods until relatively recently.[108] Even today fish and shellfish are consumed at Christmas. Prawn cocktails kick-start the meal in many households, and smoked salmon has become something of a Christmas favorite over the last few decades in Britain and Ireland.[109] These foods no longer have a ritual or even symbolic function. They are now enjoyed as festive foods because they are seen as special and celebratory, but they are not an integral part of a codified Christmas meal in the way that turkey, ham, and plum pudding are.

If we compare the place of seafood on the British Christmas table with other European countries, we see a marked difference. Given the limitations of this book, we cannot explore these variations in detail here, but it is important to recognize that Continental traditions helped shape how Christmas was marked among immigrant communities in the United States profoundly.[110] One of the most iconic Christmas fish traditions among a migrant community is undoubtedly the annual lutefisk dinner marked by Americans and Canadians from Scandinavian, and particularly Norwegian, backgrounds. Lutefisk is made by soaking dried whitefish, commonly cod, in water and lye (sodium hydroxide). Popular legend has it that lutefisk originated when Viking fishermen hung cod to dry on birch racks. The racks were partially burned down when neighbors attacked, but a storm struck and extinguished the fire. The fish then lay in a pool of water and birch ash before being discovered by some hungry Vikings. Another legend holds that St. Patrick attempted to poison Viking raiders in Ireland with lye-soaked fish, but they survived and proclaimed it a delicacy. Given that St. Patrick lived centuries before the Vikings came to Ireland, this story is problematic, but it certainly makes for a good origin myth.[111]

Lutefisk is now enjoyed at Christmastime, although not necessarily on Christmas day. It is commonly eaten in regions of America and Canada settled by Scandinavians, particularly around the American Midwest.

Madison, Minnesota, is the self-proclaimed lutefisk capital of the world. Lutefisk still retains a place in the Christmas festival in Scandinavia, but, as is commonly the case, it holds more significance among immigrant communities than it does in its countries of origin. Among these communities the tradition of lutefisk dinners began. Minnesota's Mount Olivet Lutheran Church has hosted a lutefisk dinner since 1929. This is attended by fifteen hundred people annually, who feast on a range of Scandinavian dishes, including twelve hundred pounds of lutefisk. The dish is generally served with potatoes, vegetables, lefse (a Norwegian flatbread), and melted butter or white sauce.

Today, it is a dish that Scandinavian Americans love to hate. The pungency of the dish gave rise to the humorous festive song "O Lutefisk," sung to the tune of "O Christmas Tree":

O Lutefisk, O Lutefisk, how fragrant your aroma,
O Lutefisk, O Lutefisk, you put me in a coma.
You smell so strong, you look like glue,
You taste just like an overshoe,
But lutefisk, come Saturday,
I tink I eat you anyvay.
O Lutefisk, O lutefisk, I put you in the doorvay.
I wanted you to ripen up just like they do in Norvay.
A dog came by and sprinkled you.
I hit him with my overshoe.
O lutefisk, now I suppose
I'll eat you while I hold my nose.
O Lutefisk, O lutefisk, how well I do remember.
On Christmas Eve how we'd receive our big treat of December.
It wasn't turkey or fried ham.
It wasn't even pickled Spam.
My mother knew there was no risk
In serving buttered lutefisk.
O Lutefisk, O lutefisk, now everyone discovers
That lutefisk and lefse make Norwegians better lovers.
Now all the world can have a ball.
You're better than that Geritol.

O lutefisk, with brennevin [Norwegian brandy]
You make me feel like Errol Flynn.
O Lutefisk, O lutefisk, you have a special flavor.
O Lutefisk, O lutefisk, all good Norvegians savor.
That slimy slab we know so well
Identified by ghastly smell.
O Lutefisk, O lutefisk,
Our loyalty won't waver.[112]

The Feast of the Seven Fishes is an Italian American festival held on Christmas Eve that, like the lutefisk dinner, shows just how many complex cultural strands make up the contemporary American Christmas meal. Also known as *La Vigilia*, the meal marks the wait for Christ's birth at midnight. Although it undoubtedly has roots in Italy, particularly in Sicily and the south, like the lutefisk dinner, it now has a greater following among immigrant communities than it does in its country of origin. The Feast of the Seven Fishes includes a minimum of seven fish dishes, although some families will serve more, often twelve in honor of the Apostles. Species commonly included are anchovies, whiting, lobster, sardines, baccalà (dried salted cod), smelts, eels, squid, octopus, shrimp, mussels, and clams. It is not entirely clear what the meaning of the number seven is exactly, but multiple theories have been put forward to suggest what the theological implications may be. The most plausible is that it relates to the seven sacraments, but there are other theories suggesting that it should be seen as God's number. From a food studies perspective, it is important to note that there is a crossover with the stargazy pie ritual from Cornwall that must also contain seven species of fish.

Moving across the globe, to the Antipodes, we can see the development of new seafood-based Christmas traditions in another of Britain's former colonies. Throughout the nineteenth century and for most of the twentieth, Australians clung to a traditional British Christmas meal, based on turkey (although chicken was commonly served in its place), ham, and plum pudding. Colonial Australians often ate their Christmas dinner as a picnic, enjoying the warm weather, and they adapted elements of the meal, substituting ingredients as necessary. For example, in 1804 one hundred native swans were caught and cooked for the convicts' Christmas dinner and members of the newly established penal colony.[113] Notwithstanding the use of a native bird, the basic structure of the meal—roast meats and pudding—was maintained. Even at an early stage the inappropriateness of this was remarked upon, though. Noted Australian food historian Colin Bannerman has commented that the debate surrounding whether Australians should hold fast to English tradition or embrace their environment by serving a cold meal has "been going on for more than a century and still gets a run in the media each year."[114]

It was not until the late twentieth century that things started to change. A growing sense of national pride, identity, and independence, coupled with the increasing influence of a more multicultural population, meant that many Australian families started to embrace a festive meal that was not just more appropriate for the weather but also a celebration of both the season and its abundant fresh summer produce. Real change began in the 1980s and gathered pace in the 1990s, so that, today, the seafood barbecue is quintessential Christmas fare for many Australian families. A range of fish and shellfish are served, but the most popular is undoubtedly prawns. These may be served precooked to be peeled by diners at the table—generally accompanied by an ice-cold beer or white wine. Others barbecue them, and recipes are increasingly influenced by the flavors of multicultural Australia and tastes of Asia. To keep up with the demand, for the last nineteen years the Sydney Fish Market has hosted the seafood marathon, staying open for thirty-six hours from 23 December until 5:00 p.m. on Christmas Eve. During this time more than one hundred thousand people flood through the markets, buying 750 metric tons of seafood, including two hundred metric tons of prawns and seventy thousand oysters.[115]

3

PUDDINGS
AND DESSERTS

Now bring us some figgy pudding,
Now bring us some figgy pudding,
Now bring us some figgy pudding,
And bring some out here.
Good tidings we bring
To you and your kin;
We wish you a merry Christmas
And a happy New Year.

—Excerpt from traditional Christmas carol
"We Wish You a Merry Christmas"

In the true spirit of excess, all the roast meat of the Christmas feast has traditionally been followed up with a serious hit of sugar. As the following three chapters will demonstrate, Christmas delivers sweet calorific goodness in abundance. Chapters 4 and 5 will discuss cakes, cookies, and confectionery, but this chapter is exclusively devoted to Christmas desserts—that is, what is served immediately after all that turkey and ham, delivering the final knockout punch that sends us into a food-induced coma for the rest of the evening.

The majority of the chapter will focus on the evolution of what is undoubtedly the most iconic of all festive desserts, Christmas pudding. Featured on countless Christmas greeting cards, other than the decorated tree and a present-laden Santa Claus, no image immediately says Christmas more than a jolly round pudding dripping with brandy sauce, topped with a sprig of holly. Unlike the main course, where the turkey reigns supreme but is closely followed by its beloved supporting act, the Christmas ham, there is simply no contest at the dessert course in Britain and Ireland. The award goes to the Christmas pudding, and the nearest runner-up, the sherry trifle, is a long way off. In the New World, though, the story is a little more complex. While the Christmas pudding has had a proud tradition in the Antipodes, it does not occupy the same iconic position on the American Christmas table, where there is no single designated Christmas dessert. The reasons behind this divergence will be explored here, as they tell us a great deal about the role of Christmas in each nation's psyche.

THE EVOLUTION OF THE CHRISTMAS PUDDING

Although the Christmas pudding as we know it today came into being in the nineteenth century, the recipe is on the same evolutionary tree as its distant relative, the medieval plum pottage. A pottage was quite simply a dish that was cooked in a pot. There was a countless variety of pottages made with different ingredients and techniques, ranging from humble everyday fare to luxury, high-status dishes.[1] The term "plum" specifically refers to dried prunes, but from an early period it was used to describe any type of dried fruit. The dish commonly contained chopped beef or mutton, onions, root vegetables, dried fruits, and spices, and it was thickened to a soup-like consistency with oatmeal and breadcrumbs.[2] The combination of meat, with expensive goods from the East such as dried fruits and spices, lent the plum pottage its luxury, celebratory status. Early fifteenth-century pottage recipes provide traces of dishes that show a similar flavor profile to the later Christmas pudding. Food historian C. Anne Wilson identified one such recipe named "Stewet Beef to Potage," which was not associated with Christmas exclusively at this stage but would have been enjoyed as a celebratory or dish for the elite classes more generally. It instructed the cook to seethe beef in water and wine with onion, herbs, bread, "saunders" or sandalwood, cinnamon ("canel"), mace, raisins ("raisynges"), and currants ("corance").[3]

By the mid-seventeenth century, plum pottage (or porridge, as it had come to be known) was sufficiently associated with Christmas that it was a target for the Puritans during the years of the Commonwealth, as we will discuss in more detail later in this chapter.[4] Despite the Puritans' best efforts, though, on Christmas Day in 1662 Samuel Pepys recorded in his diary that he celebrated with "a mess of brave plum porridge and a roasted pullet for dinner."[5] By the early eighteenth century, plum porridge appears to have been a widespread Christmas dish. In 1728, the French traveler César de Saussure stated that

> everyone from the King to the artisan eats soup and Christmas pies. The soup is called Christmas porridge, and is a dish few foreigners find to their taste. I must describe it to you for it will amuse you. You must stew dried raisins, plums and spice in broth, rich people add wine and others beer, and it is a great treat for English people, but I assure you, not for me . . . you never taste these dishes except for two or three days before and after Christmas, and I cannot tell you the reason why.[6]

So we see that by the eighteenth century plum porridge was eaten by a wide section of English society during Christmas. In 1736, Queen Caroline dined on "plum broth" as part of the first course of her Christmas banquet,[7] but, as de Saussure states, more humble adaptations of this now exclusively festive dish were prepared by a broad range of households as well. Hannah Glasse, the doyenne of domestic cooks in the mid-eighteenth century, naturally included a recipe for "Plum Porridge for Christmas" in *The Art of Cookery*.

To make plum-porridge for Christmas

Take a leg and shin of beef. Put them into eight gallons of water, and boil them till they are very tender, and when the broth is strong strain it out; wipe the pot and put in the broth again; then slice six penny loaves thin, cut off the top and bottom, put some of the liquor to it, cover it up and let it stand a quarter of an hour, boil it and strain it, and then put it into your pot. Let it boil a quarter of an hour, then put in five pounds of currants clean washed and picked; let them boil a little, and put in five pounds of raisins of the sun, stoned, and two pounds of prunes, and let them boil till they swell; then put in three quarters of an ounce of mace, half an ounce of cloves, two nutmegs, all of them beat fine, and mix it with a little liquor cold, and put them in a very little while, and take off the pot; then put in three pounds of sugar, a little salt, a quart of sack, a quart of claret, and the juice of two or three lemons. You may thicken with sago instead of bread, if you please; pour them into earthen pans, and keep them for use. You must boil two pounds of prunes in a quart of water till they are tender, and strain them into the pot when it is boiling.[8]

Plum porridge continued to be made in the early nineteenth century, but it is clear that by the late Georgian period the popularity of these pottages had waned. One of the last published recipes for plum porridge appeared in *The Cook & Housewife's Manual* (1826), by Margaret Dods.[9] As these amorphous dishes declined in popularity, though, the new boiled plum pudding was in the ascendancy. For a period of time, both dishes appeared in cook books, each fulfilling a different role. One reflected England's culinary past, the other its future. For example, Hannah Glasse provides a recipe for a boiled plum pudding a few pages after the Christmas porridge recipe cited above. Her boiled pudding makes no reference to Christmas, and we know that it was originally eaten alongside roast beef at many a celebratory meal, whereas the more traditional porridge is explicitly connected to the festival.

The story of these new solid, boiled puddings began with the popularization of the pudding cloth in the seventeenth century.[10] Ivan Day and his researchers have undertaken extensive work tracing some of the earliest references to both "plumb pudding" and "Christmas pudding." They found that Colonel Norwood's diary from his 1649 voyage provides one of the earliest references to a dish named "Christmas pudding." The reference appears in the following account of an improvised shipboard festive meal:

> Many sorrowful days and nights we spun out in this manner, tille the blessed feast of Christmas came upon us, which we began with a very melancholy solemnity; and yet, to make some distinction of times, the scrapings of the meal-tubs were all amassed together to compose a pudding. Malaga sack, sea water, with fruit and spice, all well fryed in oyl, were the ingredients of this regale, which raised some envy in the spectators; but allowing some privilege to the captain's mess, we met no obstruction, but did peaceably enjoy our Christmas pudding.[11]

On Christmas Day in 1675, Henry Teonge, a British naval chaplain, wrote the following in his journal:

> Our Captaine had all his officers and gentlemen to dinner with him, where wee had excellent good fayre: a ribb of beife, plumb-puddings, minct pyes,

&c. and plenty of good wines of severall sorts; dranke healths to the King, our wives and friends; and ended the day with much civill myrth.[12]

Despite the early reference to "Christmas pudding," "plum pudding" was the more standard term in the seventeenth and eighteenth centuries. It is possible that the earlier quotation is describing a pudding eaten at Christmas, rather than employing the specific name of a known dish. In any case, both sources refer to the consumption of these solid puddings on Christmas Day and highlight their importance in the makeshift Christmas meal on the ship.

In terms of published recipes named "plum pudding," Mary Kettilby's *A Collection of above Three Hundred Receipts in Cookery, Physick and Surgery* (1714) contains the earliest example located during the course of this research:

An excellent Plumb-Pudding.

Take one pound of Suet, shred very small and sifted, one pound of Raisons ston'd, four spoonfuls of Flower, and four spoonfuls of Sugar, five Eggs, but three Whites; beat the Eggs with a little Salt: Tie it up close, and boil it four Hours at least.[13]

This recipe and others, such as John Nott's example from 1723,[14] demonstrate that, with the exception of suet, meat was now rarely a component of these early eighteenth-century plum puddings. These were now essentially sweet dishes, and during the eighteenth century they started being moved to the end of the meal, becoming a dessert course, rather than an accompaniment to roast beef.[15]

Over the course of the nineteenth century, these festive boiled plum puddings became richer and sweeter still, using a wider variety of dried fruits, including candied peel. John Mollard's 1802 recipe demonstrates the use of more dried fruits, nuts, and brandy:

A rich Plum Pudding.

TAKE one pound of raisins stoned, one pound of currants washed and picked, one pound of beef suet chopped, two ounces of jordan almonds blanched and pounded, citron, candied orange and lemon peel pounded, two ounces of each, a little salt, some grated nutmeg and sugar, one pound of sifted flour, a gill of brandy, and eight eggs well beaten. Mix all together with cream or milk, and let it be of a good thickness; then tie it in a cloth, boil it five hours, and serve it up with melted butter over.[16]

By the first half of the nineteenth century, cookery authors started to refer to "plumb pudding" as "Christmas pudding." Whereas it had once been celebratory fare in a more general sense, this change in nomenclature indicates that the dish was now exclusively associated with the Yuletide meal. The classic icon of the round blazing pudding dripping with brandy sauce and decked with holly also became popular in the Christmas imagery of this period, as Dickens famously described in 1843:

> Mrs Cratchit left the room alone—too nervous to bear witnesses—to take the pudding up and bring it in. . . . Hallo! A great deal of steam! The pudding was out of the copper which smells like a washing-day. That was the cloth. A smell like an eating-house and a pastrycook's next door to each other, with a laundress's next door to that. That was the pudding. In half a minute Mrs. Cratchit entered—flushed, but smiling proudly—with the pudding, like a speckled cannon-ball, so hard and firm, blazing in half of half-a-quarter of ignited brandy, and bedight with Christmas holly stuck into the top. Oh, a wonderful pudding! Bob Cratchit said, and calmly too, that he regarded it as the greatest success achieved by Mrs. Cratchit since their marriage.[17]

The pudding enjoyed by the Cratchits would likely have been similar to the recipe Eliza Acton provided in her 1845 *Modern Cookery in All Its Branches*:

Ingoldsby Christmas Puddings.

Mix very thoroughly one pound of finely grated bread with the same quantity of flour, two pounds of raisins stoned, two of currants, two of suet minced small, one of sugar, half a pound of candied peel, one nutmeg, half an ounce of mixed spice, and the grated rinds of two lemons; mix the whole with sixteen eggs well beaten and strained, and add four glasses of brandy. These proportions will make three puddings of good size, each of which should be boiled six hours.

Bread-crumbs, 1 lb.; flour, 1 lb.; suet, 2 lbs.; currants, 2 lbs.; raisins, 2 lbs.; sugar, 1lb.; candied peel, ½lb.; rinds of lemons, 2; nutmegs, 1; mixed spice, ½ oz.; salt, ¼ teaspoonful; eggs, 16; brandy, 4 glassesful: 6 hours.

Obs.—A fourth part of the ingredients given above, will make a pudding of sufficient size for a small party: to render this very rich, half the flour and bread-crumbs may be omitted, and a few spoonsful of apricot marmalade well blended with the remainder of the mixture.*

*Rather less liquid will be required to moisten the pudding when this is done, and four hours and a quarter will boil it.[18]

In addition to several plum pudding recipes, Mrs. Beeton includes two specifically for Christmas. The first is a simpler version, titled "A Plain Christmas Pudding for Children," and a second, richer option is "Christmas Plum Pudding." Beeton recommends using a mold for the pudding and suggests that it be brought to the table alight, topped with holly, and served with brandy sauce. The recipe for this delicious sauce is as follows:

499. PLUM-PUDDING SAUCE

INGREDIENTS—1 wineglassful of brandy, 2 oz. of very fresh butter, 1 glass of Madeira, pounded sugar to taste.

Mode.—Put the pounded sugar in a basin, with part of the brandy and the butter; let it stand by the side of the fire until it is warm and the sugar and butter are dissolved; then add the rest of the brandy, with the Madeira. Either pour it over the pudding, or serve in a tureen. This is a very rich and excellent sauce.

Average cost, 1s. 3d. for this quantity.

Sufficient for a pudding made for 6 persons.[19]

Throughout the twentieth century, the Christmas pudding retained its status as a central part of Christmas. Efforts to "keep Christmas" during the war years often focused on the pudding as the most iconic and indispensable component of the festive season. During World War I in Britain, collections were made to ensure that troops had their Christmas puddings, and hampers were sent to those serving at the front and prisoners of war. Christmas cards often featured the image of the pudding with the flags of the Allies stuck into it.[20] The same efforts to keep troops in good spirits were made during World War II, with puddings and critical ingredients being sent to the troops.

The need for pudding at Christmas was no different on the home front. As rationing began to pinch, recipes were published by the Ministry of Food

Christmas Day with the RAF in Tripolitania, Libya, 28 December 1942: Cooks serving Christmas pudding and mince pies for the airmen.
Courtesy of the Australian War Memorial Photograph Collection.

to help housewives scrape together the ingredients for this key element of Christmas. The following example from December 1940 shows how grated root vegetables could be used to add moisture and sweetness in the absence of eggs and limited fat:

War-and-Peace Christmas Pudding

Mix together 1 cupfull of flour, 1 cupful of breadcrumbs, half a cupful of suet, half a cupful of mixed dried fruit, and, if you like, a teaspoonful of mixed sweet spice. Then add a cupful of grated raw potato, a cupful of grated raw carrot and finally a level teaspoonful of bicarbonate of soda dissolved in two tablespoonfuls of hot water. Mix all together, turn into a well-greased pudding bowl. The bowl should not be more than two-thirds full. Boil or steam for at least two hours.[21]

Today, Christmas pudding remains a central part of Christmas in Britain, Ireland, and beyond, as we will discuss below. It is often homemade, but it is also commercially available, and many families now purchase theirs ready made. Modern recipes consist of fat (traditionally suet, but sometimes butter) creamed with brown sugar and combined with eggs, breadcrumbs, and flour. This basic mixture is then combined with spices and dried fruits that have been soaking in alcohol. Brandy is common in British recipes, while many Irish ones use whiskey. Grated apple or carrot is sometimes still added to the mix, which is unsurprising given that older generations may have memories of rationing. Elaborate pudding molds such as those favored in the nineteenth century are almost unheard of today, with puddings generally being cooked in a pudding cloth or poured into a basin and boiled for several hours. The pudding is commonly stored for weeks, or even months, and is ideally "fed" during this maturation time with brandy or whiskey. The addition of extra alcohol aids the preservation of the pudding and enhances the flavor. Today, it is commonly served with brandy sauce, Cumberland rum sauce, brandy butter, or hard sauce.

CHRISTMAS PUDDING PREPARATION AND TRADITIONS

Given the cultural significance of Christmas pudding, it is unsurprising that a set of traditions and folklore developed surrounding not just its consumption but also its preparation. Puddings are traditionally made on the Sunday before Advent, which is four to five weeks before Christmas. This day became known as "Stir-Up Sunday." The name of the day originates from the collect for the Sunday, which in the Church of England's Book of Common Prayer reads:

> Stir up, we beseech thee, O Lord, the wills of thy faithful people; that they, plenteously bringing forth the fruit of good works, may by thee be plenteously rewarded; through Jesus Christ our Lord. Amen.[22]

Traditionally, each family member in the household stirs the mixture in a clockwise direction and makes a wish for the New Year. Children come forward to make their wishes, stirring the basin with great solemnity. Kaori O'Connor argues that

> the "proper" observation of the festival was considered essential for securing success in the coming year, and this included the creation and consumption

STIRRING THE 'XMAS PUDDING.

"Stirring the 'Xmas Pudding."
From Muriel Evelyn, *Glad Hours—The Little One's Own Treasury of Pictures and Stories*. Published by
Ward Lock & Co., London and New York, 1886. iStock/whitemay.

of foods that had become emblematic of the holiday, often cakes. The ingredients originally had special significance—usually associated with luck and fertility—and very often there was an order in which they had to be added, and a special way in which they had to be mixed.[23]

Although the practice has now largely ceased, silver coins were once added to the pudding mixture, the finder of which was supposed to have good luck for the coming year. Sometimes tokens such as a wishbone (for good luck), a thimble (for thrift or spinsterhood), an anchor (for safe harbor), a ring (for marriage), a coin (for wealth), or a miniature horseshoe (for good luck) were hidden as an alternative to coins. Such rituals are also connected to Twelfth Night cakes, where a bean and pea were traditionally hidden, as the following chapter will discuss in greater detail. In Newfoundland, a ritual known as "blowing the pudding" celebrated the successful lifting of the Christmas pudding from the pot by firing a shot into the air.[24] Gerry Bowler argues that gunfire and fireworks are traditionally used at Christmas to frighten away evil spirits.[25] We will see this use of gunfire again in the discussion of wassailing in chapter 6.

PUDDINGS AND POLITICS

The iconic status of Christmas pudding as both the ultimate Yuletide dish and a marker of British identity means that throughout history it has been the subject of great debate and political discourse. At different times throughout its history it has been held up as a symbol of all that is good and all that is debased about Britain, the Empire, and Christmas itself.

As briefly discussed above, when Oliver Cromwell came to power in 1647, the Puritans took exception to plum porridge, along with other festive activities and foods such as mince pies. Chapter 1 outlined the Puritans' key objections to the festival, and plum pottage encapsulated all of these, being shamefully extravagant and secular and, worst of all, having an air of pagan idolatry about it. Claire Hopley has argued that part of the objection to plum porridge was because the Puritans saw the good luck rituals associated with it as being suspiciously pagan and superstitious.[26] A satirical pamphlet, *The Arraignment, Conviction and Imprisoning, of Christmas*, written by an author under the pseudonym "Cissely Plum Porridge" and published by "Simon Minc'd Pye" in 1645, highlighted the resentment felt by many toward the Puritans' assault on their most cherished traditions.[27] Another pamphlet from 1652 explained that the Puritans believed that "Plumb-Pottage was mere Popery."[28] Indeed, such resentment was felt toward the Puritans that when Charles II ascended to the throne during the Restoration in 1660, the Marquis of Newcastle reportedly advised him to support customs including "carols and wassail at Christmas, with goodly plum porridge and pies, which are now forbidden as profane ungodly things."[29] And so, like these other festive traditions, the pudding was well and truly entrenched on the table during the Restoration.

Over time, plum pudding came to represent the British nation, akin to roast beef. In Thomas Hervey's famous work *The Book of Christmas*, first published in 1836, plum pudding is called "a truly national dish."[30] The pudding also came to be associated with the Empire, given that so many of its ingredients were sourced from far-flung corners of the globe. To quote Hervey again, plum pudding "is a Blackamoor, and derives his extraction from the spice lands. His Oriental properties have however received an English education and taken an English form."[31] Victorian cartoonists repeatedly used the motif of the plum pudding as a symbol of the British Empire in their discourse on foreign politics. A cartoon by James Gillray dating to 1805 shows Napoleon Bonaparte and William Pitt sitting across the table from one another carving up the globe, which has taken the form of a plum pudding. An 1848 cartoon depicts the quintessential Englishman John Bull sitting behind an enormous pudding on a table spread with the Magna Carta. The pudding carries labels referring to all of Britain's proudest achievements, such as "Liberty of the Press," "Trial by Jury," "Common Sense," and "Order." The heads of foreign states look on powerlessly as John Bull asserts his right to the globe—carving it up into chunks as he sees fit.[32]

During the Victorian period, the Christmas pudding became both a symbol of and a cipher for discussions about nationalism, trade, and empire. A fascinating short story published in Charles Dickens's weekly journal *Household Words* illustrates the significance of the pudding in these debates.[33] The first Christmas issue of the two-penny journal contained a story in which a man falls asleep on Christmas Eve and is visited by a range of spirits or genii of each of the ingredients of the Christmas pudding, notably the Genius of

James Gillray. "The plumb-pudding in danger; or, State epicures taking un petit souper."
1805. Hand-colored etching 25.5 x 35.7 cm (image) 26.1 x 36.3 cm (plate) 26.6 x 37.0 cm (sheet) BM
Satires 10371; Wright & Evans 295, National Gallery of Victoria, Melbourne Felton Bequest, 1944
(1264-4). Courtesy of the National Gallery of Victoria.

the Raisin from Moorish Iberia, the Genius of the Currant from the Levant, the Genius of Bread from Kent, the Spirit of Suet, the Genius of Sugar (a freed slave from the West Indies), the Genius of Nutmeg, the Egg Collector from Cork, and the Spirit of Salt from India. A lively debate about the Empire and trade takes place, with each of the spirits introducing moral, economic, and political issues such as the export of ingredients, the exploitation of workers in foreign lands, protectionism, animal welfare, commodity prices and fluctuations, slavery and abolition, taxes, tariffs, free trade, and the effects of monopoly. For example, when the Genius of the Raisin challenges him over the fact that English ships carry away his country's richest produce, the man defends the hard work of those throughout the Empire, in all ends of trade, arguing:

> The sun which ripens your grapes and your oranges makes the people lazy and the priests rapacious. We come to your ports with the products of our

looms and furnaces, and we induce a taste for comforts that will become a habit. When our glass and porcelain find their way into your peasant's hut, then your, then will your olives be better tended and your grapes be more carefully dried. Man only worthily labours when he labours for exchange with other labour. Behold that pudding!—It is our England's annual luxury. It is the emblem of our commercial eminence. The artisans of Birmingham and Manchester—the seamen of London and Liverpool—whose festive board will be made joyous, tomorrow, with that national dish, has contributed his labour, to make raisins of Malaga and currants of Zante—the orange of Algarve, the cinnamon of Ceylon and the nutmegs of the Moluccas—of commercial value; and he has thus called them into existence as effectually as the labour of the native cultivator.[34]

A power-loom weaver, a symbol of Britain's technological advancement and industrialization, then steps in with a pudding cloth to bind the ingredients and the Empire together. At the end of the debate, the man exclaims, "Our ancestors in their 'civil dudgeon' produced 'plum-porridge.' We, in our united interests, well bound together, produce Christmas pudding!" An enormous flaming pudding decorated with holly then materializes before them, and they all dance around it before vanishing.[35]

As the ultimate symbol of the Empire, the Christmas pudding was used in these debates about foreign politics and the market, but also in advertising campaigns that aimed to promote the trade in its goods. In 1924, when the British Empire Exhibition was hosted in London, the British Women's Patriotic League launched an appeal to "make your Christmas pudding this year an Empire pudding." It issued a leaflet with a recipe based upon ingredients entirely drawn from Empire countries. A prepackaged box of ingredients, or a ready-made Empire pudding, could also be purchased.[36] Their appeal to buy Empire products was partially a response to the 1920s push into the British market by the Californian dried-vine-fruit industry. Australian producers were incensed by this, and, with the support of the British Women's Patriotic League, they started to market themselves more aggressively, and used their status as a loyal colony to their advantage, highlighting the idea of the Empire pudding in their campaign. The emphasis on buying products from the Empire became increasingly topical in the mid-1920s, and the Christmas pudding played a starring role in the campaigns. In 1925, the theme of the Lord Mayor of London's Show was "Imperial Trade." The dominions and colonies all provided a cart overflowing with their produce for the procession through the city, and Australia's entry was an enormous Christmas pudding pulled by white horses, carrying the slogan "Make your pudding of Empire products."[37] The Empire Marketing Board, a quango established by the British government, similarly promoted trade, advertising recipes for "Empire Xmas Pudding" in 1926. The recipe appeared on a poster with an image of Britannia holding up a blazing Christmas pudding topped by a Union Jack. This recipe recommended the use of Australian or South African dried fruit, Jamaican rum, British suet, apples, eggs and breadcrumbs, and Indian spice. Importantly, the king agreed to include this recipe on his Christmas menu. On 20 December 1926, Lord Meath hosted a publicity stunt at Vernon House, the headquarters of the Overseas League, in which an Empire pudding was made with great ceremony. Indian servants presented each of the ingredients, from around the Empire. These were each carried in and formally announced to the crowd, like dignitaries arriving at a ball. The ingredients were then placed in a basin, and representatives of Canada, Australia, South Africa, India, British Guiana, and Jamaica all ritually stirred the mixture. The ceremony concluded with a toast to "The King's Empire Christmas Pudding."[38] Most important, the entire spectacle was filmed for a newsreel and was shown in cinemas across the Empire.[39] The same ritualized promotional strategy was performed in 1927, this time with an adapted version of a recipe donated by the royal chef André Cédard. The recipe was designed to utilize as many Empire ingredients as possible, and various countries lobbied to have their produce included. The campaign was hugely successful, and thousands of people wrote in from around Britain and the Empire to obtain a copy of the recipe.[40] Reporting on the Christmas dinner enjoyed by King George V and his family in 1927, Lord Meath of the Royal Colonial Institute described the pudding as "a symbol of the unity of Empire, and an example to be copied in every household throughout the length and breadth of the British Empire."[41] Because of the global mass marketing of the recipe and ingredients that year, Kaori O'Connor argues that when diners around the world sat down to eat the pudding on Christmas Day in 1927, they were participating in "a unique act of global mass consumption."[42]

BEYOND BRITAIN

Although it is eaten by some families in America, Christmas pudding does not have the same widespread popularity or iconic status there as it does in Britain. However, culinary, literary, and domestic sources tell us that it certainly existed as an important part of the nineteenth-century American Christmas table.[43] Eliza Leslie included directions for making plum puddings in her *Directions for Cookery* (1837)[44] and later works. In her 1857 *New Cookery*, Leslie provides advice on shipping plum puddings as presents and storing them. She cautions against lighting the pudding, though, sternly advising, "Do not set the pudding on fire to burn out the liquor; that practice has had its day, and is over. It was always foolish."[45] Even more disapprovingly, Sarah Josepha Hale, the great champion of Thanksgiving, conceded reluctantly that "as Christmas comes but once a year, a rich plum pudding may be permitted for the feast, though it is not healthy food; and children should be helped very sparingly."[46] Jeri Quinzio has observed that US temperance movements also took issue with the alcohol-heavy plum pudding and adapted recipes accordingly.[47] Estelle Woods Wilcox, a strong supporter of the temperance movement,[48] included several versions of plum pudding in her 1877 edition of *Buckeye Cookery and Practical Housekeeping*. Her "Christmas Plum Pudding" includes no alcohol at all and, rather depressingly, flavors the sauce with grape juice in place of brandy. Her "English Plum Pudding," however, remains authentic, using a glass of brandy. It is also certainly the more appealing of the two recipes.[49]

While, as we have seen, Christmas pudding did feature on nineteenth- and early twentieth-century American Christmas tables, its place was never cemented as it was in Britain and the Commonwealth. From the mid- to late twentieth century, Christmas pudding ceased to appear with great regularity, and it certainly never achieved the iconic status that it did in Britain. Cathy Kaufman has observed that today Christmas pudding only features on the dining tables of those most attached to and nostalgic for the idea of "Christmas as an ancient holiday."[50] For most Americans, family favorites such as pies are the most common Christmas desserts, and no single codified dish for the end of the meal exists. The festive desserts favored by Americans may draw on seasonal ingredients, or may have festive twists such as using typical spices or other flavorings, but they are not exclusively

Christmas foods in the way that the pudding is in Britain. When we consider that the Christmas pudding as we know it did not come into existence until the nineteenth century, and that it rapidly became part of nationalist and imperialist identity politics, it is not difficult to see why Americans would have struggled to embrace this element of the festival. Its development came in the postrevolutionary decades, and it was so very British to its core that it would not have been easy to weave the dish into the modern American Christmas, which, as chapter 1 discussed, was in its own critical period of formation at this time.

The ambivalent relationship with Christmas pudding in America comes into sharp and telling contrast with the status it retained in countries within the Commonwealth, where it was embraced as a central component of the festival. In Australia, Christmas pudding came to represent not just Christmas but also the incongruous nature of Antipodean identity. It symbolized Australians' complex relationship with both their own country and Britain. Having a pudding became an essential part of "keeping Christmas" in Australia and was a gastronomic reaffirmation of British identity in the colonial period. From the beginning of colonization, the pudding was paramount. Roast beef and plum pudding were served to Aboriginal people at the famous feasts hosted by Governor Macquarie in Parramatta, New South Wales, Australia. These feast days were an important point of contact between the newcomers and the original inhabitants, as well as a way of trying to draw the Aboriginal tribes into the British sphere of influence. At the feast day on 28 December 1818, after the official ceremonies had been completed, the Aboriginal guests, who were estimated to be around three hundred in number, were served that most British of meals: roast beef and plum pudding, washed down with plentiful alcohol.[51]

Even those from the convict and serving orders began to expect their puddings at Christmas. In 1832, Charlotte Welsh was incarcerated at the Female Factory in Parramatta as a punishment for insisting that her mistress provide her with brandy in her Christmas pudding.[52] Charmaine O'Brien notes in her book *The Colonial Kitchen* that when expected shipments of dried fruit did not arrive in Victoria in 1856, and when there was a shortage of flour in Van Diemen's Land (Tasmania) in 1859, there was a huge concern that colonial Australians would not be able to make their Christmas puddings.[53] Newspapers reported on the importation of fruits and spices in preparation for Christmas with great excitement. Before the domestic dried fruit industry had been established in Australia, such ingredients were hard to come by, and they represented the much-missed Christmas of Old England:

> Our blazing hearths remind us of a fireside in England, and of the cheerfulness and festivities of the frosty season there, which generally commences with Christmas. The quantity of fruit and spices lately arrived in our harbor, enables us to imitate that festive season of our countrymen, by enjoying plumpudding and pies with our roast beef, which entitles us to cry out—this is the land of health, peace, and plenty![54]

Even at an early date the oddity of preparing and eating a heavy boiled pudding in high summer was amusing to colonials. Journalist and novelist Marcus Clarke took particular issue with the Australian adoption of the Christmas pudding:

> A very merry Christmas, with the roast beef in a violent perspiration, and the thermometer at 110° in the shade! . . . It may be a rank heresy but I deliberately affirm that Christmas in Australia is a gigantic mistake . . . if the gentleman in question is sensible, and possesses digestive organs, it is quite probable that he will refuse to load his stomach with the portable nightmare known as plum pudding.[55]

John Hunter Kerr was more wistful in his longing for seasonal food, but he explains the deep-seated cultural connection to the pudding:

> Ancient roast beef and plum pudding which is forever bound up with all British memories of Christmas tide . . . It would be a desirable innovation could the hot and heavy plum pudding of the United Kingdom be replaced by some cooler and more seasonable dainty dish but long cherished associations cast a glamour over the luscious compound with its blue ghostly flame which will not readily be effaced.[56]

Historian Ken Inglis refers to a prospector in the goldfields proclaiming that he had made a fine pudding that he had boiled for twenty-four hours. He found it amusing that this hot and heavy delicacy took him a full week to digest.[57] Not everyone was so pleased with the colonial adherence to plum pudding, though. The great Australian poet Henry Lawson detested plum pudding, describing it as "the most barbarous institution of the British."[58] His following description of Christmas dinner makes his views on hot meals in Australia perfectly clear:

> We had dinner at Billy Wood's place, and a sensible Christmas dinner it was—everything cold, except the vegetables, with the hose going on the veranda in spite of the by-laws, and Billy's wife and her sister, fresh and cool-looking and jolly, instead of being hot and brown and cross like most Australian women who roast themselves over a blazing fire in a hot kitchen on a broiling day, all the morning, to cook scalding plum pudding and red-hot roasts, for no other reason than that their grandmothers used to cook hot Christmas dinners in England.[59]

Perhaps the incongruity of eating a steamed suet pudding under the blazing southern skies was part of the appeal, reflecting something of colonial identity in this strange land. Writing in the early nineteenth century, surgeon and naturalist Joseph Arnold believed that the adherence to the traditional English Christmas dinner showed that colonials had not yet made a home for themselves in Australia.[60] They were no longer British, but they were also not yet quite Australian.

The duality of Australians' summertime Christmas celebration and their very identity as Antipodeans is perfectly symbolized by the Christmas pudding. It served not just as the centerpiece of the table and the most iconic representative of the Christmas feast but also as a symbol of England and the British Empire—and their place within it. To quote Rhiannon Donaldson, "The pudding was an integral part of 'keeping Christmas,' which involved not only the celebration itself, but the opportunity to indulge in nostalgia and to connect to Empire."[61] One recipe book, written between the wars, advised readers to make a pudding "*just because* it is part of our empire [*sic*] heritage."[62] While they could not replicate snow, dark evenings, or holly bushes, they could prepare and partake in a meal on Christmas Day that connected them to the values of Britain and its Empire.[63]

Donaldson has also pointed out that even when colonial Australians began to embrace their environment and climate at Christmas by hosting festive outdoor picnics, the pudding remained central. She argues that it became a sort of linking piece: its presence on the picnic blanket helped to

"Newsletter of Australasia. A Narrative to Send to Friends. Christmas in Australia. A Happy New Year to Friends Far, Far Away."
No. 41 January 1860. Courtesy of the State Library of Victoria.

legitimize the otherwise unorthodox Christmas meal. It became a tangible connection to the past and tradition, which helped to smooth the rough corners of innovation.[64] Similar commentaries regarding the role of the pudding and images of picnics during Christmas in nineteenth-century New Zealand demonstrate that the same debates regarding both the festival and national identity were being had across the Tasman Sea.

Today, the pudding is still very common on Australian and New Zealand Christmas tables. Many families make their own, but, as in Britain, they are also available commercially. Whereas in the mid-twentieth century many families purchased puddings in a can, the Big Sister brand being particularly popular, today gourmet food stores have stepped in to improve the quality of premade puddings markedly. Nothing can compete with a family's own familiar recipe, though. Attempts have been made to develop more seasonally appropriate versions of Christmas pudding. A frozen take on the dish combines vanilla ice cream with alcohol, dried fruit, and spice. This mixture is then pressed into a mold to create a frozen, pudding-flavored masterpiece that, alas, has failed to catch on.

However, while the traditional pudding remains dominant, it is no longer unchallenged in the dessert stakes, and new, more seasonally appropriate Christmas dishes have entered the menu. Pavlova is undoubtedly the most common of these in Australia and New Zealand, with both nations claiming to have invented the dish after ballerina Anna Pavlova's 1926 tour.[65] By the 1940s, women's magazines, newspapers, and advertising campaigns were actively promoting the idea of pavlova as a suitable Christmas dessert, emphasizing the fact that it was more seasonally appropriate. A 1949 Christmas food section from the *Advocate* (Burnie, Tasmania) states that pavlova is growing in popularity as a festive dish precisely because of the hot weather.[66] Recipes like the following example from 1946 were increasingly recommended as Christmas desserts:

Pavlova Cake

Ingredients
3 fresh eggs.
6 tablespoonfuls castor sugar.
1 teaspoon vanilla.
1 teaspoon vinegar.
A pinch of salt.
A-pint of cream.
Strawberries, bananas, or passion-fruit.

Separate yolks from whites, and put whites into a basin, add a pinch of salt, and beat until very stiff. Add two tablespoonfuls of castor sugar, beating in lightly without churning, then another two, beating again, then the last two, add one teaspoonful of vanilla and one teaspoonful of vinegar, and beat in lightly keeping the mixture creamy. Only a few whisks are needed for this. Turn a sandwich tin upside down, cut buttered paper to fit the bottom of the tin, and make a band of brown paper to fit around the tin. Grease this, too. Now spoon mixture on the bottom of sandwich tin, smoothing it level. Now place a piece of paper on the buttered band, covering the cake over.

Bake 1 to 1 1/2 hours, when it will be the palest biscuit shade, and not dead white. If the oven is too slow, a colourless syrup will run into the bottom of the tin. Take out of the oven, unpin band round cake, and ease cake with a knife if any has stuck to the tin; place the plate on which cake is to be served on top of cake, turn on to plate, ease off buttered paper from cake. When cold, spread bottom of cake with whipped cream, and top with strawberries, passionfruit, or any other suitable fruit.[67]

Like the seafood barbecue, the Christmas "pav" has become a celebrated Antipodean modern festive food tradition, but one that has not yet ousted the "pud" entirely. Today, the Christmas pavlova is commonly topped with cream and the beautiful seasonal fruit available in summer, from passionfruit and berries to the much-anticipated Christmas mangoes, cherries, and stone fruits. From the late nineteenth century on, long before the invention of the pavlova, these fruits, but especially mangoes, developed an increasingly significant role in the Australian Christmas. Newspapers were filled with descriptions of dazzling displays of fruit and native flowers called "Christmas bush." Just as British families gathered to see festive window displays, Australians would make a pilgrimage to see this cornucopia laid out as Christmas approached:

The King-street Arcade was a favorite resort, with its great masses of beautiful flowers at the florists and the magnificent spread of fruit near by—the piles of oranges, lemons, mangoes, pineapples apricots, nectarines, peaches, plums, cherries, red and white currants, grapes, gooseberries and other fruits— decked with Christmas bush making a picture worth travelling to see. Flags and Chinese lanterns hung right through the arcade, with every shop making its bravest display. . . . Every shop proprietor made some effort at decoration and display. Grocers, fruit, toy and fancy shops were the most conspicuous, and some of them were to the juveniles nothing more or less than real sections of fairyland. The fruit markets were a sight worth seeing . . . there were stacks upon stacks of cases; of all kinds of fruit and the stalls were piled high with every variety.[68]

Newspapers also reported on the fluctuating Christmas fruit market, demonstrating the growing demand for tropical fruits during Christmas from the late nineteenth century on. A turn in weather could destroy the crop and send prices rocketing, so watching the market closely became something of a sport. A report from 13 February 1886 complained of the poor quality of mangoes in the Brisbane markets at Christmastime.[69] An article from 22 December 1910 warned that shoppers should expect to pay high prices for fruit on Christmas Eve, as a gale had destroyed the "Christmas peaches," with mangoes from Queensland being the only survivors.[70]

The celebration of fruit at Christmas was not entirely novel, though. Oranges, apples, and nuts had long played an important role in the British Christmas, and they would often appear in the stockings of excited children as much-appreciated gifts from Santa Claus. The celebration of tropical fruit during Christmas in Australia could be seen as an evolution of this tradition. While fruits such as mangoes do not appear to have been left by Santa, they did become a much-anticipated seasonal treat. They were generally complementary to British customs and foods, though, rather than a replacement for the traditional pudding, as the following description of a 1903 Christmas meal indicates:

I write in the afternoon, after a good dinner. A turkey, ham, and potatoes; a big plum-pudding and custard, followed by some mangoes and bananas and some muscatels and almonds. Truly, a good dinner.[71]

Giving cases of fruit, commonly mangoes, became a popular practice that continues today. Relatives from far north Queensland would send crates of the luscious fruit to their relatives in cooler climes down south. This became a very popular practice from the 1930s onward, and it was predictable enough by 1945 for one commentator to complain, "One hates to offend people, but if we get another Christmas box that includes mangoes, pineapples or a watermelon I'll scream, I know I will."[72] Notwithstanding the sentiments of this less than impressed recipient, boxes of fruit remain popular gifts during the season, and nothing says Christmas more to Australians than the heady scent of overripe mangoes mixed with perspiring pine needles.

THE CHRISTMAS TRIFLE

Having discussed the pavlova, it would be remiss to finish this chapter not having commented on Britain's number two Christmas dessert, the sherry trifle. This traditional celebratory dish is a British favorite year-round, but it does retain an association with the festival that warrants some discussion. It is also a Christmas stalwart outside of Britain as well and, like the pavlova, lends itself to a hot Southern Hemisphere, fruit-oriented celebration.

The roots of the trifle date back to the late sixteenth century, although these early predecessors were quite different from the modern trifle we know today. They were much closer to what we would call a fool, being cream-based dishes that were combined with fruit and other flavorings. The layering and textural elements that characterize modern trifles are eighteenth-century developments.[73] Thomas Dawson's recipe, published in *The Good Huswifes Jewell* of 1596, demonstrates the homogenous, creamy consistency of early trifles:

To Make a Trifle

Take a pinte of thicke Creame, and season it with Sugar and Ginger, and Rosewater, so stirre it as you would then have it, and make it luke warm in a dish on a Chafingdishe and coals, and after put it into a silver piece or bowle, and so serve it to boorde.[74]

By the mid-eighteenth century, things had begun to change, and the modern trifle was starting to emerge. Hannah Glasse was one of the first to publish a recipe resembling a modern trifle in *The Art of Cookery Made Plain and Easy* (1747). The recipe combines naples biscuits, "mackeroons," and ratafia cakes on the bottom. These were soaked with sack, topped with custard and syllabub, and then garnished with ratafia cakes, currant jelly, and flowers.[75] This layered dish soon became hugely popular, and Helen Saberi and Alan Davidson describe the 1750s as the "decade of the trifle."[76] Hannah Glasse's "A grand trifle," which appears in her *Compleat Confectioner*, includes yet another innovation, being one of the first to feature jelly in the base. The recipe is as follows:

A grand trifle

Take a very large china dish or glass; that is deep, first make some very fine rich calves-foot jelly, with which fill the dish about half the depth; when it begins to jelly, have ready some Naples biscuits, macaroons, and the little cakes called matrimony; take an equal quantity of these cakes, break them in pieces, and stick them in the jelly before it be stiff, all over very thick; pour over that a quart of very thick sweet cream, then lay all round, currant jelly, raspberry jam and some calves-foot jelly, all cut in little pieces, with which garnish your dish thick all round, intermixing them and on them lay macaroons, and the little cakes, being first dipped in sack.

Then take two quarts of the thickest cream you can get, sweeten it with double refined sugar, grate into it the rine of three fine large lemons, and whisk it up with a whisk; take off the froth as it rises, and lay it in your dish as high as you can possibly raise it; this is fit to go to the King's table, if well made, and very excellent when it comes to be all mixed together.[77]

Recipe books from the nineteenth century contain numerous trifle recipes, demonstrating that it had become a key player in the British dessert canon, but one that was not specifically connected to Christmas. Mrs. Beeton gives several variations, including the following, that notes toward the end that it is suitable for any time of year:

TO MAKE A TRIFLE.

1489. INGREDIENTS: For the whip, 1 pint of cream, 3 oz. of pounded sugar, the whites of 2 eggs, a small glass of sherry or raisin wine. For the trifle, 1 pint of custard, made with 8 eggs to a pint of milk; 6 small sponge-cakes, or 6 slices of sponge-cake; 12 macaroons, 2 dozen ratafias, 2 oz. of sweet almonds, the grated rind of 1 lemon, a layer of raspberry or strawberry jam, ½ pint of sherry or sweet wine, 6 tablespoonfuls of brandy.

Mode: The whip to lay over the top of the trifle should be made the day before it is required for table, as the flavour is better, and it is much more solid than when prepared the same day. Put into a large bowl the pounded sugar, the whites of the eggs, which should be beaten to a stiff froth, a glass of sherry or sweet wine, and the cream. Whisk these ingredients well in a cool place, and take off the froth with a skimmer as fast as it rises, and put it on a sieve to drain; continue the whisking till there is sufficient of the whip, which must be put away in a cool place to drain. The next day, place the sponge-cakes, macaroons, and ratafias at the bottom of a trifle-dish; pour over them ½ pint of sherry or sweet wine, mixed with 6 tablespoonfuls of brandy, and, should this proportion of wine not be found quite sufficient, add a little more, as the cakes should be well soaked. Over the cakes put the grated lemon-rind, the sweet almonds, blanched and cut into strips, and a layer of raspberry or strawberry jam. Make a good custard by recipe No. 1423, using 8 instead of 5 eggs to the pint of milk, and let this cool a little; then pour it over the cakes, &c. The whip being made the day previously, and the trifle prepared, there remains nothing to do now but heap the whip lightly over the top: this should stand as high as possible, and it may be garnished with strips of bright currant jelly, crystallized sweetmeats, or flowers; the small coloured comfits are sometimes used for the purpose of garnishing a trifle, but they are now considered rather old-fashioned.

Average cost: with cream at 1s. per pint, 5s. 6d.

Sufficient: for 1 trifle.

Seasonable: at any time.[78]

Over the course of the later nineteenth and early twentieth centuries, trifles came to resemble modern versions more closely. The main change in this period was that the whipped syllabub topping was replaced by cream. It remained a celebratory dish generally but did start to be connected to Christmas more explicitly than it had been in earlier periods. In 1858, a recipe called "Christmas cake" was published by Elizabeth Warren. This was not a rich fruitcake, but rather a cake to form the base of a trifle.[79] Despite its increasing association with Christmas, the dish never developed the same iconic significance in art and literature that the pudding did, nor did it ever become exclusively a Christmas dish. Regardless, it remains a mainstay of the festive tables in Britain and beyond. The doyenne of Irish cookery, Darina Allen, describes her memories of the sherry trifle at Christmas:

There's a few things, like gravy and trifle, that are very personal—your yard-stick is whatever your mammy or granny used to make. . . . Even when my brothers were in their late 40s and 50s, they seemed to revert back to childhood and squabble over the trifle, finishing it off in the middle of the night when they came home from the pub on Christmas Eve. Mummy would have to go to great lengths to hide it on the top of a cupboard or even in her wardrobe, but somehow they always managed to find it![80]

During World War II, as we saw with puddings, the government increased the tinned fruit ration before Christmas, so that people could make their cherished festive trifles.[81] Jeanette Winterson recalls the role that the sherry trifle played in her family's Christmas, and its significance to her father, who had an impoverished childhood:

Christmas brought another treat too: sherry trifle.

This was thanks to Del Monte Canned Fruit Cocktail—the cocktail name coming from the fact that, in the early days of Del Monte, this fruit mix had alcohol in it.

Dad's job down at the docks was unloading cargo of every kind . . . but the best kind of cargo was foodstuffs, and the best kinds of foodstuffs were things you could slip in a poacher's pocket and keep for later; that was cans.

So every Christmas his mother made the family sherry trifle. And when Dad married in 1947 rationing was on, but somehow he managed to eat his annual sherry trifle. . . . For me, growing up in the 1960s, sherry trifle meant Christmas.[82]

The trifle retains a cherished place on the Christmas tables of many British families and those throughout their former Empire. Its high sugar content, rich creamy layers, and colorful festive presentation make it perfect for a celebration, but, more than that, it has an essence of fun about it. Unlike Christmas pudding, as we have seen in this chapter, or mince pies, as we will discuss in chapter 5, the trifle never became a dish exclusive to Christmas. Like roast beef, it has been a constant presence at Christmas, but it also holds an importance outside of this festival. This means that it has never achieved the iconic status of the Christmas pudding, and it is rarely celebrated in Christmas art, literature, and film, but, for many, it is a central part of their memories of childhood, and a critical part of the holiday as well.

4

FESTIVE CAKES

They had holidays, too, and Twelfth cakes, and parties where they danced all night till midnight.

—Charles Dickens, "The Child's Story,"
A Round of Stories by the Christmas Fire (1853)

What would any celebration be without a cake? As with puddings and desserts, part of the festive appeal of them stems from their indulgent use of rich, calorie-laden foods such as butter, eggs, and sugar. These were also expensive ingredients in the past, making cakes a luxury food worthy of an important celebration. But there is also something about the communal nature of the rituals surrounding cakes that makes them such an important part of celebrations. Family and friends gather around the birthday boy or girl to sing "Happy Birthday" and watch them blow out the candles; the bride and groom must be photographed cutting the bottom layer of an elaborate, tiered confection in front of their guests; and, as we shall see, in the not-so-distant past, frenzied crowds of revelers tore apart giant Twelfth cakes in search of a bean and a pea. Cakes are so often front and center of our communal celebratory rituals and most cherished moments. In the words of Nicola Humble:

> Cakes are very strange things, producing a range of responses far out of keeping with their culinary significance. They are simultaneously utterly unnecessary and absolutely crucial. You can't properly have a birthday or a wedding

without a cake. Christmas cake is central to our celebration, yet its inedible hardness is legendary—the family joke about saws and the cake that will never die part of the point. Cake is one of those foodstuffs whose symbolic function can completely overwhelm its actual status as a comestible. More than anything, cake is an idea.[1]

This chapter will trace the history of some of the most famous cakes and enriched breads associated with Christmas. These do not take center stage at the festival—they are supporting acts—but without them the holiday would not be the same. Today, the most iconic of these is the rich fruitcake known simply as Christmas cake. In the past, though, when Twelfth Night held more cultural significance and was celebrated with great gusto, Twelfth Night cake, or simply Twelfth cake, reigned supreme. Traditions relating to both of these cakes, and the relationship between them, will be explored in detail below. The shift from Twelfth to Christmas cake tells the story of not just changing culinary traditions but also the changing nature of the festival itself. As the twelve days contracted, and the emphasis shifted from rowdy public festival to cozy domestic affair, the Christmas cake rose and the Twelfth cake fell into oblivion, as we shall see.

TWELFTH CAKE

Before there was Christmas cake, there was Twelfth cake. While versions of Twelfth cake traditions survive in specific regions, for most people in the English-speaking world Twelfth cake is no longer a part of their Christmas. Until the late nineteenth century, though, Twelfth cake retained immense cultural significance and played the starring role in a party that was the highlight of the season. As chapter 1 discussed, Twelfth Night was once arguably more important than Christmas Day itself. Like its distant predecessor, the Roman Saturnalia, this was a night in which the social order was inverted. Children, servants, and peasants reigned and were waited on by their superiors. And in the middle of all this chaos was the Twelfth cake.

Twelfth cake recipes changed greatly over the centuries as baking technology and techniques evolved, as we will discuss below. At its peak from the mid-eighteenth to the mid-nineteenth century, though, Twelfth cake was typically a form of rich fruitcake. Food historian Nicola Humble explains that such cakes have two main strands of development, being on the evolutionary tree of both plum puddings and enriched fruit breads. To follow the former of these lineages first, Humble argues that as plum pottages became thicker, some were boiled in cloths and became solid puddings, as we saw in the previous chapter, while ale barm was added to others to produce rich, baked fruitcakes. The cake version of the now solid plum pottage was rarer than the pudding, though, simply because bread ovens were less common. However, fruitcakes may also have evolved from the enriched spiced breads that began to appear in Britain in the 1530s and were popular in the Tudor period.[2] These became so popular that in the later sixteenth century bakers were forbidden to make or sell "spice cakes, buns, biscuits, or other spice bread" on all days except for funerals, Good Friday, and Christmas.[3] If caught, bakeries would have to forfeit the bread to the poor, which would have been a major financial setback given the expense of ingredients such as spice and dried fruit.[4] So, like many popular dishes, the history of rich fruitcakes is difficult to trace precisely, partly because they inherited form, substance, and meaning from multiple culinary strands.

Although they undoubtedly have medieval origins, from the early seventeenth century on, references to Twelfth cakes and the rituals associated with them became increasingly common. At that stage, recipes were not specifically called "Twelfth cakes" in cookery books; instead, we see generic-sounding recipes such as "a plum cake" or "a great cake." These recipes could have had multiple purposes and been used in a range of celebrations, especially weddings, where they are described as "bride cakes." What made it a "Twelfth cake" was not so much its form as its role in the festive rituals of Twelfth Night. In any case, these seventeenth-century cakes were simply enormous. Helen Leach, Mary Browne, and Raelene Inglis's detailed analysis of recipes from the seventeenth century found that the largest example in their survey used a whole bushel of flour (fifty-six pounds, or 25.4 kilograms) and eight pounds of currants, making for an absolute beast of a cake.[5] To a modern palate, these cakes would also have been much more like rich fruit breads. They used yeast as the raising agent, but they also had a far greater ratio of flour to sugar and butter than our modern fruitcakes do, which would have changed both the texture and the flavor profile of the cake considerably. In terms of fruit content, currants were universal in seventeenth-century fruitcakes, but raisins, dates, and peel were optional and appear in only some recipes. Almonds were also sometimes included, but always in a beaten or ground form, lending a depth of flavor and richness to the cake. As for flavorings, the dry spices of modern Christmas cakes such as cinnamon, cloves, mace, nutmeg, and ginger were all common, but they were also scented with orange flower, rose water, musk, and ambergris. Brandy was not yet included in Twelfth cake recipes, with sack being the most common alcohol represented.[6] The following recipe comes from Sir Kenelm Digby's famous work dating to 1669:

To make a plumb-cake

Take a peck of flower, and put it in half. Then take two quarts of good Ale-yest, and strain it into half the flower, and some new milk boiled, and almost cold again; make it into a very light paste, and set it before the fire to rise; Then take five pound of Butter, and melt it in a skillet, with a quarter of a pint of Rose-water; when your paste is risen, and your oven almost hot, which will be by this time, take your paste from the fire, and break it into small pieces, and take your other part of flower, and strew it round your paste; Then take the melted butter, and put it to the past, and by degrees work the paste and flower together, till you have mingled all very well. Take six nutmegs, some Cinnamon and Mace well beaten, and two pound of sugar, and strew it into the paste, as they are working it. Take three pounds of Raisins stoned, and twelve pounds of currants very well washed and dryed again; one pound of Dates sliced; half a pound of green Citron dryed and sliced very thin; strew all these into the paste, till it have received them all; Then let your oven be ready, and make up your cake, and set it into the oven; but you must have a great care, it doth not take cold. Then to Ice it, take a pound and half of double refined sugar beaten and searsed, and put to your sugar; Then strew your sugar into the Eggs, and beat it in a stone Mortar with a Woodden Pestel, till it be as white as snow, which will be by that time the cake is baked; Then draw it to the ovens mouth, and drop it on, in what form you will; let it stand a little again in the oven to harden.[7]

In the eighteenth century, fruitcakes continued to be made for important celebrations, including Twelfth Night. This was a century of great change in baking, though, and the rich fruitcakes we know today began to take form. By the mid-eighteenth century recipes began to change, coming one step closer to the cakes we know today. First and foremost, this century saw the removal of yeast from British cake recipes: a revolution that transformed the texture of cakes and the future of cake making. Whereas seventeenth-century recipes, which commonly used ale barm to raise them, instructed the cook to rub butter into the flour, or to add melted butter to the mixture, during the eighteenth century, creaming butter and sugar together developed and transformed the texture of cakes.[8] The other hugely significant eighteenth-century cake-making development was the technique of beating and separating eggs to raise and lighten cakes. Elizabeth Raffald advised her readers to "beat your eggs well" and to be sure to beat the butter "to a fine cream."[9] These innovations ultimately led to the development of the pound cake system, which used a pound each of butter, flour, sugar, and eggs. The pound cake's crumb was soft, but the egg content created a structure that could still rise despite the presence of heavy dried fruit. The development of the kitchen range in 1780 allowed cooks to control temperature more accurately for the first time, again leading to lighter cakes.[10] In terms of flavor profile, eighteenth-century cakes had become significantly sweeter, thanks in no small part to the ever-reducing cost of sugar. The proportion of sugar used in these eighteenth-century fruitcakes was significantly higher than any in the seventeenth century.[11] The following recipe from Eliza Smith's *The Compleat Housewife* demonstrates the method of creaming butter and sugar together. It is not yet a pound cake in terms of the ratio of ingredients, but it uses more butter than flour and would have had a "mouth feel" much closer to a modern cake. It also uses brandy rather than sack, giving a depth of flavor that is similar to a contemporary Christmas cake:

Another Plum-cake with almonds

Take four pounds of fine flour dried well, five pounds of Currants well picked and rubbed, but not washed; five pounds of butter washed and beaten in Orange-flower water and sack; two pounds of almonds beaten very fine, four pounds of eggs weighed, half the whites taken out; three pounds of double refined sugar, three nutmegs grated, a little ginger, a quarter of an ounce of mace, as much cloves finely beaten, a quarter of a pint of the best Brandy: The butter must be beaten to Cream; then put in your flour, and all of the rest of your things, beating it till you put in your Oven; four hours will bake it, the oven must be very quick; put in Orange, Lemon peel candied, and Citron as you like.[12]

Although recipes were still not yet labeled "Twelfth cakes" in the eighteenth century, James Jenks's *The Complete Cook* included one that drew a specific connection between these rich fruitcakes and the feast day. His recipe for "A Rich Cake," which involves creaming the butter with your hands and incorporating beaten eggs into the mixture, states that "this is called a twelfth cake at London."[13] One of the first printed recipes for a cake actually called a "Twelfth cake" appeared in John Mollard's *The Art of Cookery* (1802). Interestingly, this recipe is actually for an earlier yeasted fruit bread–style cake, demonstrating that this earlier style prevailed into the nineteenth century:

> Take seven pounds of flour, make a cavity in the centre, set a sponge with a gill and a half of yeast and a little warm milk; then put round it one pound of fresh butter broke into small lumps, one pound and a quarter of sifted sugar, four pounds and a half of currants washed and picked, half an ounce of sifted cinnamon, a quarter of an ounce of pounded cloves, mace, and nutmeg mixed, sliced candied orange or lemon peel and citron. When the sponge is risen, mix all the ingredients together with a little warm milk; let the hoops be well papered and buttered, then fill them with the mixture and bake them, and when nearly cold ice them over with sugar prepared for that purpose as per receipt; or they may be plain.[14]

During the nineteenth century, the innovations in cake making continued, with the development of chemical raising agents. First there was pearl ash, which was invented in the 1790s and did a good job of raising cakes but had a distinctly soapy flavor. Pearl ash was followed by bicarbonate of soda, and then finally, in the 1850s, by baking powder, which was a mixture of bicarbonate of soda, cream of tartar, and cornstarch. This development led to lighter and spongier cakes that were faster to make, as the laborious hand beating of eggs—which, along with the creaming of butter and sugar, could literally take hours—was no longer required.[15] Examples of such recipes will be included in the Christmas cakes section to follow.

One of the other most important qualities of celebratory cakes is their visual appearance. From novelty children's birthday cakes to tiered wedding cakes, culturally we are still very familiar with the idea of cake as spectacle at feasts. This was, of course, no different with Twelfth cakes, and as the cake recipe itself developed, so, too, did the techniques of cake decorating. The earliest form of icing involved painting a hot cake with a mixture of whisked egg white and a flavoring such as rose water. Sugar was then strewn on top, and the cake was returned to the oven to glaze. The advice given in *The Closet of Sir Kenelm Digby Opened* (1669) is that the icing should look "pure, white and smooth like silver, between polished and matte, or like a looking glass."[16] Great care needed to be taken to ensure that this icing would not burn. Digby's book includes several recipes for cakes that may have been used as Twelfth cakes—including one cited above. He also includes the following recipe, with detailed instructions for icing at the end:

Another very good cake

Take four quarts of fine flower, two pound and half of butter, three quarters of a pound of Sugar, four Nutmegs; a little Mace; a pound of Almonds finely beaten, half a pint of Sack, a pint of good Aleyest, a pint of boiled Cream, twelve yolks, and four whites of eggs; four pound of Currants. When you have wrought all these into a very fine past, let it be kept warm before the fire half an hour, before you set it into the oven. If you please, you may put into it, two pounds of Raisins of the Sun stoned and quartered. Let your oven be of a temperate heat, and let your Cake stand therein two hours and a half, before you Ice it; and afterwards only harden the Ice. The Ice for this Cake is made thus: take the Whites of three new laid Eggs, and three quarters of a pound of fine Sugar finely beaten; beat it well together with the whites of the Eggs, and Ice the Cake. If you please you may add a little Musk of Ambergreece.[17]

As with the innovations in cake making, the eighteenth century saw major developments in the areas of icing and decoration. The quantity of sugar involved in icing increased hugely in the eighteenth century, and it started to be beaten with the egg whites and flavorings before being applied. In the late eighteenth century, the layer of marzipan now common on fruitcakes started to be added. Bridget Ann Henisch has traced this innovation to the 1760s.[18] This was a significant change, as there is no evidence to suggest that fruitcakes were elaborately decorated or covered in a layer of marzipan in the seventeenth century.[19] This technique may stem from the earlier practice of serving a large, round cake of pure marzipan that had been decoratively iced at feasts. Adding this marzipan layer to the cake itself helped to keep cakes fresh and airtight, but it also separated the delicate white icing from the moist, dark cake beneath. Elizabeth Raffald is one of the first published authors to recommend adding a layer of marzipan under the icing. Following on from her recipe for a bride cake, she includes the following instructions:

To make Almond-Icing for the Bride Cake

Beat the whites of three eggs to a strong froth, beat a pound of Jordan almonds very fine with rose-water, mix your almonds with the eggs lightly together, a pound of common loaf sugar beat fine, and put in by degrees; when your cake is enough, take it out, and lay your icing on, then put it in to brown.

To make Sugar Icing for the Bride Cake

Beat two pounds of double refined sugar, with two ounces of fine starch. Sift it through a gauze sieve, then beat the whites of five eggs with a knife upon a pewter dish half an hour; beat in your sugar a little at a time, or it will make the eggs fall, and will not be so good a colour, when you have put in all your sugar, beat it half an hour longer, then lay it on your almond icing, and spread it even with a knife; if it be put on as soon as the cake comes out of the oven it will be hard by the time that cake is cold.[20]

In addition to the layers of marzipan and icing, Twelfth cakes also started to be adorned with increasingly ornate festive decorations over the course of the eighteenth century. In the nineteenth century, the fashion for elaborately decorated Twelfth cakes only gained momentum, and they became a spectacle in the windows of pastry and confectioners' shops, which were lit up after dark on Twelfth Night. Going to see the window displays of Twelfth cakes became a Christmas pastime. As we saw in the last chapter, in relation to grocers' exhibits in nineteenth-century Sydney, elaborate displays of food have been an important tradition during the festive season for centuries, helping to excite the senses, whet the appetite, and situate food at the heart of the building anticipation. In 1825, William Hone, the English writer and satirist, described the displays in pastry shops:

In London, with every pastry cook in the city, and at the west end of the town, it is "high change" on Twelfth-Day. . . . Before dusk the important arrangement of the window is completed. Then the gas is turned on with supernumerary argand lamps and manifold wax-lights, to illuminate countless cakes of all prices and dimensions, that stand in rows and piles on the counters and sideboards, and in the windows. The richest in flavour and the heaviest in weight and price are placed on large and massy salvers; one, enormously superior to the rest in size, is the chief object of curiosity; and all are decorated with all imaginable images of things animate and inanimate. Stars, castles, kings, cottages, trees, fish, palaces, cats, dogs, churches, lions, milkmaids, knights, serpents, and innumerable other forms in snow white confectionary, painted with variegated colours, glitter by "excess of light" from mirrors against the walls festooned with artificial "wonders of flora." This "paradise of dainty devices," is crowded by successive and successful desirers of the seasonable delicacies.[21]

The desire to see ever more elaborately decorated cakes was met and fed through these retailers' window displays, but also through print media and newspapers, which reported extensively on the elaborate cakes of the elites. As with so many other areas of Christmas, Queen Victoria and Prince Albert's traditions were commented on regularly. Special attention was given to the reporting of their Majesties' spectacular Twelfth cakes:

The cake was of regal dimensions, being about 30 inches in diameter, and tall in proportion: round the side the decorations consisted of strips of gilded paper, bowing outwards near the top, issuing from an elegant gold bordering. The figures, of which there were 16, on top of the cake, represented a party of beaux and belles of the last century enjoying a repast al fresco under some trees: whilst others, and some children, were dancing to minstrel strains. The repast, spread on the ground, with its full complement of comestibles, decanters and wineglasses (the latter, by the way, were real brittle ware, not sugar) was admirably modelled as were also the figures, servants being represented handing refreshments to some of the gentlemen and ladies, whilst some of the companions of the latter were dancing. The violinist and harpist seemed to be thoroughly impressed with the importance of their functions, and their characteristic attitudes were cleverly given. As a specimen of fancy workmanship, the ornaments of the cake do credit the skill of Mr Mawditt, the Royal confiseur.[22]

These elaborate designs became spectacles for average families to marvel over and to admire from afar, but they were out of reach for most and certainly could not be re-created in your average domestic kitchen. An excerpt

"The Queen's Twelfth Cake."
William Little, *Illustrated London News and Sketch Ltd.*, London, 13 January 1849, 21. Courtesy of the
National Library of Australia.

from 1850 contrasts the unobtainable Twelfth cake of the elites with the Christmas pudding of the masses:

> The spectators of Twelfth-Night luxuries have, for the most part, every reason to believe that their participation will be confined to the sense of sight. Fine combinations of saccharine splendour for the eyes; Kings and Queens, ill-formed but gorgeously gilt and frosted for the eyes; pippin-paste involved into curious scrolls—all for the eyes. But the interest in the Grocer's shop on Christmas Eve penetrates far more deeply into the soul of the surveying crowd. Many, many of them far beyond the limits of twelfth-cake consumers, hope to share practically in the boiled luxury. While the twelfth cake is more an aristocratic type, the plum pudding is a national symbol. It does not represent a class or caste, but the bulk of the English nation. There is not a man, woman or child raised above what the French would call the prolétaires, that does not expect to taste a plum-pudding of some sort or other on Christmas Day.[23]

The trend for elaborate decoration may have led, in part, to the ultimate downfall of the Twelfth cake. Confectioners produced a variety of elaborate decorations for Twelfth cakes, but some of the food coloring used was found to be poisonous, and there were reported cases of children becoming extremely ill, even dying, after consuming the decorations.[24] *Punch* magazine took aim at these mercenary confectioners in 1851, complaining about "the Confectioner-Imp, who paints Twelfth Cakes with emerald green (a beautiful change for coppers, in an arsenite development), and—especially in holiday-times—plays Herod among the innocents."[25]

The most fascinating part of the Twelfth cake tradition, though, is not the evolution of the recipe, or the changing styles of decoration, but rather the accounts of the raucous festive rituals and games in which they played a central role. Until the later seventeenth century, a bean and a pea were traditionally hidden inside the Twelfth cake. The finder of the bean became the king and the finder of the pea became the queen for the night, reigning over the chaos.[26] Robert Herrick, a clergyman who wrote many poems about Christmas, detailed the traditions of the bean and the pea:

> Now, now the mirth comes
> With the cake full of plums,

Where Beane's the King of the sport here;
Beside we must know
The Pea also must revel,
as Queene, in the court here.[27]

Sometimes additional tokens were inserted, such as a rag for the "slut," a clove for the knave, and a forked stick for the cuckold; the finders of each of these would play their part for the rest of the evening.[28] Henry Teonge's account on board a ship in 1676 provides the following recollection:

> Wee had a lot of myrth on board, for wee had a great cake made in which was a bean for the king, a pease for the queen a cloave for the knave a forked stick for the coockold, rag for the slutt. The cake was cutt into severall pieces in the great cabin, and all put into a napkin out of which one took its piece, as out of a lottery then each piece was broken to see what was in it, which caused much laughter to see our lieutenant prove the coockold.[29]

Claire Hopley claims that the tradition of the bean king in Twelfth cakes dates back to Saturnalia, during which a bean was hidden in festive dishes and alcohol-fueled pranks were central to the celebration.[30] In any case, this element of role-play, luck, and inverting the normal social order seems to have been a long-running theme in winter festivals.

Sources from the late sixteenth to early seventeenth centuries describe enormous cakes being ripped to shreds by frenzied guests searching for the pea or bean. Samuel Pepys's diary of the 1660s refers to Twelfth cakes and their associated rituals over many years, and these annual entries allow us to see some significant changes taking place in this period. In 1660, Pepys celebrated Twelfth Night at his cousin's house, where "we had a brave cake brought us, and in the choosing, Pall [Pepys's sister Pauline] was queen and Mr. Sedgwick was king."[31] The following year he explained that the pea had been cut in two, and so both his wife and Mrs. Ward were crowned queen for the evening's festivities. The bean itself had been lost, and so the doctor was chosen to be king.[32] In 1668, Pepys wrote that their cook Jane made "an excellent cake" that cost almost 20 shillings.[33] From the second half of the seventeenth century on, sources, including Pepys's diary, show that change was afoot. It seems that Twelfth cakes were increasingly cut and served to guests in a more orderly fashion, and the pea and bean were becoming relics of the past.[34] Pepys wrote that for Twelfth Night in 1669, "I did bring out my cake—a noble cake, and there cut it into pieces . . . and after a new fashion, to prevent spoiling the cake, did put so many titles into the hat and so drow [drew] cuts."[35] Here we see that instead of ripping the cake apart in search of the tokens, the characters' names were simply drawn from a hat. It was both more civilized and more economical to cut and serve the cake in an orderly fashion and prevent waste. This shift is also demonstrated by the increasing popularity and printing of cards representing Twelfth Night characters. By the late eighteenth century, one could buy booklets with cards for different characters to be drawn on Twelfth Night.[36] In the nineteenth century, small figures made from card or marzipan representing the king, queen, and other characters also developed.[37] And so, while the cake was maintained, its place in the wild role-play was increasingly sidelined. In 1825, William Hone gave directions for proceedings on Twelfth Night:

First, buy your cake. Then, before your visitors arrive, buy your characters,—each of which should have a pleasant verse beneath. Next, look at your invitation list, and count the number of ladies you expect, and afterwards the number of gentlemen. Then, take as many female characters as you have invited ladies, fold them up exactly of the same size, and number each on the back, taking care to make the king No. 1, and the queen No. 2. Then prepare and number the gentlemen's characters. Cause tea and coffee to be handed to your visitors, as they drop in. When all are assembled, and tea over, put as many ladies' characters in a reticule as there are ladies present; next, put the gentlemen's characters in a hat. Then call on a gentleman to carry the reticule to the ladies as they sit; from which each lady is to draw one ticket, and to preserve it unopened. Select a lady to bear the hat to the gentlemen for the same purpose. There will be one ticket left in the reticule, and another in the hat,—which the lady and gentleman who carried each is to interchange, as having fallen to each. Next, arrange your visitors, according to their numbers; the king No. 1, the queen No. 2, and so on. The king is then to recite the verse on his ticket, then the queen the verse on hers; and so the characters are to proceed, in numerical order. This done, let the cake and refreshments go round; and hey! for merriment![38]

The Twelfth cake tradition was by no means unique to Britain—versions of it were celebrated across Europe—and continue to this day. The northern parts of France have the *Galette des Rois*, made with puff pastry and

"Park's New Twelfth Night Characters."
Copyright 2018, Hordern-Dalgety Collection. http://puzzlemuseum.org.

frangipane, while the *Gateau des Rois*, made with brioche and candied fruits, is more common in the south. Versions of this cake were mentioned in medieval France, but its royalist-sounding name made it the subject of tension in the wake of the Revolution.[39] In the French tradition, a child hides under the table and calls out the name of each guest in a random order to come and collect their slice of cake. One of these pieces will contain the hidden trinket. Nicola Humble has suggested that this inversion of order, in which a child becomes the authority for the evening and determines the fates of the adults assembled, harkens back to the social inversion of Saturnalia, in which slaves became masters.[40] Similarly, the Spanish have the *Rosca de Reyes*, a citrus-flavored brioche ring that is decorated with sugar, almonds, and colorful glacé fruit. A figurine of baby Jesus or a bean is inserted into the cake, to be found by the luckiest guest. And, of course, emigrants leaving Europe took these traditions with them to the New World, where they are celebrated to this day. Most famous is the New Orleans king cake, which was brought to America by French immigrants. Its name stems from its connection to the visit of the three kings to the infant Jesus. This brioche-like cake is decorated with green, purple, and gold icing and colored sugars, and it is eaten from Epiphany through to Mardi Gras. As we have seen with all cakes associated with Epiphany, the king cake traditionally contained a hidden bean, but it is now more common to use a small plastic baby figurine. The finder of the baby is obliged to host the next party of the season.[41]

CHRISTMAS CAKE

From the second half of the nineteenth century, the Twelfth cake went into decline in Britain, and soon it was relegated to the dining halls of Christmas past. Today, at least in most of the English-speaking world, very few people have heard of Twelfth cake, let alone eaten it or participated in a wild game of festive role-play. Given its huge cultural significance in the past, this relatively rapid descent into culinary oblivion is remarkable. The British Christmas has not been left cakeless, though. The void that was left was filled by Christmas cake: similar to the Twelfth cake in so many ways, but regrettably less fun. Like its predecessor, Christmas cake is a rich fruitcake, and it is often elaborately iced and decorated. Unlike the Twelfth cake, though, it is not associated with any specific day in the festival, and it does not have any ritualized games or activities surrounding it. Rather than being the centerpiece of a wild night of frivolities in which the social order is upended, Christmas cake is quite simply there to sit on the sideboard looking cheerful and to be offered to guests with a cup of tea. So, while it inherited aspects of Twelfth cake's legacy, it did not assume many of its most defining elements. Some of these traditions, such as role-play and, indeed, the celebration of Twelfth Night, largely disappeared, while other elements were subsumed into the rituals of other Christmas foods. For example, the fortune-telling trinkets did not disappear altogether but went into the plum pudding, and the corny jokes and mock crowns found their way into the Christmas crackers (see chapter 5).[42]

It is difficult to pinpoint the exact reason for Twelfth cake's decline and its replacement with a considerably more sedate descendant. Helen Leach, Mary Browne, and Raelene Inglis argue that the Twelfth cake's reputation had been irreversibly damaged after a series of widely reported scandals that tarnished its image. As discussed above, confectioners began to use toxic substances in their decorations, and a number of children died as a consequence of eating tainted cakes.[43] The most obvious and convincing reason for the demise of the Twelfth cake, though, is quite simply the demise of Twelfth Night itself in Britain. As chapter 1 discussed, as Christmas Day rose in prominence over the course of the Victorian period, it absorbed many of the rituals of the traditional twelve days. The festival contracted and many traditions were lost altogether, while others were welded onto 25 December. This meant that the Christmas cake took on the primary culinary responsibilities of the Twelfth cake, but as the Epiphany itself was no longer widely marked outside the church, elements such as the bean king, Lord of Misrule, and character cards simply disappeared.

The transition from Twelfth cake to Christmas cake was not immediate, though, and there was a period of overlap in which the two coexisted. Leach, Browne, and Inglis have traced some of the earliest references to "Christmas cakes" in a range of sources from newspaper archives to recipe books globally. They found, perhaps surprisingly, that some of the earliest references to Christmas cakes come from 1830s Sydney, Australia, and, critically, that these early references consider them as distinct from the still extant Twelfth cake. An advertisement dated 30 December 1835 specified that the pastry cook, M. Gill, had "a splendid variety of ornamental CHRISTMAS CAKES and in a few days will be seen a most extensive display of grand TWELFTH-NIGHT CAKES."[44] By the mid-nineteenth century, Christmas cakes were becoming more prominent than Twelfth cakes in Australia and New Zealand, but sources suggest that the rate of change was considerably slower in Britain.[45]

By the early 1860s rich fruitcake recipes named "Christmas cake" began appearing in published recipe books throughout the English-speaking world. One of the earliest (if not the first) published fruitcake recipes to use the name "Christmas cake" in the title actually appeared in an American cookbook, *The Practical Housekeeper: A Cyclopaedia of Domestic Economy* (1857), by Elizabeth Ellet:

The Housewife's Christmas Cake.

Take two pounds of pounded sugar-candy, two pounds of butter, thirty-six eggs, four pounds of currants, a pound of raisins stoned and chopped, half a pound of almonds blanched and chopped, half a pound of citron, a pound of candied orange-peel, the same of candied lemon-peel, a large nutmeg pounded, half an ounce of powdered all-spice, half an ounce of powdered mace, ginger, cinnamon, and coriander, and half a pint of brandy.

All the ingredients should be well dried, the white of the eggs well beaten up separately from the yolks, the butter stirred and beaten almost to a cream; then add the rest gradually, taking care they are well beaten and mixed. Have ready a large tin, well lined with buttered paper, pour in the cake, and bake in a slow oven for at least four hours.

Smaller proportions may be adopted.[46]

The first fruitcake recipe published in Britain called "Christmas cake" appears to be Mrs. Beeton's 1861 offering. Interestingly, the recipe does not follow the pound cake system or creaming method that was already well established by this stage, and which is typical of the standard Christmas cake today:

Christmas Cake

1754. Ingredients.—5 teacupsful of flour, 1 teacupful of melted butter, 1 teacup full of cream, 1 teacupful of treacle, 1 teacupful of moist sugar, 2 eggs, 1/3 oz. of powdered ginger, ½ lb of raisins, 1 teaspoonful of carbonate of soda, 1 tablespoonful of vinegar.

Mode.—Make the butter sufficiently warm to melt it, but do not allow it to oil; put the flour into a basin; add to it the sugar, ginger, and raisins, which should be stoned and cut into small pieces. When these dry ingredients are thoroughly mixed, stir in the butter, cream, treacle, and well-whisked eggs, and beat the mixture for a few minutes. Dissolve the soda in the vinegar, add it to the dough, and be particular that these latter ingredients are well incorporated with the others; put the cake into a buttered mould or tin, place it in a moderate oven immediately, and bake it from 1 ¾ to 2 ¼ hours.[47]

Shortly after Mrs. Beeton's work was published, Edward Abbott included a recipe for "Christmas Yule Cake" in *The English and Australian Cookery Book* (1864). This recipe was considerably closer to a modern Christmas cake than Beeton's offering, using brandy, more spices, and mixed peel.[48] Abbott's, Ellet's, and Beeton's recipes collectively demonstrate that within a very short period of time, from the late 1850s to the early 1860s, fruitcakes now described as "Christmas cakes" began to appear in recipe books across the English-speaking world. Suddenly, the Christmas cake had well and truly arrived, at precisely the moment that the Twelfth cake was starting to fade.

As the nineteenth century progressed, more and more fruitcakes were rebranded as Christmas cakes. These were generally smaller than earlier cakes, so they were far easier for the domestic cook or housewife to prepare at home. The recipes now almost always followed the pound cake principle and used baking soda as a raising agent. Other minor changes to recipes include the adoption of "mixed spice," and the use of sliced or slivered rather than pounded almonds, adding a textural element to the cake. Mixed peel also became a popular addition, and essences were developed that added flavor at a more affordable price.[49] Like Twelfth cakes, Christmas cakes continued to be festively decorated, but the style became simpler and decorations more straightforward, especially as home cooks started to tackle them in domestic kitchens. The layer of marzipan and royal icing remained throughout the twentieth century, though, and is still used on cakes today. However, many modern consumers no longer appreciate the flavor of marzipan, opting for alternatives such as fondant icing or simply glazed nuts, glacé fruits, and festive tartan ribbons.

Of course there are many national and regional varieties of rich fruit Christmas cakes. Scotland in particular has specialties associated with the New Year's festival of Hogmanay. Dundee cake and black bun, or Scotch bun, are two favorites there. The former of these is a light, crumbly style of fruitcake topped with almonds arranged in a decorative pattern. It was invented by the Keiller Marmalade Company and was mass-produced by them from the nineteenth century on. Dundee cake is a festive food, and reportedly a favorite of Queen Elizabeth II, but it is not exclusively related to Christmas, being eaten year-round. Black bun, also known as Scotch bun, by contrast, is strongly connected to Hogmanay. This is a very dark fruitcake, so rich and moist that it is almost plum pudding–like in texture and flavor. The cake itself is encased in pastry and served in either a round or a loaf shape. One of the earliest published recipes for Scotch bun that connects it to Christmas appears in a later edition of Margaret Dods's *The Cook and Housewife's Manual*:

A Scotch Christmas Bun, from Mrs Fraser's Cookery.—Take half a peck of flour, keeping out a little to work it up with; make a hole in the middle of the flour, and break in sixteen ounces of butter; pour in a mutchkin (pint) of warm water, and three gills of yeast, and work it up into a smooth dough. If it is not wet enough, put in a little more warm water; then cut off one-third of the dough, and lay it aside for the cover. Take three pounds of stoned raisins, three pounds of cleaned currants, half a pound of blanched almonds cut long-wise; candied orange and citron peel cut, or each eight ounces; half an ounce of cloves, an ounce of cinnamon, and two ounces of ginger, all beat and sifted. Mix the spices by themselves, then spread out the dough; lay the fruit upon it; strew the spices over the fruit, and mix altogether. When it is well kneaded, roll out the cover, and lay the bun upon it; then cover it neatly, cut it round the sides, prickle it, and bind it with paper to keep it in shape; set it in a pretty quick oven, and, just before you take it out, glaze the top with beaten egg.[50]

This exact recipe also appears in Dods's first edition, dating to 1826, under the title "A Scotch Half-peck Bun, from Mrs Fraser's Cookery."[51] The dish and directions for its preparation are identical, but this earlier edition simply does not connect it with Christmas explicitly. Along with haggis, shortbread, and Yule cakes or bannocks, which will be discussed in the following chapter, Scotch bun is commonly associated with Scottish "first footing" rituals, in which visitors to a house come bearing gifts and good luck for the New Year. The first person across the threshold is an omen for things to come, as we will discuss in more detail in the following chapter, and that person must bring, but also be offered, suitable foods like Scotch bun by the host.[52] Robert Louis Stevenson described the lead-up to Hogmanay in 1879, stating that "currant-loaf is now popular eating in all households. For weeks before the great morning, confectioners display stacks of Scotch bun—a dense, black substance inimical to life."[53] Although it is now associated with Hogmanay, Scotch bun appears to have been a Scottish variety of a Twelfth cake and, according to Alan Davidson, preserves elements of its prophetic powers.[54]

Like many foods so central to the British, Irish, and Commonwealth festive season, Christmas cake has never gained the same iconic status in America. Nineteenth-century sources such as Ellet's recipe, included above, show that it has always been on the menu, but it is not nearly as popular or as mandatory a part of the festival there. The famous quote by comedian and television host Johnny Carson gives a humorous American view of Christmas cake: "The worst gift is fruitcake. There is only one fruitcake in the entire world, and people keep sending it to each other." Nicola Humble has argued that "in the American context the problem with fruit cake is that it is the opposite of what now registers as 'cake' in the popular imagination. If 'cake' is soft, tall, light, fluffy and ephemeral then a cake that is solid, dense and seemingly everlasting poses a conceptual problem."[55]

Despite Christmas cake not being quite as much fun as its predecessor, it retains an important role in the festive traditions of Britain, Ireland, and many countries within the Commonwealth. It may not be quite as popular in America, but it is still commonplace enough for jokes to be made at its expense. Christmas cakes will commonly be made weeks in advance, often on "Stir-Up Sunday" alongside the puddings. The cakes will then be "fed" with brandy or whiskey over the following weeks to allow the flavor to develop and the cake to mature. If Twelfth cake represented the bawdiest and most frivolous side of Christmas past, Christmas cake possibly typifies the Victorians' taming and domestication of the festival. Where once the fruitcake played a central role in a night of raucous role-play, it is now passed around with tins of shortbread as a last unnecessary morsel after the Christmas dinner, offered to houseguests with a cup of tea, or perhaps on a plate with a small dram for Santa. More than anything, it represents both the raucous side of Christmas past and the domestic, cozy side of Christmas present.

CONTINENTAL CHRISTMAS CAKES

Volumes could be written on the many festive cakes of Continental Europe. Most countries, if not regions, have their own cakes or enriched breads that make the Christmas season special and that are connected to specific days or rituals. There is not space to do justice to all of these cakes here; they each have their own rich history, which is embedded in the culinary story of Christmas in each of these places. Rather, we will focus on some of the European cakes that have penetrated the Christmas menu of the Anglophone world the most and helped to create an increasingly varied culinary experience at this time of year. Cakes and other baked goods appear to be one of the areas of festive food where Continental influences have taken root more easily and become a part of the British Christmas. Whereas the main parts of the meal (that is, the turkey, ham, brussels sprouts, and pudding) remain steadfastly English, there seems to have been a greater receptiveness to experimentation with the sweet optional extras. And while some of these cakes have only penetrated the menu in the last two decades at most, as a result of immigration and travel, their established roots in Europe give these newcomers to the otherwise traditional British Christmas an air of ancient ritual and authenticity.

Foremost among Continental baked goods that have found a place in the modern Christmas outside their country of origin is panettone: an enriched and spiced fruit bread traditionally prepared in Italy. Milan is considered the capital of panettone, but other regions offer different varieties for the festive season. It has only been since the late twentieth century that panettone penetrated the British market in any significant way. Nineteenth-century English sources do mention panettone, but they make it clear that it was an exotic, foreign oddity, rather than a foodstuff that was produced or consumed in Britain. In the late twentieth century, panettone started to appear in shops and households in the lead-up to Christmas in Britain and many other places in the English-speaking world. Of course, Italian migrants had brought it with them to America and Australia long before the wider communities embraced these baked goods. References from the 1940s in New York proudly describe its manufacture there, but outside of Italian communities it gained little traction for decades.[56] In a relatively short space of time, though, this traditional Italian specialty has become firmly entrenched in the Christmas repertoire of Britain, America, and beyond. Today, the cheerful, distinctively shaped festive boxes of panettone hitting the shelves of delicatessens and grocers is one of the first signs that Christmas is on its way. Panforte has also finally gained a well-deserved place at Christmas tables beyond Italy. A specialty of Siena, panforte is a very dense, solid cake made of dried fruits and nuts mixed with spices and cocoa.[57] Sold in beautiful packaging, it has become a popular Christmas gift for many people globally.

German stollen is another famous European Christmas cake that is being celebrated outside of its homeland more than ever before. Stollen is made from an enriched sweetened yeast dough, mixed dried fruits, and almonds. It is flavored with lemon, rum, or brandy and filled with marzipan. After it is baked, it is dredged in icing sugar before being served. Stollen is particularly associated with the city of Dresden in Germany, where every year a three-metric-ton cake is paraded through the streets as part of Stollenfest. Although there has not been a strong tradition of stollen in Britain, food historian William Woys Weaver demonstrates that it has a considerable legacy in the parts of America most heavily settled by German immigrants. Stollen is closely related and extremely similar to "Dutch Christmas cake," which is popular in the middle Atlantic States.[58] Finally, the last of the imported festive fruit breads needing some commentary is bishop's bread, or *bischofsbrot*. This is a variety of cake so densely packed with dried fruit that when it is sliced its colors are revealed in section. When held up to the light, a slice should look like a stained glass window, earning it the alternative names of broken or stained glass cake. Bishop's bread likely originated in northern and central Europe and was brought to America with immigrant communities.

Finally, no discussion of Christmas cakes would be complete without mentioning the famous Yule log, or *Bûche de Noël*. As the name suggests, *Bûche de Noël* is of French origin, but it has been a Christmas favorite far beyond its native shores for some time. *Bûche de Noël* is essentially a rolled sponge cake decorated to resemble a tree log. Both the name and the concept refer to the traditional Yule log that was burned during the winter festival. In many parts of Europe a great log was brought into the house and lit on the hearth, where it stayed burning for the twelve days and could not be extinguished. Part of the wood was retained at the end of the twelve days and kept throughout the year, being used to light the Yule log the following year. Practices vary across Europe, but the emphasis on keeping the light burning in the depths of midwinter and preserving an element of it from year to year is consistent and likely stems from earlier pagan rituals.[59] While the Yule log no longer appears in Britain and many other parts of Europe during Christmas, it is remembered with a festive cake, which provides a welcome relief from the enriched spiced fruit breads and cakes that otherwise dominate at Christmas.

5

SWEET TREATS

*I passed through the seven levels of the candy cane forest, through
the sea of swirly-twirly gum drops, and then I walked through the
Lincoln Tunnel.*

—Will Ferrell, as Buddy the Elf, *Elf* (2003)

Given what we have seen in the last two chapters, which have addressed
the story of festive desserts and cakes in detail, you would be forgiven
for thinking that the sugar hit of Christmas has been dealt with in full, but
we are really only just beginning. This chapter will discuss the myriad of
indulgent sweet treats that are enjoyed throughout the festival. Mince pies,
cookies, chocolates, and candy may not hold pride of place at the dining table, but they are the treats decking the tree, enjoyed by the fire, and given as
gifts that make Christmas a truly indulgent, days-long experience. Christmas
would not be Christmas without these last totally unnecessary, delectable
morsels, all of which have their own stories to tell. William Woys Weaver
includes the following quote from 1877, which illustrates the role that these
sweet treats play at Christmas perfectly:

Christmas is coming, and the holidays are coming, and all the Children are
coming, and all the grandchildren are coming, and all their country-cousins
are coming, and all their uncles and aunts are coming, and every one of these
wants their share of Christmas goodies, the Christmas eating and Christmas

drinking, the Christmas pies, cakes, puddings and Christmas confections; its bon-bons, nicknacks, and its forty thousand sweet things.[1]

BAKED GOODS

In the weeks before Christmas many a household becomes a hive of baking activity. Sweet treats are prepared to share with the increased number of houseguests over the holiday period. These are also packaged up in jars and cellophane bags as homemade gifts. Shops begin to stock gift boxes of mince pies and decorative tins of biscuits, or cookies, to ensure that the collective annual sugar high is maintained for all of December and at least part of January. For many families, Christmas would just not be the same without a seemingly endless supply of mince pies, cookies, and shortbread on offer. What makes these supposedly supporting acts so important is that each of these dishes has its own festive story to tell. Many have a history that extends back to the medieval period, if not earlier, meaning that their legacy has deep cultural roots. They also commonly have their own traditions in families and are connected to some of the most cherished memories of childhood. The lead-up to Christmas is a time when many families bake together more than at any other time of year. Making tree decorations, sweet-laden gingerbread houses, and small cellophane bags of star-shaped biscuits to give as gifts is an important part of the season for many families. Children may recall seeing their mother struggle to fit the turkey in the oven, but they are more likely to actively participate in and remember the scent, feel, and taste of raw cookie dough while helping to stamp out shapes for the Christmas tree. These experiences of producing these foods annually with their parents help children to incorporate them into their own memory, culture, and sense of tradition. And it is through the ritual of annual domestic production that the significance of these otherwise culinary bit parts is elevated.

Mince Pies

Mince pies are without a doubt one of Christmas's most iconic dishes. In the world's biggest mince pie factory, run by the British household name Mr. Kipling, approximately 180 million are produced over the festive season, using seven thousand metric tons of dried fruit.[2] Like plum pudding, they are medieval in origin and were once consumed at many celebratory feasts, but they are now exclusively associated with Christmas. Today, the "mince-meat" filling is typically a mixture of dried fruits, nuts, apples, suet, spices, and alcohol (most commonly brandy). This is contained in a small, sweet, shortcrust pastry base and is covered with either a fully closed lid or a decorative top, such as lattice or a star. Like many other Christmas foods, their cultural significance and connections to the festival mean that a rich folklore has developed around the history of mince pies. One popular legend is that their shape was originally fashioned after the Christ's crib. Another story explains that their high spice content symbolized the Eastern origins of the three Wise Men.[3] There is only limited (if any) evidence to support these stories, but they have become so entrenched in the popular imagination that they add yet another layer to the history of these intriguing little pies.

Like the plum pudding, the medieval predecessors of modern mince pies contained meat. They demonstrated a distinctly different flavor profile from today's mince pies, combining both sweet and savory elements with spice. Pies originally contained larger whole pieces of flesh, but by the fourteenth century new fillings of finely minced and spiced meat had emerged.[4] Early ancestors of contemporary mince pies include the medieval "chewette," which was a small pastry filled with chopped meat or liver, hard-boiled eggs, ginger, and dried fruits. By the sixteenth century, these were known as "minced" or "shred" pies, and they were already associated with Christmas.[5] In 1573, Thomas Tusser included "Beef, mutton, and pork, shred pies of the best" as an important part of "Christmas Husbandly Fare."[6] Robert Herrick's seventeenth-century poem commemorated the pies and again connects them to Christmas:

> Drink now the strong beer,
> Cut the white loaf here,
> The while the meat is a-shredding;
> For the rare mince-pie
> And the plums stand by
> To fill the paste that's a-kneading.[7]

Gervase Markham's recipe from *The English Huswife*, first published in 1615, demonstrates the combination of meat, fruit, and spice that would be quite unusual to a contemporary palate but was quite typical of high-status food during this period:

> Take a Leg of Mutton, and cut the best of the best flesh from the bone, and parboyle it well: then put to it three pound of the best Mutton suet, and shred it very small: then spread it abroad, and season it with pepper and salt, cloves and mace: then put in good store of currants, great raysons and prunes clean washt and pickt, a few dates slic't, and some orange pills slic't: then being all well mixt together, put it into a coffin, or into divers coffins, and so bake them: and when they are served up, open the liddes and strow store of Suger on the top of the meate and upon the lid. And in this sort you may also bake Beef or Veal, onely the Beef would not be parboyld, and the Veal will ask a double quantity of Suet.[8]

As we saw with plum porridge, the strong connection between mince pies and Christmas made them a direct target for Puritans in their war against the festival. Not only were they luxurious and indulgent, but they also had a suspicious air of popish idolatry about them.[9] In 1652, the *Flying Eagle* reported that "the poore will pawn all to the Cloaths of their back to provide Christmas pies for their bellies, and the broth of Abominable things in their Vessels."[10] In a Commons debate on Christmas Day 1656, Puritan MPs fretted over the fact that Christmas was still being observed by the masses. Lord Lambert cautioned that the cavaliers were "now merry over their Christmas pies, drinking the king of Scots health, or your confusion."[11] Here we see mince pies again linked to suspicions of popish, royalist plots. R. Fletcher published the following scathing satire of the Puritans' paranoia in 1656, taking aim at their absurd suspicion of mince pies:

> Christ-mass? give me my beads: the word implies
> A plot, by its ingredients, beef and pyes.
> The cloyster'd steaks with salt and pepper lye
> Like Nunnes with patches in a monastrie.
> Prophaneness in a conclave? Nay, much more,
> Idolatrie in crust! Babylon's whore
> Rak'd from the grave, and bak'd by hanches, then

Serv'd up in Coffins to unholy men;
Defil'd, with superstition, like the Gentiles
Of old, that worship'd onions, roots, and lentiles!"[12]

Sources from the late seventeenth century indicate that the Puritans' objections had had very little impact and that foods like mince pies had more than survived the Commonwealth and were celebrated during the Restoration. Monsieur Misson, a French visitor to England in the late seventeenth century, observed that "every family against Christmas makes a famous Pye: It is a great Nostrum the composition of this Pasty; it is a most learned mixture of Neats' [calves'] tongues, Chicken, Eggs, Sugar Raisins, Lemon and Orange Peel, various kinds of spicery."[13]

In 1660, Robert May included a range of mince pie recipes using various meats in his famous work, *The Accomplisht Cook*, as well as a series of important illustrations demonstrating the different elaborate shapes they could be made in.[14] Although mince pies are almost exclusively round today, early modern versions experimented with different shapes and more elaborate decoration. These would sometimes fit together on a plate to form a complicated decorative pattern. Designs also appear in manuscript receipt

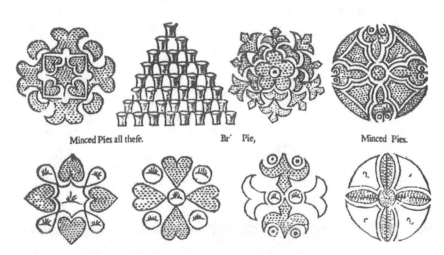

Minced Pies all thefe.   Br Pie,   Minced Pies.

"Dishes of minced pies for all manner of Flesh or Fowl, according to these Forms."
From Robert May, *The Accomplisht Cook, or the Art and Mystery of Cookery*, 1685 edition, published by Obadiah Blagrave, London.

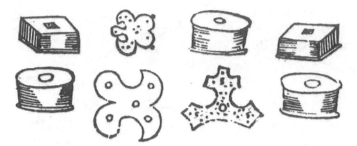

"Forms of minced Pyes."
From Robert May, *The Accomplisht Cook, or the Art and Mystery of Cookery*,
1685 edition, published by Obadiah Blagrave, London.

books of the period. For example, Hannah Bisaker's book, started in 1692, contains a beautiful illustration of the variety of mince pies designs that could be made.[15]

Minced pies remained a hugely popular Christmas treat throughout the seventeenth century. On Christmas Eve night in 1666, Samuel Pepys's wife stayed up until four o'clock on Christmas morning to supervise her maids preparing mince pies. Her husband enjoyed these as an accompaniment to roast beef for his Christmas dinner the next day.[16] *The Closet of Sir Kenelm Digby Opened*, first published in 1669, contains multiple recipes for minced pies, including the following showing a distinctly sweet flavor profile, with the addition of ambergris sugar on top:

Minced Pyes

My Lady Larsson makes her finest minced Pyes of Neats-tongues; But she holdeth the most savoury ones to be of veal and mutton equal parts very small minced. Her finest crust is made by sprinkling the flower (as much as it needeth) with cold water, and then working the past with little pieces of raw Butter in good quantity. So that she useth neither hot water, nor melted butter in them; And this makes the crust short and light. After all the meat and seasoning, and Plums and Citron Peel, &c. is in the Coffin, she puts a little Ambred-sugar upon it, thus; Grind much two grains of Ambergreece and half a one of musk, with a little piece of hard loaf sugar. This will serve six or eight pyes, strwed all over the top. Then cover it with the Liddle, and set it in the oven.[17]

Meat remained a part of most recipes throughout the eighteenth century, but it began to reduce considerably, and mince pies took on an increasingly sweet flavor profile. Elizabeth Raffald's recipe from 1769 maintains a meat component but demonstrates that the ratio of meat to fruit had changed. Note also the use of "puff paste," which was common throughout the Victorian period as well:

A Mince Pie

Boil a neat's tongue two hours, then skin it and chop it as small as possible. Chop very small three pounds of fresh beef suet, three pounds of good baking apples, four pounds of currants clean washed, picked, and well dried before the fire, one pound of jar raisins stoned and chopped small, and one pound of powdered sugar. Mix them altogether with half an ounce of mace, the same of nutmeg grated, cloves and cinnamon, a quarter of an ounce of each, and one pint of French brandy, and make a rich puff paste. As you fill the pie up put in a little candied citron and orange cut in little pieces, what you have to spare, put close down in a pot and cover it up.[18]

By the nineteenth century, many recipes no longer included meat, with the exception of suet.[19] Meat versions of the dish did survive in the Victorian period, though. Queen Victoria's famous chef Charles Elmé Francatelli reportedly prepared the following meat-based recipe each Christmas, although he also included meat-free versions in his work *The Modern Cook*:

Mince Meat, A La Royale

To equal proportions of roast-beef; raisins, currants, suet, candied citron, orange, lemon, spices and sugar, add a proportionate weight of stewed pears and preserved ginger, the grated rind of three dozen oranges and lemons, and also their juice, one bottle of old rum, one bottle of brandy, and two of old port.[20]

Mrs. Beeton also included a recipe for mincemeat using one and a half pounds of lean beef in addition to three pounds of beef suet in the first edition of *Household Management*. She includes a second version called an "excellent mincemeat" that contains no meat bar suet, but it is the former that she recommends for use in mince pies.[21] The recommendation had changed in later editions of her book, though. The 1907 edition of Mrs. Beeton's book includes a recipe with beef tongue titled "American mincemeat," but the version it recommends for use in mince pies is distinctly sweet and contains only suet:

1740. Mincemeat.

Ingredients.—1 lb of finely-chopped suet, 1 lb of currants washed and picked, 1 lb. of raisins stoned and quartered, 1 lb of chopped apples, 1 lb of castor sugar, ½ lb of sultanas, ¼ of an lb of shredded mixed candied peel, 2 lemons, ½ a gill of brandy, ½ a saltspoonful each of nutmeg, mace and cinnamon.

Method.—Pare the lemons thinly, simmer the rinds in a little water until perfectly tender, then pound them or rub them through a fine sieve. Mix all the ingredients well together, press into a jar, cover closely, and keep in a cool dry place for at least 1 month before using.[22]

Beloved in Britain to this day, mince pies also became mandatory festive fare throughout the Empire. And while they are not as popular in America, they were always on the menu there as well. The famous American cookbook author Eliza Leslie includes extensive instructions and several recipes for making mincemeat and mince pies, including some based on beef tongue and heart.[23] One of the earliest Canadian-authored cookbooks, *The Frugal Housewife's Manual* (1840), shows this same adherence to the older meat-based dish, including directions for making mince pies with two pounds of beef.[24] This work also includes advice for supplementing expensive dried fruits and sugar with preserved cherries and apples, demonstrating how cooks adapted their recipes in order to "keep Christmas" in the colonies.[25] Notwithstanding these early recipes, these dishes never gained the same level of popularity, or centrality to the season, in the United States. Cathy Kaufman observes that the first American edition of Hannah Glasse's *Art of Cookery*, published in 1805, actually removed the recipes for "Christmas Pye" and "Christmas Plumb Porridge." Kaufman suggests that one explanation for this decision may be that such dishes were strongly associated with southern Loyalists and thus were seen as inherently British.[26]

As we have seen previously, in relation to both puddings and cakes, against all odds, the Antipodeans were more determined than anyone in this endeavor. In spite of the challenges of making pastry in a colonial kitchen in high summer, Australian cooks faithfully maintained the tradition of mince pies. In 1837, the same pastry cook and confectioner, M. Gill, who posted early advertisements for Christmas cakes in Sydney, boasted to have coming into stock "some of the finest mince pies ever made in the colony."[27] Those living off the land, outside urban centers, needed to fend for themselves. Annabella Boswell, of Lake Innes, New South Wales, wrote that she rose early on the morning of 23 December 1850 to prepare fruit for her mince pies.[28] As always, though, from an early date social commentators queried the Australian adherence to such heavy festive foods, with one writer asking, "Who would give a fig for a hot mince pie, with the rays of a nearly tropical sun resting on it?"[29] Notwithstanding these colonial complaints, mince pies remain a common festive food in Australia and New Zealand to this day.

Cookies

Many of the Christmas food traditions discussed thus far have focused on Britain, but the discussion of cookies will have a decidedly American flavor. It is not that cookies, or rather biscuits, do not feature during Christmas in Britain—shortbread is a well-loved Christmas specialty and tins of biscuits make welcome gifts—but they do not occupy the same festive status that they retain on the other side of the Atlantic, where they are a central part of the holidays.

European immigrants introduced their festive baking traditions to the New World in the seventeenth century, and, in doing so, they left their culinary mark on the American Christmas. Indeed, the very term "cookie" reflects this Continental European influence in America. It emerged during the eighteenth century and comes from the New Netherlands Dutch *koekje*.[30] A huge range of cookie recipes were brought to America by the various communities from across Europe who arrived and settled there. Dutch communities famously made elaborately shaped cookies to serve on New Year's Day. These "New Year's cakes" were considered a delicacy particularly associated with New York and the Hudson Valley.[31] Eliza Leslie's recipe for New Year's cake is as follows:

New-Year's Cake

Stir together a pound of nice fresh butter, and a pound of powdered white sugar, till they become a light thick cream. Then stir in, gradually, three pounds of sifted flour. Add, by degrees, a tea-spoonful of soda dissolved in a small tea-cup of milk, and then a half salt-spoonful of tartaric acid, melted in a large tablespoonful of warm water. Then mix in, gradually, three table-spoonfuls of fine caraway seeds. Roll out the dough into sheets half an inch thick, and cut it with a jagging iron into oval or oblong cakes, pricked with a fork. Bake them immediately in shallow iron pans, slightly greased with fresh butter. The bakers in New York ornament these cakes, with devices or pictures raised by a wooden stamp. They are good plain cakes for children.[32]

Gingerbread is perhaps the most iconic Christmas cookie of all, though. Medieval gingerbreads, recorded in sources from the thirteenth century on, were mixtures of ginger, spices, honey, breadcrumbs, and sometimes saffron or powdered sandalwood, known as sanders, for color.[33] The dough was pressed into elaborate shapes and molds, and the finished product covered in gold leaf. These spiced, scented, and gilt cookies were given as luxury and highly desirable gifts within elite circles. Versions of gingerbread became popular across Europe. The Norwegians had *pepperkaker*, the Swedish *pepperkakor*, the Danish *brunkagor*, the Dutch *speculoos*, and, of course, the German *lebkuchen*. Nuremberg became particularly famous as a center for gingerbread production, with guilds of makers being established from the fifteenth and sixteenth centuries. This was also the home of the gingerbread house, which became popular in Germany by the nineteenth century and is now a celebrated part of Christmas in many countries.[34] Decorating a ginger-bread house with royal icing and sweets has become a common activity for children and parents to do together in the lead-up to Christmas.

The introduction of these and a host of other cookie varieties too nu-merous to name started a strong tradition of Christmas baking in the New World. According to Cathy Kaufman, the first recipe published in America that was explicitly connected to Christmas appeared in the 1796 edition of Amelia Simmons's *American Cookery*. It was for a "Christmas cookey," spiced with coriander:

Another Christmas Cookey

To three pound of flour, sprinkle a tea cup of fine powdered coriander seed, rub in one pound of butter, and one and a half pound sugar, dissolve one tea spoonful of pearlash in a tea cup of milk, kneed all together well, roll three quarters of an inch thick, and cut or stamp into shape and slice you please, bake slowly fifteen or twenty minutes; tho' hard and dry at first, if put in an earthen pot, and dry cellar, or damp room, they will be finer, softer and better when six months old.[35]

The malleability of cookie dough, which lent itself to being made into an almost unimaginable number of shapes and designs, was part of the appeal of festive cookies—that is, if their sweet spiciness was not reason enough. As discussed above, from the medieval period on, elaborately shaped biscuits were popular across Europe, but as another German tradition, the Christmas tree, took root in America, the decorative qualities of cookie dough were more celebrated than ever. As they rose in popularity from the 1820s, as chapter 1 outlined, so, too, did the fashion for making decorated, shaped cookies and confectionery to adorn them.

As William Woys Weaver discusses, until the later nineteenth century most families would not have had access to specialized tin cookie cutters, so simple or hand-cut shapes sufficed for a time. From the 1870s on, though, cheap, imported baking utensils and wares from Germany entered the market in the United States, and so cookie cutters became widely available. These allowed domestic cooks to create highly stylized images that were specifically designed to hang on the Christmas tree.[36] Wooden molds were an alternative way to produce decorative shapes and could be used to stamp intricate patterns or images onto cookies. Springerle boards are among the most beautifully crafted of such molds, and they were used to create a specific type of German festive cookie called springerle. The boards themselves were often brought with immigrants to the New World as cherished family heirlooms, but they were also imported to cater to the growing demand for festive cookies in America.[37] Eventually commercial businesses began to produce decorative cookies specifically designed for Christmas trees. Animal crackers, which developed in the nineteenth century, became one of the most iconic varieties of these. In 1902, boxes of "Barnum's Animals" started to be manufactured by the National Biscuit Company. They were packaged in a decorative, festive box designed specifically for the Christmas season, which included a string for hanging from the tree.[38]

Shaped cookies were made even more festive with elaborate decoration. Icing, gold and silver leaf, sweets, and ribbons created striking decorations for the tree. From the mid- to late nineteenth century, scrap pictures were

Reproduced nineteenth-century cookie.
Courtesy of Winterthur Museum, Shipley Room, Yuletide 2017, photo by James Schneck.

also added to cookies to create truly ornate gifts and decorations that reflected a particularly Victorian, romantic aesthetic.[39] "Yule dollies," as they were known, often had elaborately iced dresses and faces completed with scrap pictures that were produced cheaply through chromolithography.[40] These Yule dollies were hugely popular in the nineteenth century and were a Victorian revival of medieval Yule dows or doughs: shaped pastries, normally depicting animals, humans, or the baby Jesus. These were also sometimes known as "baby cakes."[41]

The significance that cookies have had in the development of the American Christmas is reflected by the modern ritual of the cookie exchange (or swap). This is a festive event whereby each guest at an exchange brings a batch of their favorite homemade Christmas cookies. Each batch is passed around so that every guest takes home an assortment of all the cookies to share with their family. Newspapers from the twentieth century indicate that these cookie swaps were increasingly popular from the 1960s on.[42] The most famous of these is undoubtedly the Wellesley cookie exchange, which Mary Bevilacqua and Laurel Gabel began in 1971. The annual tradition ultimately inspired Susan Mahnke Peery to write *The Wellesley Cookie Exchange Cookbook* (1986), based upon some of the most popular recipes. The cookie exchange highlights the significance of baking at this time of year, the love of sweet and often spicy flavors throughout the festival, and the role that food plays in this communal celebration. Today, Christmas cookies retain a central place in the American Christmas. Festive iced cookies in a range of flavors and shapes are still used as decorations and gifts and are frequently left out for Santa Claus with a customary glass of milk (or something stronger).

Shortbread

In a British context, the cookie, or rather biscuit, most celebrated at Christmas is undoubtedly shortbread. Shortbread is made across Britain, but it is strongly associated with Scotland, where it is something of a national food. It has a particular connection to the New Year festival Hogmanay and the tradition of the "first footing." As briefly discussed in chapter 4, in relation to black bun, this is where the first person to cross a household's threshold after midnight is said to determine the family's fortune in the New Year. Dark-haired men are said to bring luck, but women and redheads are not good omens. As part of the ritual the first footer must be shown hospitality, with shortbread or oatcakes being a common offering.[43] Upon visiting people for the first time after Hogmanay, guests will commonly bring a gift with them, and, again, shortbread is a traditional choice. In 1879, Robert Louis Stevenson described Hogmanay preparations in Edinburgh. He wrote that the bakers' windows boasted "full moons of shortbread adorned with mottoes of peel or sugar-plum, in honour of the season and the family affections."[44]

The origins of shortbread lie in sixteenth-century "shortcakes," which were a type of flat, although sometimes leavened, shortcrust pastry.[45] As sugar was made more widely available and affordable during the eighteenth century, shortbread became increasing sweet, beginning to resemble modern recipes for it more closely. Today, traditional Scottish shortbread is quite simply a layer of sweet shortcrust pastry. Due to its high fat content, its texture should be crumbly and light. Its main flavor profile comes simply from the richness of the butter and the sweetness of the sugar, but some regional variations use dried peel, almonds, and spices. The biscuits are now served in a range of shapes, but "petticoat tails" are a traditional form. This refers to baking the pastry in a round with crimped edges, which is sliced into wedges upon serving.[46] This same shape was also used in the traditional Yule bannocks or brünies: a Christmas flat bread or cake made from oats or other meal and served with a special sort of cheese called kebbuck. Bannocks were made in a round with notches pressed around the edges—a shape said to represent the sun. A Yule bannock was given to each member of the family on Christmas or Hogmanay Eve and needed to be kept intact until the time came to eat it. If the cake was broken too early, this was a bad omen for the coming year.[47] Christmas Eve was sometimes known as *Oidhche nam Bonnagan*, or Bannock Night, stemming from the ritual of baking the cakes on this night. A carol called "Duan Nollaig" recalls this connection:

> Hey the hannock ho the bannock,
> Hey the bannock, air a' bhco,
> Telling us that Christ is born,
> King of Kings and Lord of Lords.[48]

Shortbread has become a Christmas staple beyond Britain and Ireland, and it is a popular gift throughout the Commonwealth and former Empire.

Annabella Boswell, whose memories of preparing the fruit for mince pies has already been discussed, also recalled making Christmas shortbread early in the morning on 23 December 1850 on the family property in Lake Innes, New South Wales.[49] One can only imagine the difficulties of preparing butter-rich shortbread in a colonial kitchen during the height of the Australian summer. From around this same date, New Zealand newspapers held numerous advertisements for shops selling Christmas shortbread[50] and ran editorials suggesting recipes for the biscuits alongside those for Christmas cakes, plum puddings, and other goodies.[51] Nineteenth-century Antipodean newspapers also reported on the festive displays of shortbread in shop windows.[52]

Today, shortbread makes a common gift at Christmas and is served to household guests throughout the festival. It is still frequently homemade but also widely available commercially, often packaged in attractive festive tins. The Walkers Shortbread brand, founded by Joseph Walker in 1898, has become particularly well known for its tartan-patterned decorative gift tins and boxes.

CONFECTIONERY

After Santa Claus and the sack full of toys he brings, the abundance of confectionery available during Christmas is one of the most exciting parts of the festival for children. No stocking would be complete without some sugary offering—a tradition stretching back centuries. Fruit, nuts, and sweets were typical offerings in Victorian children's stockings. Today, very few children would be impressed to find a piece of fruit on Christmas morning, but confectionery stocking fillers remain a constant. As we have seen, sugar has always been and remains a central part of the celebration. Once upon a time the use of excess sugar was a luxury because it represented great expense; today it may be cheap, but it is a luxury because it signifies sheer indulgence. Either way, confectionery and chocolate continue to mean celebration. The role of confectionery in the modern Christmas is demonstrated brilliantly in the movie *Elf* (2003), in which Will Ferrell plays Buddy, a man who has been raised in the North Pole as one of Santa's elves. After learning his true identity, Buddy sets out to New York to find his real father. When his new family is shocked by his act of drenching spaghetti with maple syrup, he explains the culinary culture of Santa's elves: "We elves try to stick to the four main food groups: candy, candy canes, candy corns, and syrup."

As we saw with cookies, another part of the role of confectionery at Christmas is decorative. The long shelf life, bright colors, and potential to create a range of intricate shapes make confectionery ideal for decorations. Early descriptions of Christmas trees in Britain and America refer to various types of confectionery on the tree. According to William Woys Weaver, the second half of the nineteenth century saw a proliferation in the sheer variety of foods used as decorations. Confectionery led the way in this area, and a reduction in sugar prices, coupled with the industrialization of the process, created almost limitless possibilities.[53] Paper cornucopias were one of the most common forms of tree decorations. These brightly colored paper cones held bonbons and various candies. These could be homemade, but paper companies also produced little kits that could be easily assembled. A description of Charles Follen's tree in Cambridge in 1832 refers to decorations including paper cornucopias filled with comfits, lozenges, and barley sugar.[54] Trees would also commonly be decorated with spun sugar, bird's nests, nougat baskets, candy canes, clear toys, candy fruits, barley sugar, and figures made from blown sugar.[55]

As we have already seen, retailers went to great efforts to attract customers with elaborate window displays of produce over Christmas, and confectioners led the way in this fashion.[56] William Hone's description of Georgian confectioners' shops on Twelfth Night demonstrates this vividly:

> Their upright cylinder shaped show-glasses, containing peppermint drops, elecampane, sugar-sticks, hard-bake, brandy-balls, and bulls' eyes are carefully polished; their lolly-pops are fresh encased, and look as white as the stems of tobacco-pipes; and their candle-sticks are ornamented with fillets and bosses of writing paper.[57]

The types of confectionery eaten during Christmas are countless, and so the following section will explore the history of just some of the most iconic festive staples.

Candy Canes

Unlike many other forms of confectionery enjoyed as part of the festival, candy canes are exclusively Christmas fare. These traditional peppermint-flavored stick candies, with their distinctive hook shape and red and white stripes, have become such an iconic Christmas food that, like plum puddings and Christmas trees, their very image is used to represent the holiday. They regularly feature as motifs and symbols for the season on greeting cards or in Christmas light displays.

Stick candy of this kind traces its roots to medieval Europe, where sugar was valuable and confectionery was manufactured primarily for medicinal purposes. Medieval Europeans believed that sugar, which was thought of as a spice, was a suitable treatment for a variety of ailments. The confectionery used to treat such ailments sometimes took the form of little twisted sticks called *penida* in Latin, later Anglicized to "pennets."[58] The tradition of these survives in forms of confectionery like candy canes that are twisted and flavored with therapeutic essences, herbs, and spices.[59]

The iconic status of candy canes, particularly in the American Christmas, means that they have naturally accumulated their own share of folklore and popular mythology. The most famous legend tells of a seventeenth-century German choirmaster in Cologne Cathedral who handed them out to young choristers in order to keep them quiet during a long church service. It is difficult to establish any basis for this story, but it is true that hard stick candy was available in Germany at this time.[60] Several stories also maintain that the shape has religious significance. The idea that it represents a shepherd's staff is a reoccurring theme. In other versions, the shape is supposed to be an upside-down "J" for Jesus, while the red color represents his blood. It is impossible to establish the true "meaning" of the shape, or the precise origins of the connection between the candy cane and Christmas, but these stories enhance their status as a festive food, and add a layer of mystery and romanticism. The one thing that is certain about the shape is that it makes it an ideal Christmas tree decoration.[61]

Although very little is known about their earlier history, we do know that candy canes had become a part of the American Christmas tradition by the mid-nineteenth century.[62] One of the first American stories connecting the candy cane explicitly to Christmas tells of when August Imgard, a German immigrant to Wooster, Ohio, reportedly used them to decorate his Christmas tree in 1847.[63] A recipe dating from around this time, although slightly earlier, to 1844, gives us some indication of what these early candy canes may have been like. The recipe in question is for stick candy flavored with ginger, clove, or peppermint. It is not crooked, or explicitly connected to Christmas, but in other respects it is similar to candy canes as we know them:

Clove, ginger or peppermint candy

These are all made in the same way as raspberry, using the essential oil of each flavour. For clove, the mixture whilst boiling, is coloured with cochineal; ginger with saffron; but the peppermint must be kept perfectly white, except the stripes, which is done by cutting off as many pieces from the bulk as you have colours, which should be in powder; put a sufficiency in each piece to give the desired tint, and keep them warm. When the remaining portion of the sugar is pulled, lay them over the surface in narrow stripes, double the roll together, and the face each way will be alike. Pull them out into long sticks, and twist them; make them round by rolling them under the hand, or they may be cut into small pieces with a pair of shears or scissors.[64]

Throughout the second half of the nineteenth century, candy canes appear to have become an established part of the American Christmas tradition, but, as they remained a handmade product, their consumption was somewhat limited in relative terms. Over the course of the first half of the twentieth century, though, technological innovations in the manufacturing and packaging process allowed them to become much more widespread. Whereas once local cooks and confectioners made small quantities of the fragile sweets, which needed to be bent by hand, the twentieth century brought mass production, superior packaging, and a stronger product that was able to reach more consumers. The Bunte brothers of New York were the first to mass-produce them in the 1920s.[65] Then Bobs Candies, founded by Robert E. McCormack, became the first to use the Keller machine, patented in 1957, which could twist, cut, and bend the stick into a cane. McCormack also made innovations in packaging by wrapping them in cellophane. By the 1950s, candy canes had become an emblematic part of the American Christmas.[66] Today, 26 December is designated as National Candy Cane Day in America. Approximately 1.7 billion candy canes are currently sold each year in the United States alone.[67]

Sugarplums

Clement Moore's much-loved Christmas poem "A Visit from St Nicholas" forever enshrined the word "sugarplum" in our Christmas vocabulary. It famously begins:

'Twas the night before Christmas, when all through the house
Not a creature was stirring, not even a mouse;
The stockings were hung by the chimney with care,
In hopes that St. Nicholas soon would be there;
The children were nestled all snug in their beds;
While visions of sugar-plums danced in their heads.[68]

As if the last evocative line about excited children dreaming of the good things to come were not enough, the sugarplum's place in the Christmas culinary canon was cemented by Tchaikovsky's *Nutcracker* ballet, first performed in 1892. When the protagonist, Clara, and her beloved Nutcracker travel to the Land of Sweets in Act 2, they find an enchanted kingdom populated by various forms of confectionery. The land is ruled by the Sugarplum Fairy, who performs a dance to an iconic and much-celebrated piece of music. Going to see the ballet has become an important Christmas ritual in its own right, particularly in America.

The name "sugarplum" is somewhat misleading, with most people understandably imagining them to be quite literally sugarcoated plums. However, they were actually an early form of boiled confectionery that were colored and flavored in many different ways. Their name is believed to stem from their size and oval shape, rather than from any real relationship with plums. They can also be thought of as part of the comfit family and sometimes had an aniseed or caraway seed at their center, which had been coated in multiple layers of sugar.[69] In any case, they were hugely popular from the seventeenth to the nineteenth centuries but had generally ceased to be manufactured or consumed by the early twentieth century. Despite fading from the menu, the word "sugarplum" still instantly triggers thoughts of Christmas for many, thanks largely to the writing of Clement Moore and Tchaikovsky's famous score.

Marzipan

Marzipan has had a long and enduring association with Christmas. It is essentially a paste made from ground almonds, sugar, egg whites, and sometimes additional flavorings. While mixtures of honey and nuts have been known for millennia, the ancestors of marzipan as we know it today appear to have come into Europe from Persia in the Middle Ages.[70] Originally called "marchpane" in English, it became hugely popular in the medieval and early modern period, where it was an expensive luxury food enjoyed within elite circles. This indulgent status was the reason for its association with Christmas, one of the most important feasts of the medieval calendar.

As we saw with cookies and other forms of confectionery, from the Middle Ages to the present, marzipan has been admired for its decorative qualities and visual appeal as much as for its flavor. In the medieval period it was used to create extraordinary confectionery creations known as "subtleties," but even today it is still molded into small colored fruits, figures, and animals. These decorative sweetmeats have been popular Christmas gifts for centuries. Elizabeth I reportedly received marzipan as a gift from her cook on New Year's Day.[71]

While traditional marzipan figures or marzipan-stuffed dates still make the occasional appearance at Christmas, its main role during the festive season today is as a thick layer under the icing on Christmas cakes. As discussed in chapter 4, marzipan has traditionally been added as a layer to protect the snow-white icing from the dark fruitcake and moisture below. Using marzipan in this way began in the mid-eighteenth century but may stem from the earlier tradition of serving a large round of iced marzipan. Today, it is still used as a sweet, fragrant filling in the middle of Germany's Christmas stollen, as also discussed in the previous chapter. Its flavor is now somewhat divisive in the English-speaking world, with many people—particularly in younger generations—disliking the strong flavor of almond essence that is commonly added to recipes, but it remains popular in Germany and Continental Europe at Christmas.

Christmas Crackers

The history of Christmas crackers is intimately connected to the Victorian confectionery industry in Britain, and so it warrants some discussion here.

Although they are less popular in America, crackers are an indispensable part of the Christmas meal in Britain, Ireland, and many parts of the Commonwealth. Christmas dinner is just not Christmas dinner without them. A Christmas cracker is quite simply a cardboard tube that has been wrapped in brightly colored paper, twisted at both ends. Inside is a chemically impregnated card strip that makes a loud crack when pulled at each end. Inside the cracker is a colored paper crown, a motto, or a joke (which has to be as corny as possible) and a tiny gift such as a small toy. The cracker is pulled by the guest seated next to you at the dining table, and the winner of the pull gets the section of the cracker containing the prizes. The paper crowns, bad jokes, and trinkets add an extra layer of fun and frivolity to the meal.

The earliest form of Christmas crackers is generally believed to have been invented by the London confectioner Tom Smith by 1847.[72] His earliest versions did not include a bang but simply involved adding a motto to his wrapped sugared almond bonbons.[73] By 1850, the sugared almonds had been replaced by small toys or trinkets and a paper hat.[74] By 1860, after years of experimentation, Smith had perfected the banger, to produce the all-important "crack." Popular legend has it that he was inspired by the sound made when he threw another log on his fire one cold winter's evening.[75] They were originally sold as "cosaques"[76] but soon became known as "crackers." Over time they became more decorative, and a collectible image called a "cracker scrap" was added to the front. Even today, such an embellishment is a common feature, especially on more upmarket varieties.[77] This feature was linked to the Victorian fashion for collecting scrap pictures, which has already been touched on above in relation to cookies. The boxes themselves were also elaborately decorated and marketed the crackers based on current affairs across the Empire, covering issues such as women's suffrage, the construction of the Channel Tunnel, and World War I, among more frivolous themes.[78] Crackers gained huge popularity during the nineteenth century. By the 1890s, Tom Smith's company alone was producing thirteen million each year.[79] They have retained their status in Britain and beyond and, notwithstanding a few minor modern tweaks, remain a relatively unchanged and critical Christmas tradition for many families.

Chocolate

No feast would be complete without chocolate; the very word has become synonymous with indulgence and celebration. As one of the world's most beloved foods, much has been written about chocolate, from its pre-Columbian history and importance in Aztec culture to its importation into Europe and adoption from the sixteenth century on.[80] Most of this scholarship is outside the scope of this discussion, but what is important here is that although it had been incorporated into the culinary cultures of most European countries by the seventeenth century, it was not until the nineteenth century that chocolate became a widespread part of Christmas.

Although it had been popular in Europe for centuries, primarily as a drink, technological innovations of the nineteenth century created new horizons for chocolate. A Dutchman by the name of Coenraad Van Houten patented a screw press in 1828, which separated out the fat, or cocoa butter, from the beans and left a product that could be pulverized to form cocoa powder. Van Houten also developed a process known as "Dutching," or alkalizing, which led to a milder flavor and a stronger color. These technological breakthroughs led to the development of chocolate as we know it today and created endless possibilities for chocolate confectionery. The block chocolate that emerged as a result of these innovations, when the pressed cocoa butter was reblended with the cocoa powder, could be molded into an almost limitless number of shapes, but, most important, it was solid at room temperature and would melt sinfully in the mouth.[81] This innovation led to the rapid development of the craft of chocolatiers from the mid-nineteenth century on. They created individual chocolate-based sweetmeats, known as pralines in parts of Europe, which were made by coating fillings such as nuts, caramel, flavored fondant, or marzipan in chocolate.

The mid-nineteenth century also saw the establishment of some of the major British companies that would become household names through the mass production and marketing of chocolate confectionery.[82] John Cadbury, a Quaker, was manufacturing drinking chocolate by 1831, but he developed a range of individual chocolates by 1866.[83] Another famous confectioner who became an important name in the history of British chocolate was Joseph Storr Fry, also a Quaker. Fry specialized in bars of chocolate, and his company was later acquired by Cadbury. Finally, there was Henry Isaac Rowntree, who bought William Tuke and Sons of York, a company that had been selling chocolate since 1785.[84] These businesses soon developed special, beautifully packaged selections of chocolates targeting the Christmas market, which became hugely popular gifts and remain so to this day.[85] While these products were still out of reach for many families in the nineteenth century, in the first half of the twentieth century these companies worked hard to create affordable options to take to the mass market. In the 1920s, they invented "selection boxes" of bars for Christmas, with Rowntree creating a facility for people to pay them off in installments throughout the year as part of their Christmas club. This was the beginning of a great British Christmas tradition. Originally these were luxury gifts, containing not just chocolate but also a range of other goods. Rowntree included items such as sets of cutlery, clocks, and vases. In the 1930s, selection boxes were increasingly marketed toward children and began to include toys and games.[86] Today, selection boxes are a cheaper affair and are common stocking fillers for children, containing an assortment of chocolate bars in festive packing, but they are the direct descendants of these earlier upmarket versions. Beautifully packaged boxes or tins of individual chocolates were also developed by these companies and were Christmas essentials by the first half of the twentieth century. "Quality Street," created by the famous toffee company Mackintosh in 1936, is one of the most iconic assortments. Mackintosh later merged with Rowntree but was acquired by Nestlé in 1988.[87] Equally famous is Cadbury's "Roses," created in 1938.[88] Of course, America had domestic brands that developed their own iconic status on the other side of the Atlantic. Chief among them was Whitman's, which developed its hugely popular "Whitman's Sampler" box in 1912.[89] These famous chocolate assortments are not exclusively Christmas fare—they are available all year round—but the vast majority of their sales takes place over Christmas, and they continue to market themselves as popular and affordable gifts. Families in Britain tend to maintain a firm allegiance to either Cadbury's Roses or Quality Street, with individual members battling it out annually for their favorite varieties in each tin.

6

DRINK

Our wassail cup is made
Of the rosemary tree,
And so is your beer
Of the best barley.
Love and joy come to you,
And to you your wassail too;
And God bless you and send you a Happy New Year
And God send you a Happy New Year.

—Excerpt from traditional Christmas carol
"Here We Come A-wassailing"

As we have seen in this book, a persistent theme throughout the history of Christmas has been excess: excess in all good things. This is a theme that holds true in this last area for discussion. An extensive body of anthropological literature exists relating to the social function of alcohol. Since its development in the Neolithic to the present, alcohol has played a major role in feasting for cultures across the globe.[1]

Imbibing is undoubtedly a part of the modern Christmas. Having one too many at the office Christmas party, and a general decline in sobriety over December, are part of the adult side of the festival for many. While the more temperate among us may rue the increased dissipation at this time of year, if we look to the history of Christmas, we see that overindulgence has always been a constant element. The other constant has been anxiety about this excess, as it comes into conflict with the more religious elements of the holiday.

To tell the story of Christmas boozing, we need to go right back to the pre-Christian origins of the festival. It is highly likely that alcohol played a central role in the midwinter festivals of Europe. It may well have had a ritual function, as a form of libation, but, as with meat, this was also quite simply the time of the year when alcohol was plentiful, as it was starting to be ready to drink postharvest. As discussed in chapter 1, public feasting and frivolity were central to the ancient Roman festival of Saturnalia. After the main public feast, the evening was devoted to reciting bawdy poetry, gambling, gaming, and drinking to excess.[2] Even after Europe was Christianized, these elements persisted, with drinking becoming a central part of the Christmas feast. Many a medieval carol refers to drinking, as this Anglo-Norman example demonstrates:

Lordings, Christmas loves good drinking.
Wines of Gascoigne, France, Anjou,
English ale that drives out thinking,
Prince of liquors, old or new.
Every neighbour shares the bowl,
Drinks of the spicy liquor deep,
Drinks his fill without controul,
Till he drowns his care in sleep.

And now—by Christmas, jolly soul!
By this mansion's generous sire!
By the wine, and by the bowl,
And all the joys they both inspire!
Here I'll drink a health to all:
The glorious task shall first be mine:
And ever may foul luck befall
Him that to pledge me shall decline.[3]

As we have seen elsewhere in the story of Christmas food, the excesses of the festival became a major source of tension during the early modern period. Given that they took exception to puddings and mince pies, it hardly needs to be said that the Puritans of England and New England condemned the drunkenness of Christmas in their war against the festival.[4] Despite this tension, and a gradual movement toward greater moderation, Stephen Nissenbaum argues that in the early nineteenth century the Twelve Days of Christmas remained a rowdy public occasion. The emphasis was still placed on public frivolity, and the Victorian family-oriented conceptualization of the festival had not yet taken hold. Public drunkenness was common over Christmas in the Georgian period, with groups of youths out celebrating on the streets. Men visited friends and expected to be served alcohol throughout the day. John Pintard, a New Yorker writing in the early nineteenth century briefly introduced in chapter 1, recalled that in his youth people roamed the streets on New Year's Day to "drink drams at every house as of old."[5] As the nineteenth century progressed, this became increasingly unacceptable, and temperance movements promoted a more sober, family-oriented Christmas.[6] Sources from earlier in the century depict an interesting crossover phase, though, when new child-centered elements like the modern Santa Claus combined with these adult traditions for a time. Nissenbaum cites an 1828 poem *Ode to Saint Class, Written on New Year's Eve*, by an author called "Rip Van Dam." The poem depicts Santa bringing toys and sweets, but also "mull'd cider, cherry bounce, [and] spiced rum." The author imagines him then staying to join the party, declaring, "And let us bouse it [booze it] till we die!"[7] The idea of Santa staying to get drunk with the adults after completing his toy delivery duties has long since faded, although, even today, children will often leave out a wee dram for him alongside his mince pie.

As Mark Connelly has discussed, given the way in which the Victorians remade Christmas as a child-centered domestic holiday, and the growing momentum of temperance movements during the period, it is unsurprising that the festival's long history of excess was troubling to them. The Victorians' anxiety about the drunkenness of Christmas past came into conflict with their attempt to find cultural and historical legitimacy for their remodeled festival in an idealized medieval world. This tension is best demonstrated by an excerpt from A. T. Wright, who was delivering an address to the Eccleston Young Men's Association:

> Another peculiarity of our Christmas is that it is essentially a drinking season, has been so from time immemorial. . . . However high may have been the

character of the Saxons for thorough honesty, the sad fact remains that they were very deep drinkers.[8]

WASSAILING

Wassailing is undoubtedly the most iconic drinking ritual of Christmas past, celebrated in countless carols. While a number of different wassailing traditions existed, which will be discussed in more detail below, in its essence, it was the communal sharing of alcohol, intended to ensure health and prosperity in the New Year. The origins of the word, which literally means "good health," are found in a common greeting shared by Old Saxon (*wis hel*), Old English (*wes hal*), and Old Norse (*ver hell*). Over time this greeting became a drinking toast.[9] According to Richard Sermon, one of the earliest recorded references to the word "wassail" being used in this way dates to around 1140 and is found in Geoffrey of Monmouth's *Historia Regum Britanniae.* Geoffrey describes an encounter between Renwein, the daughter of the Saxons' leader, and Vortigern, king of south Britain:

> While he was being entertained at a royal banquet, the girl Renwein came out of an inner room carrying a goblet full of wine. She walked up to the king, curtsied low and said: Laverd King, was hail! . . . He asked his interpreter what it was that the girl had said and what he ought to reply to her. She called you Lord King answered the interpreter, and did you honour by drinking your health. What you should reply is drinc hail. Vortigern immediately said the words drinc hail and ordered Renwein to drink. Then he took the goblet from her hand, kissed her and drank in his turn. From that day to this the tradition has endured in Britain that the one who drinks first at a banquet says was hail to his partner and he who takes the next drink replies drinc hail.[10]

Folklorists generally agree that wassailing is a remnant of ancient fertility rites, undertaken to ensure that the following year's harvest would be abundant.[11] Although source material for the more distant past is obviously limited, historical and ethnographic records provide fascinating accounts of such rituals taking place over Christmas and, most commonly, on Twelfth Night.[12] The precise details of the rituals vary from region to region, but consistent elements are wassailers going into orchards to toast and sing to the trees to ensure their fertility and safeguard the New Year's harvest. The trees would sometimes be hit to awaken good spirits and then splashed with cider or ale. Cider-soaked toast was also left as an offering at the roots of apple trees.[13] Rituals associated with fire and gunfire were also common, and were possibly used to drive out potentially malevolent spirits bent on ruining the next harvest. According to Linda Raedisch, during the apple wassail in the cider-producing regions of Britain, songs were often addressed to the oldest tree, or the apple-tree man who lived in it, and whose goodwill was essential to safeguard the fruit.[14] Clement Miles gives an account of a Devonshire farmer who would go into the orchard with a large jug of cider and drink a toast at the foot of the best apple tree on Twelfth Night.[15] He also cites a wassail song from that county:

> Here's to thee old apple tree,
> Whence thou mayst bud, and whence thou may'st blow!
> And whence thou may'st bear apples enow!
> Hats full! Caps full!
> Bushels! Bushels, sacks full,
> And my pockets full too! Huzza![16]

After drinking cider and reciting this verse to the trees, the wassailers would fire their guns and return home. There they were met by the female members of their families, who would prevent them from entering the house until they guessed what type of meat was being roasted for the festive meal. The man who guessed correctly would then have the honor of presiding over the evening's festivities.[17] Each region had its own variations of the ritual, but all were intended to safeguard the New Year's harvest. In Cornwall, for example, the fruit trees were splashed with cider and beaten with sticks. There the traditional song was as follows:

> Huzza, Huzza, in our good town
> The bread shall be white, and the liquor be brown
> So here my old fellow I drink to thee
> And the very health of each other tree.
> Well may ye blow, well may ye bear
> Blossom and fruit both apple and pear.

So that every bough and every twig
May bend with a burden both fair and big
May ye bear us and yield us fruit such a store
That the bags and chambers and house run o'er.[18]

Other regions saw animals included as well. Oxen were sung to and a cake was placed on a beast's horns. If the beast remained silent, or did not throw the cake off when splashed with cider, these were good omens for the year ahead.[19] The famous "Gloucestershire Wassail," recorded by Samuel Lysons in the late eighteenth century, toasts Dobbin (the horse), Smiler (the mare), and Fillpail (the cow):

Wassail, wassail, all over the town
Our toast it is white and our ale it is brown
Our bowl it is made of the white maple tree
With the wassailing bowl we'll drink to thee
So here is to Cherry and to his right cheek
Pray God send out master a good piece of beef
And a good piece of beef that we all may see
With the wassailing bowl we'll drink to thee
And here is to Dobbin and to his right eye
Pray God send our master a good Christmas pie
And a good Christmas pie that we may all see
With the wassailing bowl we'll drink to thee
So here is to Broad May and to her broad horn
May God send our master a good crop of corn
And a good crop of corn that we may all see
With the wassailing bowl we'll drink to thee
And here is to Fillpail and to her left ear
Pray God send our master a happy new year
And a happy new year as e'er he did see
With the wassailing bowl we'll drink to thee
And here is to Colly and to her long tail
Pray God send our master, he never may fail
A bowl of strong beer, I pray you draw near
And our jolly wassail, it's then you shall hear

Then here's to the maid in the lily white smock
Who tripped to the door and slipped back the lock
Who tripped to the door and pulled back the pin
For to let these jolly wassailer's in
Wassail, wassail, all over the town
Our toast it is white and our ale it is brown
Our bowl it is made of the white maple tree
With the wassailing bowl we'll drink to thee
Drink to thee, drink to thee
With the wassailing bowl we'll drink to thee.[20]

This ritual of wassailing the crops and livestock was retained in parts of Britain, especially in the West Country, but it largely went into decline in the nineteenth century.[21] However, the communal sharing of alcohol and wishing for prosperity in the New Year continued in a distinct and markedly different branch of the wassailing tradition. This was where groups of wassailers would call from house to house, demanding money or hospitality. In returning for filling their bowl, they would wish you and your kin well in the New Year. Poor families would also take a wooden bowl and go a-wassailing to collect money for Christmas.[22] The Tudor carol, commonly called "Drive the Cold Winter Away," describes this practice and the connected tradition of mumming. The carol first appeared in print in a broadside dating to 1625 under a different title. Its lyrics discuss Christmas festivities and depict the wassail as being central to hospitality and community at this time of year:

To maske and to mum kind neighbours will come
With Wassels of nut-browne Ale,
To drinke and carouse to all in this house,
As merry as bucks in the dale;
Where cake, bread and cheese is brought for your fees
To make you the longer stay;
At the fire to warme will do you no harme,
To drive the cold winter away.[23]

Over the course of the sixteenth and seventeenth centuries, the tradition of "wassail wenches," or "wassail virgins," became popular. Groups of

"The Wassail Bowl at Christmas."
English illustration, 1860. Courtesy of the World History Archive/APRL.

women stopped at houses to sing carols and bless families in return for gifts of money. The lawyer John Selden bemoaned these "wenches" with "wassails" in the seventeenth century. An apparent real-life precursor to Scrooge, Selden resented that they made you "drink of the slabby stuff" and then give them "moneys ten times more than it is worth."[24] Refusing to participate in the wassail and lacking generosity was believed to bring poor fortune for the New Year, though, so only the brave or foolish would turn them away.[25] Samuel Pepys recorded visiting an alehouse on 26 December 1661, where a "washeallbowle woman and a girl came to us and sung to us."[26] Payments made to wassailers also appear in household accounts from the seventeenth and eighteenth centuries.[27]

Another common ritual, particularly popular in stately or aristocratic settings, was the domestic wassail, in which the bowl or cup was brought into the hall with great ceremony. As it appeared, the word "wassail" was chanted by all present, as a wish for good health. As discussed above, the traditional response to this call was *drinc hail*, meaning "drink, be well."[28] A version of the domestic wassail ritual continued throughout the medieval and early modern period. The Household Ordinances of 1494 describe the wassail at Henry VII's court:

> Item as for the voide on twelfth day at night, the King and Queene ought to take it in the halle, and as for the wassell, the Steward and the treasurer shall come for it with their staves in their hands . . . when the Steward cometh into the hall doore with the wasssell he must crie three times, wassell, wassell, wassell and then the chappell to answere with a good songe.[29]

Decorative wassail bowls were kept specifically for this ceremony by many families.[30] These bowls were adorned with ribbons, holly, mistletoe, flowers, and even apples.[31] In Ben Jonson's 1616 *Christmas, His Masque*, the introductory procession is described, and the brown bowl is decorated with ribbons and rosemary.[32]

In terms of the actual contents of the wassail bowl, it could be wine, cider, or ale, depending on the main produce of the region. In England, cider and ale were the most common wassails by far.[33] Sometimes the alcohol was warmed, spiced, and fortified in a variety of different ways. A recipe known as "lambswool" was one of the most common of these. This was a warm spiced cider or ale in which roasted apples were stewed. Pieces of toast were sometimes soaked in the lambswool, or, alternatively, cream and eggs could be added to enrich it further. Robert Herrick refers to lambswool in his 1648 poem *Twelfth Night; or, King and Queen*:

> Next crown the bowl full
> With gentle lamb's wool
> Add sugar, nutmeg and ginger,
> With store of ale too;
> And thus ye must doe
> To make the wassaile a swinger.[34]

Sir Watkin Williams Wynne's recipe for wassail, dating to 1722, recommends a spiced beer and sherry. This combination undergoes a second fermentation using bread and is served with roasted apples:

> Take one lb. of brown sugar, 1 pint of hot beer a grated nutmeg, and a large lump of preserved ginger root cut up. Add 4 glasses of sherry, and stir well.

When cold, dilute with 5 pints of cold beer, spred suspicion of yeast on to hot slices of toasted brown bread, and let it stand covered for several hours. Bottle off and seal down, and in a few days it should be bursting the corks, when it should be poured out into the wassail bowl, and served with hot, roasted apples floated in it.[35]

Such drinks were still popular in the nineteenth century. Dickens's *Pickwick Papers* describes "hot elder wine, well qualified with brandy and spice" and "a mighty bowl of wassail, something smaller than an ordinary wash-house copper, in which the hot apples were hissing and bubbling with a rich look and a jolly sound that were perfectly irresistible."[36]

Although wassailing trees is no longer widely practiced, it has persisted in some regions, particularly in the cider districts of England's West Country. Since the 1970s it has also been experiencing something of a revival, but is still far from widespread.[37] Far more common throughout the twentieth century and even today is caroling. This practice preserves elements of the door-knocking version of wassailing, as neighbors go from house to house offering songs and good wishes in return for food, money, or hospitality. The act of sharing hot spiced beverages at communal gatherings such as Christmas markets also preserves something of the spirit of wassailing, as people gather to enjoy these warming festive drinks together.

MULLED WINE

As discussed above, heated spiced wine, known as mulled wine, was undoubtedly used in wassailing, but it is such an established part of the modern Christmas, with its own distinct story, that it requires more focused discussion.

The history of sweetening and spicing wine goes back to the ancient Greeks and their famous medicinal tonic hippocras. Versions of this survived in Britain into the early modern period, and recipes for it show up regularly in receipt books. Thomas Dawson includes the following in his 1596 *The Good Huswifes Jewell*:

To make Hypocrase

Take a gallon of white wine, sugar two pounds, of cinnamon, ginger, long pepper, mace not bruised, grains, galingall and cloves not bruised. You must bruise every kind of spice a little and put them in an earthen pot all day. And then cast them through your bags two times or more as you see cause. And so drink it.[38]

As the recipe shows, hippocras was served cold and commonly used white wine. It eventually left the British cook's repertoire, but the tradition of sweetening and spicing wine did not.

The term "mulled wine" emerged in the seventeenth century,[39] and the beverage became wildly popular as a festive tipple over the next two centuries. The following recipe for mulled wine enriched with eggs appears in Elizabeth Raffald's *The Experienced English Housekeeper* (1769):

To mull Wine

Grate half a nutmeg into a pint of wine and sweeten it to your taste with loaf sugar. Set it over the fire and when it boils take it off to cool. Beat the yolks of four eggs exceedingly well, add to them a little cold wine, then mix them carefully with your hot wine a little at a time. Then pour it backwards and forwards several times until it looks fine and bright. Then set it on the fire and heat it a little at a time for several times till it is quite hot and pretty thick, and pour it backwards and forwards several times. Then send it in chocolate cups and serve it with dry toast cut in long narrow pieces.[40]

The use of eggs in this recipe makes it similar to a caudle, and modern consumers would find it markedly different from the mulled wine consumed today. Published a century later, Mrs. Beeton's recipe would have been far more familiar to a contemporary palate:

TO MULL WINE

Ingredients—To every pint of wine allow 1 large cupful of water, sugar and spice to taste.

Mode.—In making preparations like the above, it is very difficult to give the exact proportions of ingredients like sugar and spice, as what quantity might suit one person would be to another quite distasteful. Boil the spice in the water until the flavour is extracted, then add the wine and sugar, and bring the whole to the boiling-point, then serve with strips of crisp dry toast, or with biscuits. The spices usually used for mulled wine are cloves, grated nutmeg, and cinnamon or mace. Any kind of wine may be mulled, but port and claret are those usually selected for the purpose; and the latter requires a very large proportion of sugar. The vessel that the wine is boiled in must be delicately cleaned, and should be kept exclusively for the purpose. Small tin warmers may be purchased for a trifle, which are more suitable than saucepans, as, if the latter are not scrupulously clean; they spoil the wine, by imparting to it a very disagreeable flavour. These warmers should be used for no other purposes.[41]

By the Victorian period, when Mrs. Beeton penned the above, mulled wine had become so popular over Christmas that a number of variations had emerged. The most famous of these were the family of "ecclesiasts": smoking archbishop (made with claret), smoking beadle (made with ginger wine and raisins), smoking cardinal (made with Champagne or Rhine wine), smoking pope (made with burgundy), church warden (made with ginger wine and tea), and lawn sleeves (made with madeira or sherry and jelly), but the most iconic of all was smoking bishop.[42] Smoking bishop, or more commonly just "bishop," was made from port, red wine, sugar, spices, and, importantly, roasted caramelized citrus fruits. One of the earliest references to smoking bishop is made in a poem by Jonathan Swift:

Come buy my fine oranges, sauce for your veal,
And charming, when squeezed in a pot of brown ale;
Well roasted, with sugar and wine in a cup,
They'll make a sweet bishop when gentlefolks sup.[43]

Richard Cook's 1827 *Oxford Nightcaps* includes one of the earliest published recipes for bishop:

Make several incisions in the rind of a lemon, stick cloves in the incisions, and roast the lemon by a slow fire. Put small but equal quantities of cinnamon, cloves, mace, and all-spice, and a race of ginger, into a saucepan, with half a pint of water; let it boil until it is reduced one half. Boil one bottle of port wine; burn a portion of the spirit out of it, by applying a lighted paper to the saucepan. Put the roasted lemons and spice into the wine; stir it up well, and then let it stand near the fire ten minutes. Rub a few knobs of sugar on the rind of a lemon, put the sugar into a bowl or jug, with the juice of half a lemon, (not roasted,) pour wine upon it, sweeten it to your taste, and serve it up with the lemon and spice floating in it.[44]

"Scrooge and Bob Cratchit."
Illustrated by John Leech. In Charles Dickens, *A Christmas Carol* (1843). Courtesy of Lebrecht Authors/ Bridgeman Images.

The drink became hugely popular in the nineteenth century, but it was catapulted to fame by Dickens. After Scrooge's reawakening on Christmas morning, he greets the hardworking Bob Cratchit with the following offer:

> "A Merry Christmas, Bob!" said Scrooge with an earnestness that could not be mistaken, as he clapped him on the back. "A merrier Christmas, Bob, my good fellow, than I have given you for many a year! I'll raise your salary, and

endeavour to assist your struggling family, and we will discuss your affairs this very afternoon over a bowl of smoking bishop, Bob!"[45]

Here the bowl of smoking bishop becomes a central part of Scrooge's new-found Christmas spirit and goodwill, and it symbolizes his acceptance of his social responsibilities. Ivan Day has argued that Dickens may have in fact coined the term "smoking bishop," the beverage being referred to previously as simply "bishop."[46]

Although smoking bishop is not widely known today, mulled wine is still a Christmas favorite. Revelers will also be familiar with mulled wine's numerous cousins from across Europe, where most countries have their own variations and distinct traditions. German *glüwein* and the Nordic *glögg* (also *gløgg*, *glögi*) have been made particularly famous. These are commonly served at Christmas markets and, despite some minor differences, are broadly similar to English mulled wine. One notable specialty of Germany is the famous *Feuerzangenbowle* (literally, "fire-tongs punch"), in which a rum-soaked sugarloaf is emblazoned and allowed to drip into the wine below.

PUNCH

Despite no longer having a central place on the Christmas table, punch was a firm festive favorite for hundreds of years following its development in the seventeenth century.[47] Generally thought of as a sweetened alcohol mixed with fruit juice and other flavorings, punch encompasses a wide family of drinks, with national and regional variations existing around the globe.[48] Its role in festive gatherings stems from its indulgent use of multiple strong liquors, as well as from the fact that it could be prepared in large quantities, meaning that it was excellent for a crowd of people.

The origin of the term "punch" is fiercely debated. Some argue that the word reflects the drink's Eastern origins, stemming from *panch*, the Hindi word for five. This is supposedly a reference to the fact it contained just five ingredients (water, alcohol, juice, sugar, and spice). Others argue, perhaps more convincingly, that it stems from the word *puncheon*, which is a term referring to a barrel used for storing alcohol on a ship.[49] The origins of punch are indeed strongly connected to shipping and the expansion of the British

Empire. Sailors drank "grog," a mixture of rum and water, on long voyages, and they brought the exotic tastes of the East back to Britain with them. As the Empire and trade networks expanded, sugar, spice, and spirits became more readily available in Britain, and so these sweetened and flavored drinks became increasingly popular. The first recorded reference to punch is found in a letter written to an East India merchant, Thomas Colley, in 1632, highlighting the maritime connection once again. The letter, from the merchant Robert Adams, encourages Colley to "drincke punch by no allowance."[50]

In the 1670s the first published recipe for punch appeared in Hannah Woolley's *The Queen-like Closet*. Woolley instructs readers to "take one Quart of Claret Wine, half a pint of brandy, and a little nutmeg grated, a little sugar, and the juice of a limon, and so drink it."[51] The similarity to mulled wine is evident here, and it is true to say that mulled wine is undoubtedly a part of the punch family.

Elizabeth Gabay, who has written extensively on the subject of punch, has observed that over the course of the eighteenth century recipes became markedly less alcoholic, as well as increasingly codified. Punch tended to be based on an acidic component such as citrus juice, sugar, alcohol (commonly brandy, rum, arrack, or wine), and a mixing element such as water, tea, milk, or eggs.[52] In the case of the latter two, these were called milk or egg punch: varieties of eggnog that will be discussed in more detail in the following section. This basic template, consisting of alcohol, acid, sugar, and a mixer, can be seen in the following recipe for *Punch Royal*, which appears in John Nott's *Cook's and Confectioner's Dictionary*, first published in 1723:

To Make Punch-Royal

Take three Pints of the best Brandy, as much Spring-water, a Pint or better of the best Lime-juice, a pound of double refin'd Sugar. This Punch is better than weaker Punch, for it does not easily affect the Head, by reason of the large Quantity of Lime-juice more than common, and it is more grateful and comfortable to the stomach.[53]

Punch continued to evolve over the nineteenth century, with recipes generally becoming sweeter and richer. Nonalcoholic varieties also emerged, in line with Victorian temperance sensibilities. Nonetheless, hot alcoholic punch had its heyday as a central component of Christmas in the nineteenth century. Scrooge sees a vision of "seething bowls of punch, that made the chamber dim with their delicious steam" in Dickens's famous work. Indeed, Dickens left behind his own recipe for punch in a letter from 1847:

> Peel into a very common basin (which may be broken in case of accident, without damage to the owner's peace or pocket) the rinds of three lemons, cut very thin and with as little as possible of the white coating between the peel and the fruit, attached.
>
> Add a double handful of lump sugar (good measure), a pint of good old rum, and a large wine-glass of good old brandy—if it be not a large claret glass, say two.
>
> Set this on fire, by filling a warm silver spoon with the spirit, lighting the contents at a wax taper, and pouring them gently in. Let it burn three or four minutes at least, stirring it from time to time. Then extinguish it by covering the basin with a tray, which will immediately put out the flame.
>
> Then squeeze in the juice of the three lemons, and add a quart of boiling water. Stir the whole well, cover it up for five minutes, and stir again.
>
> At this crisis (having skimmed off the pips with a spoon) you may taste. If not sweet enough, add sugar to your liking, but observe that it will be a little sweeter presently. Pour the whole into a jug, pour a leather or coarse cloth over the top, so as to exclude the air completely, and stand it in a hot oven ten minutes or on a hot stove one quarter of an hour. Keep it until it comes to table in a warm place near the fire, but not too hot. If it be intended to stand three or four hours, take half the lemon peel out or it will acquire a bitter taste.
>
> The same punch allowed to grow cool by degrees, and then iced, is delicious. It requires less sugar when made for this purpose. If you wish to produce it bright, strain it into bottles through silk.
>
> These proportions and directions will, of course, apply to any quantity.[54]

Over the Victorian period, punch became a ritualized part of Christmas and New Year festivities. Like decorating the tree or stirring up the pudding, families developed set rituals and heirlooms specifically associated with punch, giving its production and consumption a sense of sacred tradition and timelessness. Families would use the same recipe and would serve it in the same cherished bowl each year, kept especially for the occasion. Upon serving, the punch was then ladled into specialized ceramic, glass, or metal punch cups. The rind of a citrus fruit, commonly an orange, was sometimes carefully peeled into a spiral and draped over the edge of the bowl in a decorative fashion.[55]

The emphasis placed on the communal ceremonial bowl shows a connection to wassailing, and there is no doubt that Christmas punch rituals are a modern variation on these older traditions. The shared experience and wish for good health is central to the meaning of Christmas punch. This element, as well as the connection to the New Year in particular, is highlighted in the following quote from 1850 by the Anglo-German writer Elpis Melena:

> We greeted the entrance of the New Year in the good old English fashion. A bowl of punch was prepared, and whilst the clock, striking the hour of midnight, tolled the knell of the expiring year, we drank to the health of our dear distant friends, with fondest wishes for their welfare and happiness.[56]

The handing down of punch bowls and recipes, as well as the importance of ritualized production and consumption, is beautifully illustrated in the following Canadian Christmas story dating to 1872:

> We were a merry party when we drew our chairs round the fire in Davy's dining-room. The flames gave forth a ruddy cheerfulness, the kettle sang snugly on the trivet, the decanters, glasses, and golden lemons glistened on the table, and we were prepared to make a night of it. The centre-piece was a large china Bowl, with an old fashioned punch-ladle, which had descended to our host through several generations of Douglases.
>
> This was the bowl.
>
> "Now," said David, tenderly taking down from a shelf a manuscript receipt-book, that had been compiled in bye-gone days by his great grandmother, a dame famous far and wide for her confections, "I'll read the directions; and, Gerald, will you brew?"
>
> "With all my heart," I replied, turning back my sleeves and preparing for action.
>
> "Rub the sugar over the lemon until it has absorbed all the yellow part of the skin, then put the sugar into the bowl; add the lemon-juice (free from pips), and mix these ingredients together."
>
> "Mixed they are, Sir."
>
> "Pour over them the boiling water."
>
> "How much?"
>
> "About a pint, and take care that it boils."

"Take care that it boils! Why, the kettle is fuming and fretting and puffing out volumes of steam, as if it dared me to lay hold of it and make it do its duty."

"Add a tumbler of rum, a tumbler of brandy, some nutmeg—half a teaspoonful!—and mix discreetly. Then spice it according to taste."

It was finished at last.

There it stood upon the table, its hot breath heavy with the odours of Indian spices, and offering up its incense of vapour, while it ladened the air with delicious aromas.

Again and again the ancient ladle did its duty. Then the sparks glowed in the bowls of the mist-compelling meerschaums, and there rolled to the ceiling thick, wreathing clouds of fragrant tobacco smoke.[57]

Such scenes of Christmas conviviality were popular subjects for Victorian greeting cards and postcards. From the late nineteenth to the mid-twentieth century, jolly scenes of family and friends gathered round the punch bowl became a central theme.[58]

Punch is in no way exclusive to Britain and North America. Varieties of the drink are found across the former British Empire and particularly throughout the Caribbean, where each country has a distinct rum-based punch specialty.[59] While most people are still familiar with punch in some form, and may have enjoyed it at large gatherings such as dances and so on, it no longer retains a central place at Christmas. It is also commonly now served as an alcohol-free mix of juices, fruit, and soda, so it has come a long way from its original boozy maritime origins.

EGGNOG

One of the drinks most commonly associated with the modern Christmas, especially in America and Canada, is eggnog. Today, eggnog is made with milk, cream, sugar, eggs, and spices such as nutmeg or cinnamon. It can be served without alcohol but is at its most festive when fortified by a spirit, commonly brandy, rum, whiskey, or bourbon. It is most commonly served chilled, sometimes topped with whipped cream, but it can also be served warmed.

The precise history of eggnog is debated, but it is clear that it developed from the established English culinary tradition of rich creamy alcoholic drinks and desserts including syllabubs and caudles, but more specifically possets. Possets developed in medieval England and were popular until the nineteenth century. Today, the term "posset" refers to a creamy dessert, but the original posset was made with hot milk that was curdled with an acid, sometimes citrus, but more commonly wine or ale. Possets were sweetened, and they could be flavored with a range of spices. Eggs and cream were sometimes added to enrich the drink, and eventually more solid "eating possets" developed by mixing the curds with breadcrumbs, almonds, and crushed Naples biscuits.[60] *The Closet of Sir Kenelm Digby Opened* (1669) includes several posset recipes, including the following one for a sack posset:

A Sack Posset.

Take three pints of Cream; boil in it a Little Cinnamon, a Nutmeg quartered, and two spoonfuls of grated bread; then beat the yolks of twelve eggs very well with a little cold Cream, and a spoonful of Sack. When your Cream hath boiled about a quarter of an hour, thicken it up with the Eggs, and sweeten it with Sugar; and take half a pint of Sack and six spoonfuls of Ale, and put into the basin or dish, you intend to make it in, with a little Ambergreece, if you please. Then pour your Cream and Eggs into it, holding your hand as high as conveniently you can, gently stirring in the basin with the spoon as you pour it; so serve it up. If you please you may strew Sugar upon it. You may strew Ambered sugar upon it, as you eat it; or Sugar-beaten with Cinnamon, if you like it.[61]

Multiple posset recipes also appear in manuscript receipt books of the period. The following example comes from an early eighteenth-century Irish receipt book started by Catherine O'Brien, wife of Lucius O'Brien and the first cousin of both Queen Anne and Queen Mary:

Sack poset wch I like best My Grand Mother

Take 18 eggs beat ym & strain ym & put to ym a pint of sack & half a pound of good suger or better; a quartered nutmeg put it altogether into a bason & sett it on the fire tell tis so hot yu can bear yr finger in the bottom of the bason stur it all one way: take a pint of cream & a pint of Milk & byle it & pour it

boyling hott into yr eggs & wine stur it once or twice gently round & take it
& cover it.[62]

A well-made posset was supposed to have three distinct layers, and special pots emerged that were designed to highlight these different textures.
The top layer was a foam known as "the grace," and under this was a spicy
custard. These two layers were eaten with a spoon. The bottom layer was an
alcoholic liquid, which was drunk through the spout or "pipe" of the posset
pot.[63] Like its descendant, eggnog, posset was celebratory fare, but it was
also recommended for invalids.

Once the posset family of drinks and desserts crossed the Atlantic, new
variations evolved, one of which was eggnog. The term "eggnog" did not
appear in America until the late eighteenth century, and the origins of the
name are debated. The most plausible explanations are that it is derived
either from the word "nog," meaning "ale,"[64] or from the term "noggin,"
which refers to a type of wooden vessel traditionally used to serve alcohol.[65]
The earliest uses of the term "eggnog" all date to the last quarter of the
eighteenth century. One of the first references is in a poem written by a
clergyman from Maryland in 1775, which was published posthumously at
a much later date:

Fog-drams i' th' moro, or (better still) egg-nog,
At night hot-suppings, and at mid-day, grogg,
My palate can regale.[66]

Another early reference appears in an account of a breakfast enjoyed
at the City Tavern, Philadelphia, in February 1796.[67] A final and hugely
significant late eighteenth-century reference to eggnog was left by George
Washington, who provided the following recipe:

One quart cream, one quart milk, one dozen tablespoons sugar, one pint
brandy, ½ pint rye whiskey, ½ pint Jamaica rum, ¼ pint sherry—mix liquor
first, then separate yolks and whites of eggs, add sugar to beaten yolks, mix
well. Add milk and cream, slowly beating. Beat whites of eggs until stiff
and fold slowly into mixture. Let set in cool place for several days. Taste
frequently.[68]

Whereas possets in England generally contained wine or sack, in the colonies these were not as easy to obtain, and they were certainly less affordable. Rum from the Caribbean proved an appealing and accessible substitute, and it became widely consumed by American colonists during the seventeenth century. It was first distilled from West Indian sugarcane in the 1640s and soon made its way to the northern colonies through trade. It was cheap and strong and had a pleasant taste, so Anglo-Americans embraced it quickly. Rum's reign was short lived, though. As domestically produced bourbon started to be made widely available, it became the most popular spirit, a change that gathered momentum during the War of Independence.[69]

Precisely when and why eggnog became associated with Christmas in America is another question. Elizabeth Gabay has argued that it is likely that it was seen as festive because cream and eggs were not readily or cheaply available in winter. Various sources indicate that the connection between the beverage and the festival had been made by the early nineteenth century. In 1815, a British observer wrote that Americans served their friends eggnog on Christmas Day. This account also states that eggnog was favored in the North all year but was indispensable during Christmas in the South.[70] This early association with Christmas in the South is borne out by other sources. Various accounts refer to making eggnog as a family and taking it for breakfast over each of the twelve days. In 1842, a bride from Philadelphia, who was living in Alabama, noted that eggnog was drunk every morning over Christmas there.[71] Accounts of Christmases on plantations also refer to eggnog and depict a festival with heavy alcohol consumption. Eggnog, punch, and toddy were reportedly consumed heavily by slave owners, slaves, and children alike.[72] Eggnog parties were central to the concept of open house during Christmas in the South, as neighbors from all social ranks would be invited in to make and drink eggnog communally.[73] Further evidence of the cultural importance of a boozy eggnog at Christmas in the South can be found in the infamous eggnog riot of 1826. This rebellion occurred when the cadets at the West Point military academy were informed that the eggnog would be alcohol-free that Christmas. In response, they smuggled whiskey into the academy and had a drunken party that ended in a riot. Among the nineteen cadets court-martialed for the mutiny was Jefferson Davis, future Confederate president.[74]

From the nineteenth century, American cookbooks began to include multiple recipes for eggnog, generally consisting of cream, sugar, eggs, nutmeg, and alcohol. Sherry and spirits such as brandy, rum, or bourbon were the most common fortifiers, sometimes in combination. In 1839, Lettice Bryan published the following recipe, combining both rum and brandy, in *The Kentucky Housewife*:

Egg Nogg

Break six eggs, separating the whites from the yolks; beat the whites to a stiff froth, put the yolks in a bowl and beat them light. Stir into it slowly, that the spirits may cook the egg, half a pint of rum, or three gills of common brandy; add a quart of rich sweet milk and half a pound of powdered sugar; then stir in the egg froth, and finish by grating nutmeg on the top.[75]

The famous bartender Jerry Thomas published several eggnog recipes in his 1862 *Bar-Tender's Guide*, where he also stated that the beverage was a favorite all year in the North but indispensable at Christmas in the South.[76] His 1887 revised and expanded version of the book provided yet more eggnog recipes, including the following directions for making three and a half gallons of the stuff:

Egg Nogg for a Party

(Three-and-a-half gallons.)

Take 20 fresh eggs.
2 1/2 quarts fine old brandy.
1 pint of Santa Cruz Rum.
2 1/2 gallons of rich milk.
2 pounds of white sugar.

Separate the whites of the eggs from the yolks, beat each separately with an egg-beater until the yolks are well cut up, and the whites assume a light fleecy appearance. Mix all the ingredients (except the milk and the whites of the eggs) in a large punch bowl. Then pour in the milk gradually, continually stirring, in order to prevent the milk from curdling with the eggs. Grate sufficient nutmeg on the mixture, and lastly, let the whites float on top, and ornament with colored sugars. Cool in a tub of ice, and serve.[77]

While freshly made eggnog is still enjoyed in many homes, commercially produced versions are now commonly consumed throughout the holidays across America. The popularity of these mass-produced ready-made versions stems from their convenience, as well as from fears surrounding the consumption of raw egg. Eggnog is also now a popular flavoring for a range of commercially produced seasonal offerings, such as "Eggnog Lattes" at Starbucks. Christmas Eve has been designated as National Eggnog Day in the United States, but versions of the drink are enjoyed globally, and particularly throughout the Caribbean.

REGIONAL SPECIALTIES

Thus far this chapter has tackled the iconic and widespread festive drinks—wassail, mulled wine, punch, and eggnog—but there are naturally countless national and regional specialties when it comes to Christmas imbibing.

Among those that have become fashionable again in recent years is sloe gin. This is an aromatic, ruby-red liqueur made from the berries, or drupes, of the blackthorn bush, which is native to Britain and Ireland and commonly grows in hedgerows. Sloes come into season in autumn and are traditionally picked after the first frost.[78] Once harvested, you need to prick each berry to help them release their flavor and color. This is traditionally done with the thorn of the bush on which they grew, or a silver fork. The berries are then placed into a clean jar, to which you add both gin and sugar. The ratio of sugar can be altered to taste, but enough is required to extract the full juice and flavor from the berries. The jar should be left for a minimum of three to four months and shaken regularly, after which time you will have a deeply colored and aromatic liqueur. Slow gin has become a popular homemade gift and celebratory tipple in Britain and Ireland, primarily because it reaches maturity around Christmas.[79]

The story of sloe gin is relatively recent and tied to the expansion of the Empire and changes to landscape in the early modern period. As land was enclosed in Britain and Ireland, the number of field boundaries and hedgerows across the countryside increased dramatically, which meant that there was more blackthorn available than ever before.[80] Then, during the eighteenth century, at around the time when enclosure was gathering pace, cheap gin flooded the British market and became a hugely popular drink.[81] The increased availability of gin, sloe, and ultimately sugar led to the development of this liqueur, which made the best of what are otherwise unpalatable berries.

Although today sloe gin is a sought-after product, connected to the renewed interest in foraging, in the past sloe gin was far from elite or fashionable. Edward Lanzer Joseph wrote disparagingly of the "mixture of sloe-juice and gin . . . which the inhabitants of London swallow for port."[82] Sloe berries were also associated with wine adulteration, as seen in the following poem of 1717:

> Besides rare Wines of e'ery sort,
> White, Claret, Sherry, Mountain, Port,
> Tho'none of't e'er had cross'd the Seas
> Or from the Grape deriv'd its Lees,
> But made at Home, 'twixt chip and Dash
> Of Sugar, Sloes, and Grocer's Trash,
> Of cyder dy'd with Cochineal.[83]

Today, though, the nostalgic return to foraging and the fad for artisanal gin has led to a sloe gin resurgence, and it has become a fashionable element of many festive cocktails.

Atholl brose is another festive tipple that hails from Scotland.[84] It is traditionally a whisky-, oatmeal- and honey-based concoction, although cream is sometimes added to enrich the drink further. It can be consumed year-round, but is most specifically associated with the Scottish Hogmanay (New Year), and the "first footing" tradition. As discussed previously, this is where the first person to cross a house's threshold after midnight is said to determine the family's fortune in the New Year. As part of the ritual, the first footer must be offered a drink, traditionally either an atholl brose or a "het pint," which is a frothy mixture of ale, whisky, sugar, eggs, and nutmeg.[85] This is clearly a version of an eggnog or "egg flip." Some accounts tell of a large bowl or kettle of "het pint" being paraded through the city streets just before midnight at Hogmanay and being given to all encountered as a form of wassailing ritual.[86]

While the "brose" component of the name is relatively straightforward, meaning a mixture of uncooked water and oatmeal, the association with "atholl" is the stuff of popular legend. Folklore maintains that it is named after the First Earl of Atholl, who stopped a Highland rebellion against King James III in 1475 when he filled a well with honey and whisky; the rebel leader, John MacDonald, Earl of Ross and Lord of the Isles, allegedly became so drunk on the delicious waters of the well that he was easily captured.[87] Another story attributes this to the rebellion of Bonnie Prince Charlie in 1745.

In the Georgian and Victorian periods, monarchs often seem to have been treated to atholl brose when visiting Scotland. An account of George IV's 1822 visit to Scotland stated that "during dinner the King drank two glasses of Atholl brose, which had become his Majesty's most common beverage at table, and to which he declared himself partial."[88] Twenty years later, on Queen Victoria's first visit to Scotland, she was served atholl brose on the grounds of Dunkeld Castle.[89] And if a drink needed any endorsement in order for it to become part of the Christmas canon, it could not be any better than having been a favorite of Queen Victoria herself.

CONCLUSION

From its pre-Christian origins to the present, food is (and always has been) central to Christmas. The Roman Saturnalia had a grand public feast at its center. The pagan midwinter festivals of northwestern Europe included sacrificial rites involving pork, poultry, and alcohol. The medievals held grand feasts in their halls, and the Tudors followed them with twelve days of eating, drinking, and masquing. The Puritans saw the need to attack the most beloved of Christmas foods directly in order to quash the festival, but these continued to be enjoyed and made it to the Restoration relatively unscathed. However, it was the Victorians who developed the now iconic Christmas family dinner, with the set menu that we know so well today. This development drew on the legacy and dishes of all that had gone before, reworking them to forge an idealized domestic performance, and a version of this meal has been maintained ever since. Today, it continues to be enjoyed in many places most strongly associated with the old British Empire. It has become globally influential and recognized, though, as it has been celebrated in film and popular culture as an iconic scene that perfectly epitomizes the secular expression of Christmas: simultaneously symbolizing family, indulgence, and nostalgia.

Gathering the family together for Christmas dinner is the focal point and pinnacle of the day for many. Days (if not weeks) of planning and preparation go into the meal in many households. The pudding is made ceremoniously on "Stir-Up Sunday" weeks in advance and left to mature. The turkey and ham are preordered, and detailed shopping lists are written and rewritten to prepare for the meal itself and the full house over the holidays. Shopping trips are timed to factor in crowds, freshness, and availability. Once home, organizing fridge space becomes a detailed exercise in precision engineering. Then comes the challenge of actually cooking the meal. From making condiments such as brandy butter and cranberry sauce days in advance to getting an enormous turkey and potatoes to fit in the oven on the day itself and be cooked on time, preparing a grand Victorian feast in a small modern kitchen is no mean feat. The table itself is also beautifully laid with special festive tablecloths, centerpieces, napkins, and (most critically) Christmas crackers. Setting the scene is part of the performance. Once everyone is seated, the ritual of cracker pulling begins, papers crowns are donned, and cheesy jokes are told. Then the feast gets under way.

But the role of festive food does not stop with Christmas dinner. For the extended season, covering most of December and early January, special celebratory food and drinks surround us. Gifts of food, such as the sophisticated store-bought panettone, homemade cookies, or the ubiquitous boxes of Cadbury Roses, are common. Chocolates, mince pies, and slices of marzipan-topped Christmas cake are passed around to guests who drop by. The tree itself is decked with candy canes, and selection boxes of chocolates and sweets are left in children's stockings. A mince pie or cookie and a glass of milk (or perhaps something a little stronger) is left out as a thank-you to Santa, helping to keep him fueled for the night's important work. Office Christmas parties and New Year's celebrations are awash with our favorite festive tipples. These treats, which are not a part of the dinner itself, are no less essential; they tell us that this is a time of plenty, indulgence, and fun. Being surrounded by this suite of festive offerings makes it clear that this time of year is like no other.

While Christmas food has certainly not remained static, this book has demonstrated that there are some significant patterns and reoccurring themes that have been consistent over the centuries, the first being that meat matters. Notwithstanding the valiant efforts made by vegetarians to establish the nut roast on the festive table, Christmas is and always has been a meat-heavy affair. Folklorists and archaeologists suggest that midwinter feasts in pagan Europe, particularly among Germanic peoples, may have involved sacrificing boar and migratory fowl as part of fertility rituals. Meat was also quite simply at its most plentiful at this time of year. The animals were at their fattest and needed to be slaughtered for winter, and the hunting season was at its peak, so the heavy meat consumption was as seasonal as it was ritual. While there is undoubtedly an element of conjecture relating to this earlier period, we know for certain that meat played an important role in the medieval and Tudor Christmas festival, representing a welcome celebration after the long fast of Advent. Tenants traditionally bought gifts of meat to their lords, and open-house hospitality witnessed hundreds, if not thousands, of animals served up over the twelve days. While roast fowl had always been traditional, it was not until the sixteenth century that turkey, having been introduced from the Americas, came to grace the Christmas table in Britain. By the nineteenth century, it had become part of a codified Christmas menu that was celebrated, idealized, and popularized by Charles Dickens. It was not until the second half of the twentieth century that turkey could be afforded by the masses, but today it is undoubtedly the dominant main in Britain, Ireland, and much of the Commonwealth, being closely supported by the Christmas ham.

The other foodstuff critical to Christmas is sugar. Three chapters of this book have been devoted to sweet dishes alone. Sugar, spice, and dried fruits were expensive ingredients in the medieval world, and so recipes like plum pottage (or porridge) and mince pies were indulgent, luxury foods befitting such a significant celebratory feast. By the mid-seventeenth century, these dishes were sufficiently associated with the festival to make them a target for Puritans, and so they can consequently be seen as two of the earliest specifically designated Christmas foods. While these may be the most iconic, as chapters 3–5 demonstrated, they are not the only sweet dishes enjoyed over the festive season. Christmas is a time when bakers, confectioners, and chocolatiers do a busy trade. From the eighteenth century onward, sugar became more affordable and was forever embedded in our culinary experience of Christmas, with an endless and ever-increasing supply of desserts, cakes, cookies, candy, and chocolate entering the menu. As food and industrial production technologies rapidly developed from the late nineteenth century onward, chocolate and confectionery also became important as popular gifts and decorations.

After meat and sugar, the final critical element is alcohol. Imbibing to excess has always been an important part of the midwinter festival. Ancient fertility rites involving libations can be identified in later wassailing traditions, which continue in some form to this day and ensure prosperity in the New Year. Drinking together has also been a way to cement kinship networks and reinforce social obligations. The simple need to "let off steam" collectively has, and always will have, an important social function. Although some of the more archaic traditions and old-fashioned recipes discussed in this book no longer form part of most families' Christmases, the role that alcohol plays in the adult side of the festival remains: modern Christmas drinking rituals include having one too many at the office Christmas party to gathering at the pub on Christmas Eve, leaving a nightcap by the chimney for Santa, and enjoying a wild night out on New Year's. There is a long and established tradition of drinking to excess at Christmas, which, despite the concerns of the more puritanical among us, shows no signs of stopping.

The story of festive food that this book has traced has shown us that after centuries of festive feasting, we arrived in Victorian Britain with a very familiar-looking Christmas dinner. This menu was centered around a large roast fowl—ideally a turkey—which was supported by a ham and trimmed with stuffing, potatoes, gravy, and brussels sprouts. This main course was followed by a flaming holly-decked Christmas pudding served with brandy or rum sauce and butters. As we have seen, almost all these dishes had earlier origins—this is why they mattered so much to the nostalgic Victorians—but it was in the mid-nineteenth century that this very set and stylized British menu emerged and began to be repeated annually by all who had the means. Those who did not made do, and in times of hardship alternatives and substitutes were found, but this framework was always faithfully maintained. This meal, and the tension of being able to afford it, was immortalized by Dickens in his description of the Cratchit family feast (see chapters 2 and 3). Cathy Kaufman observes that "Dickens did not single-handedly invent the signature Cratchit meal; his legacy was in popularizing a very specific menu to the exclusion of other foods historically served at Christmas."[1] In any case, his writing helped to codify the menu that we know today, embedding it with a powerful cultural resonance and meaning.

The astonishing thing about this Christmas menu is not so much its substance—it is, after all, quite simply a very traditional British roast dinner and pudding—but rather how faithfully it has been maintained over time. Eating this series of particular foods annually became a sort of ritualized gastronomic performance of nostalgia. It ties us to our past annually, and to a period that, for Britain and many of its former colonies, is hugely culturally significant. This Victorian menu drew on older traditions and created a meal that became a sort of romantic idealized performance that was repeated annually. Judith Flanders writes of Christmas generally that "there is that wonderous, nostalgically flawless day that is seared in our memories, the day that we can never quite recapture, the perfect Christmas."[2] And this quote equally applies to the meal itself; many of us have this vivid (if not necessarily accurate) recollection of a perfect family dinner that we seek to reenact each year.

This meal has been maintained not just over time but also over great distance, being replicated across many parts of the globe. Wherever the British went, they took their Christmas with them. Eating this meal annually on the same day across the Empire tied it together culturally, as well as tying it across time. However, differences in how accurately (or perhaps rigidly) the meal was performed can tell us a great deal about the cultural identity, changing values and meaning of Christmas in new climes. In places associated with the mass migration of the British diaspora, which remained strongly tied to the Commonwealth for much of the twentieth century, this menu was adhered to as faithfully as possible. Roasted fowl, ham, mince pies, shortbread, Christmas cake, and, above all, Christmas pudding were (and still are) prepared in households throughout Australia and New Zealand in the height of summer. As we have seen, the inappropriateness of the meal did not escape the notice of early colonial commentators. Then as now, people annually shook their heads at the absurdity of boiling a suet pudding all day in the middle of summer, and yet so many families continue to do so. This meal means something. It is not unchanging, though, and the development of distinctly Antipodean Christmas culinary traditions tells us a great deal about the growing sense of national and cultural identity and an increasingly diverse multicultural population. Today, many Australians commonly mark Christmas with an outdoor seafood barbecue. This modern tradition developed in the later twentieth century, but it has now become firmly established. Other families find a happy middle ground, preparing a buffet of cold turkey or chicken, ham, and salad: a nod to the past, but an acceptance and celebration of the climate. Pavlova and fresh fruit now rival the pudding but have not yet ousted it completely. Of course, as Australia's population has become more diverse, new traditions and flavors have also penetrated the Christmas table, from Asian-inspired ham glazes to entirely new dishes such as panettone. Still, the love of tradition and the British Christmas persists, and it has led to the modern phenomenon of Christmas in July, marked in many Southern Hemisphere countries. Christmas in July has grown in popularity every year, especially in Australia and New Zealand, where it is an opportunity to enjoy the traditional turkey, ham, and pudding in their rightful season.

In America, the culinary traditions associated with Christmas are more complex, reflecting the diversity of the population across different colonies from an early date, as well as the more marked cultural separation from Britain following independence. While turkey, ham, pudding, mince pies, and Christmas cake all feature on historical and contemporary American Christmas tables, they do not do so with the consistency seen throughout many parts of the Commonwealth. Turkey is common, and was certainly associated with Christmas from an early date, but it is not a mandatory part of the meal to the degree that it is in Britain. The dessert course may (but rarely does) include Christmas pudding, with festively flavored twists on traditional American desserts such as pies being more common. Kaufman, a leading authority on the history of Christmas food in the United States, states that

> unlike Thanksgiving, with its immutable elements of turkey, corn, pumpkin, and cranberries regardless of one's socioeconomic status, American Christmas has become an expression of class, purse and ethnic origins, with only occasional nods to unifying tradition. . . . Unlike our colonial ancestors, contemporary Americans think Christmas dinner very important: we simply cannot predict the menu.[3]

The reasons for the diversity of the American Christmas meal when compared to the British version are complex, but three main factors are readily apparent. The first is the role of Thanksgiving just weeks earlier. The national and cultural emphasis is directed toward that meal, at which turkey is paramount, and so Christmas dinner suffers from being something of a second act. This same impact may be felt in Canada, although to a lesser extent, as Thanksgiving is marked there in early October, so there is more of a buffer between celebrations. Second, as we have seen, the Christmas meal in Britain was not codified until the mid-nineteenth century, after which time it became imbued with a strong sense of national identity for the British. As this formalization did not take place until after the Revolutionary War, it is unsurprising that Americans neither inherited nor reveled in this particularly British institution. They still inherited aspects of it, as most of the dishes and traditions have earlier roots, but this exact set menu postdates independence and ultimately became a signifier of British identity. And, finally, the American Christmas was always a diverse celebration that varied much from colony to colony based on the religious and cultural makeup of its population. As a result, it never had the uniformity that the British Christmas did, and this factor carried over into the culinary experience of the festival. This diversity undoubtedly led to a very rich and textured culinary Christmas landscape in America, though, as the traditions of multiple immigrant groups were embraced. American Christmas traditions such as cookies, candy canes, and eggnog, along with Santa Claus, were exported around the world from the twentieth century on through popular film, music, and television. Thus, America has put its own culinary stamp on Christmas.

Looking at the history of Christmas, from its potentially pagan origins to the present day, tells us three important points about the festival. The first is that it survives because it means a great deal to those cultures and people who keep it. In the twenty-first-century Western world, there are precious few festivals steeped in meaning and tradition. Our world is considerably less magical than it once was, and so, for many people, Christmas is the one time of the year when food, family, and frivolity are the priorities. Second, excess has always been a central part of Christmas. This is not to diminish or underplay the spiritual dimensions of the holiday, but it has also always been a time for people to communally let off steam, to indulge, to eat, and to drink. Throughout times of hardship, people have found ways and means of celebrating, and food has commonly been central to "keeping Christmas." And, finally, for as long as there has been indulgence over the season, there have always been those who disapprove of the worldly excesses. Elements of the early church disagreed with the selection of the date, the Puritans outlawed the celebration altogether, and today commentators regularly complain about the annual spending frenzy. Christmas has always been a reflection of how we see ourselves and our past, and it has been used as a way of debating tensions in the present. In the words of historian Stephen

Nissenbaum, Christmas rituals "reveal something of what we would like to be, what we once were, or what we are becoming despite ourselves."[4] Because (or perhaps in spite) of this fact, we continue to keep Christmas, and for so many of us it remains, above all, a time to eat, drink, and be merry.

NOTES

INTRODUCTION

1. Hattie Garlick, "Is Christmas Still Christmas If You Eat Out?" *Financial Times*, 24 November 2017, https://www.ft.com/content/b0602ce2-cf0e-11e7-b781-794ce08b24dc.

2. Garlick, "Is Christmas Still Christmas?"

3. Kenneth Stanley Inglis, *The Australian Colonists: An Exploration of Social History, 1788–1870* (Carlton, Victoria, Australia: Melbourne University Press, 1974), 29.

4. Mark Connelly, *Christmas: A History* (London: I. B. Tauris, 2012), 4.

5. Clement A. Miles, *Christmas Customs and Traditions: Their History and Significance* (New York: Dover, 1976 [1912]), 283.

CHAPTER 1

1. John F. Miller, "Festivals, Roman," in *The Oxford Encyclopedia of Ancient Greece and Rome, vol. 1,* edited by Michael Gagarin (Oxford: Oxford University Press, 2010), 172.

2. Penne L. Restad, *Christmas in America: A History* (New York: Oxford University Press, 1995), 4.

3. William F. Hansen, *Ariadne's Thread: A Guide to International Tales Found in Classical Literature* (Ithaca, NY: Cornell University Press, 2002), 385; Hans Friedrich Mueller, "Saturn," in *The Oxford Encyclopedia of Ancient Greece and*

Rome, vol. 1, edited by Michael Gagarin (Oxford: Oxford University Press, 2010), 222.

4. Clement A. Miles, *Christmas Customs and Traditions: Their History and Significance* (New York: Dover, 1976 [1912]), 165–66; Hansen, *Ariadne's Thread*, 385.

5. Mueller, "Saturn," 221–22; Mary Beard, John North, and Simon Price, *Religions of Rome: Volume 2; A Source Book* (Cambridge: Cambridge University Press, 2003), 124.

6. H. S. Versnel, *Inconsistencies in Greek & Roman Religion: Transition & Reversal in Myth & Ritual* (Leiden, Netherlands: E. J. Brill, 1994), 206–7.

7. Restad, *Christmas in America*, 57.

8. Mueller, "Saturn," 221.

9. Beard, North, and Price, *Religions of Rome*, 124.

10. Steven Hijmans, "Sol Invictus, the Winter Solstice and the Origins of Christmas," *Mouseion*, Series III, vol. 3 (2003): 377–78.

11. Stephen Nissenbaum, *The Battle for Christmas: A Cultural History of America's Most Cherished Holiday* (New York: Vintage, 1997), 4.

12. Miles, *Christmas Customs and Traditions*, 24.

13. For a detailed discussion of the relationship between Sol Invictus and Christmas that outlines debates relating to why the early church chose 25 December to mark the Feast of the Nativity, see Hijmans, "Sol Invictus."

14. Restad, *Christmas in America*, 5; Hijmans, "Sol Invictus," 378.

15. Nissenbaum, *Battle for Christmas*, 8.

16. Miles, *Christmas Customs and Traditions*, 201, 203.

17. Miles, *Christmas Customs and Traditions*, 226.

18. Miles, *Christmas Customs and Traditions*, 171–72.

19. Judith Flanders, *Christmas: A Biography* (n.p.: Picador, 2017), 9–10.

20. Flanders, *Christmas: A Biography*, 9–10; Gerry Bowler, *The World Encyclopedia of Christmas* (Toronto: McClelland & Stewart, 2000), 113, https://play.google.com/books/reader?id=WGaVZ6fEjjsC, 1031.

21. For a discussion of traditions from St. Stephen's Day to Holy Innocents' Day, see Miles, *Christmas Customs and Traditions*, 311–17.

22. For a discussion of the Epiphany, see Miles, *Christmas Customs and Traditions*, 337–50.

23. Restad, *Christmas in America*, 5–6.

24. Flanders, *Christmas: A Biography*, 9–10.

25. Miles, *Christmas Customs and Traditions*, 21.

26. Restad, *Christmas in America*, 6.

27. Kaori O'Connor, "The King's Christmas Pudding: Globalization, Recipes, and the Commodities of Empire," *Journal of Global History* 4, no. 1 (2009): 130.

28. Cited in Bridget Ann Henisch, *Fast and Feast: Food in Medieval Society* (University Park: Pennsylvania State University Press, 1999), 54.

29. Cited in Henisch, *Fast and Feast*, 55.

30. Cited in Henisch, *Fast and Feast*, 12.

31. Cited in Henisch, *Fast and Feast*, 13.

32. John Stowe, *The Annals of England to 1603* (n.p., 1603), 1027.

33. Alison Weir, *Henry VIII, King and Court* (London: Vintage, 2008), 127–29.

34. Edward Hall, *Hall's Chronicle, Containing the History of England* (London: J. Johnson, 1809 [1548]), 526.

35. Peter Brears, *Cooking and Dining in Tudor and Early Stuart England* (London: Prospect Books, 2015), 584–90.

36. Henisch, *Fast and Feast*, 221–22.

37. Weir, *Henry VIII, King and Court*, 127–29.

38. Thomas Tusser, *Five Hundred Points of Good Husbandry*, ed. William Mavor (London: Lackington, Allen, 1812 [1573]), 70.

39. Brears, *Cooking and Dining in Tudor and Early Stuart England*, 402.

40. Cited in Brears, *Cooking and Dining in Tudor and Early Stuart England*, 16.

41. Hezekiah Woodward, *Christmas Day. The old heathens feasting day in honour to Saturn their idol god, the papists massing day, the prophane mans ranting day, the superstitious mans idol day, the multitudes idle day whereon because they cannot do nothing they do worse than nothing, satans, that adversaries working day, the true christian mans fasting day. Taking to heart the heathenish customes, popish superstitions, ranting fashions, fearful provocations, humble abhominations com- mitted against the Lord and his Christ oh that day and days following* (London: Henry Cripps, 1656), 28.

42. Philip Stubbes, *Philip Stubbes's Anatomy of the Abuses in England in Shakespeare's Youth, AD 1583, Part I*, ed. Frederick J. Furnivall (London: N. Trübner, 1877–1879), 174.

43. Bernard Capp, *England's Culture Wars: Puritan Reformation and Its Enemies in the Interregnum, 1649–1660* (Oxford: Oxford University Press, 2012), 8.

44. Capp, *England's Culture Wars*, 20.

45. Capp, *England's Culture Wars*, 24.

46. Nissenbaum, *Battle for Christmas*, 3.

47. Cotton Mather, cited in Restad, *Christmas in America*, 15.

48. Nissenbaum, *Battle for Christmas*, 5.

49. Nissenbaum, *Battle for Christmas*, 4.

50. Restad, *Christmas in America*, 9.

51. Restad, *Christmas in America*, 9.

52. Restad, *Christmas in America*, 12; Cathy Kaufman, "The Ideal Christmas Dinner," *Gastronomica* 4, no. 4 (2004): 17–19.

53. Nissenbaum, *Battle for Christmas*, 13.

54. O'Connor, "King's Christmas Pudding," 131.

55. Claire Hopley, *History of Christmas Food and Feasts* (Barnsley, South Yorkshire, UK: Remember When, 2009), 112.

56. Madame Van Muyden, trans. and ed., *A Foreign View of England in the Reigns of George I and George II: The Letters of Monsieur Césare de Saussure to His Family* (London: John Murray, 1902), 297.

57. Nissenbaum, *Battle for Christmas*, 13–15.

58. Nissenbaum, *Battle for Christmas*, 3.

59. Shauna Bigham and Robert E. May, "The Time o' All Times? Masters, Slaves, and Christmas in the Old South," *Journal of the Early Republic* 18, no. 2 (1998): 266–67.

60. For a discussion of Christmas in the slave South, see Bigham and May, "Time o' All Times?" 263–88; see also Restad, *Christmas in America*, 75–90.

61. *London Magazine*, July 1746 (London: T. Astley, 1746), 323, https://play.google.com/books/reader?id=jvoRAAAAYAAJ&printsec=frontcover&output=reader&hl=en&pg=GBS.PP1.

62. For a discussion of Irving's work, see Nissenbaum, *Battle for Christmas*, 57–61.

63. Washington Irving, *The Sketch Book of Geoffrey Crayon, Gent* (New York: Putnam, 1864), http://www.gutenberg.org/files/2048/2048-h/2048-h.htm#link2H_4_0023.

64. Nissenbaum, *Battle for Christmas*, 56.

65. Nissenbaum, *Battle for Christmas*, 52–54.

66. Restad, *Christmas in America*, 45–47; see also Nissenbaum, *Battle for Christmas*, 84–85.

67. Restad, *Christmas in America*, 58.

68. Restad, *Christmas in America*, 59; Nissenbaum, *Battle for Christmas*, 195.

69. Nissenbaum, *Battle for Christmas*, 177.

70. Nissenbaum, *Battle for Christmas*, 195.

71. For a discussion of the Victorians' role in the creation of the modern Christmas, see Mark Connelly, *Christmas: A History* (London: I. B. Taurus, 2012).

72. Connelly, *Christmas: A History*, 15–22.

73. Connelly, *Christmas: A History*, 29.

74. Connelly, *Christmas: A History*, 16–17.

75. William Francis Dawson, *Christmas: Its Origins and Associations* (London: Elliot Stock, 1902), 33–41.

76. Connelly, *Christmas: A History*, 18–19, 23.

77. Connelly, *Christmas: A History*, 25–28.

78. Hopley, *History of Christmas Food*, 19–20.

79. Nissenbaum, *Battle for Christmas*, 62.

80. Nissenbaum, *Battle for Christmas*, 51.

81. Henisch, *Fast and Feast*, 180.

82. Henisch, *Fast and Feast*, 183.

83. Henisch, *Fast and Feast*, 200–201.

84. O'Connor, "King's Christmas Pudding," 131.

85. O'Connor, "King's Christmas Pudding," 131.

86. Connelly, *Christmas: A History*, 28.

87. Tara Moore, "Starvation in Victorian Christmas Fiction," *Victorian Literature and Culture* 36, no. 2 (2008): 489–505.

88. Moore, "Starvation in Victorian Christmas Fiction," 498.

89. *Illustrated London News*, Christmas Number 1891, cited in Connelly, *Christmas: A History*, 100.

90. Connelly, *Christmas: A History*, 100–132.

91. Connelly, *Christmas: A History*, 100–104.

92. *New Zealand Herald*, 25 December 1872, cited in Connelly, *Christmas: A History*, 114.

93. Connelly, *Christmas: A History*, 113.

94. Hopley, *History of Christmas Food*, 189–91.

95. Hopley, *History of Christmas Food*, 145.

CHAPTER 2

1. "Christmas Stats and Traditions," British Turkey, accessed 7 February 2018, http://www.britishturkey.co.uk/facts-and-figures/christmas-stats-and-traditions.html.

2. "Turkey Facts," University of Illinois Extension, accessed 7 May 2018, http://extension.illinois.edu/turkey/turkey_facts.cfm.

3. H. R. Ellis Davidson, *Myths and Symbols in Pagan Europe: Early Scandinavian and Celtic Religions* (Syracuse, NY: Syracuse University Press, 1988), 36.

4. Davidson, *Myths and Symbols*, 38.

5. Cathy Kaufman, "Christmas," in *Entertaining from Ancient Rome to the Superbowl: An Encyclopedia, vol. 1*, ed. Melitta Weiss Adamson and Francine Segan (Westport, CT: Greenwood, 2008), 144; Maguelonne Toussaint-Samat, *A History of Food* (Chichester, UK: Wiley-Blackwell, 2009), 317.

6. Claire Hopley, *History of Christmas Food and Feasts* (Barnsley, South Yorkshire, UK: Remember When, 2009), 10.

7. Thomas Pennant, *The Antiquities of London: Comprising Views and Historical Descriptions of Its Principal Buildings; Also Anecdotes of Eminent Persons Connected Therewith* (London: Coxhead, 1818), 80.

8. Kaufman, "Christmas," 144.

9. W. A. Neilson, trans., *Sir Gawain and the Green Knight* (Cambridge, ON: In Parentheses Publications Middle English Series, 1999), 2–3, www.yorku.ca/inpar/sggk_neilson.pdf.

10. Thomas Tusser, *Five Hundred Points of Good Husbandry*, ed. William Mavor (London: Lackington, Allen, 1812 [1573]), 73.

11. Peter Brears, *Cooking and Dining in Tudor and Early Stuart England* (London: Prospect Books, 2015), 154.

12. Robert May, *The Accomplisht Cook; or, The Art and Mystery of Cookery* (London: Printed for Obadiah Blagrave, 1660), no page number.

13. Hopley, *History of Christmas Food*, 121.

14. Jane Austen, *Persuasion* (Peterborough, ON: Broadview, 2013 [1817]), 156.

15. Hopley, *History of Christmas Food*, 153.

16. Clement A. Miles, *Christmas Customs and Traditions: Their History and Significance* (New York: Dover, 1976 [1912]), 284.

17. Toussaint-Samat, *History of Food*, 317.

18. C. Anne Wilson, *Food & Drink in Britain: From the Stone Age to the 19th Century* (Chicago: Academy Chicago, 1991), 124–25.

19. Toussaint-Samat, *History of Food*, 320.

20. Tamra Andrews, *Nectar and Ambrosia: An Encyclopedia of Food in World Mythology* (Santa Barbara, CA: ABC-CLIO, 2000), 105–6.

21. Andrew F. Smith, *The Turkey: An American Story* (Chicago: University of Illinois Press, 2006), 51.

22. Hopley, *History of Christmas Food*, 109; Alan Davidson, *Oxford Companion to Food*, 2nd ed., ed. Tom Jaine (Oxford: Oxford University Press, 2006), 812; Smith, *Turkey: An American Story*, 41–42.

23. Smith, *Turkey: An American Story*, 40–41.

24. Smith, *Turkey: An American Story*, 18.

25. Smith, *Turkey: An American Story*, 40–41.

26. Brooklynne "Tyr" Fothergill, "The Husbandry, Perception and 'Improvement' of Turkeys in Britain, 1500–1900," *Post-medieval Archaeology* 48, no. 1 (2014): 207.

27. Smith, *Turkey: An American Story*, 40–44.

28. Davidson, *Oxford Companion to Food*, 813; Smith, *Turkey: An American Story*, 45; Jean-Louis Flandrin, "Introduction: The Early Modern Period," in *Food: A Culinary History*, ed. Jean-Louis Flandrin and Massimo Montanari (New York: Columbia University Press, 1999), 359.

29. Fothergill, "Husbandry, Perception and 'Improvement,'" 208.

30. Davidson, *Oxford Companion to Food*, 813.

31. Fothergill, "Husbandry, Perception and 'Improvement,'" 211.

32. Smith, *Turkey: An American Story*, 18.

33. Smith, *Turkey: An American Story*, 56–57.

34. Tusser, *Five Hundred Points of Good Husbandry*, 73.

35. Fothergill, "Husbandry, Perception and 'Improvement,'" 213–14.

36. Samuel Pepys, "The Diary of Samuel Pepys," entry from 23 December 1660, https://www.pepysdiary.com/diary/1660/12/.

37. May, *Accomplisht Cook*, no page number.

38. John Gay, *Fables by the Late Mr. Gay, in One Volume Complete* (London: W. Strahan, 1769), 83.

39. Smith, *Turkey: An American Story*, 62.

40. Nicholas Peacock, *The Diary of Nicholas Peacock, 1740–1751: The Worlds of a County Limerick Farmer and Agent*, ed. Marie Louise Legg (Dublin: Four Courts, 2005), 131.

41. Hopley, *History of Christmas Food*, 173.

42. Isabella Beeton, *Mrs. Beeton's Household Management* (Ware, Hertfordshire, UK: Wordsworth Editions, 2006 [1861]), 486.

43. Gerry Bowler, *The World Encyclopedia of Christmas* (Toronto: McClelland & Stewart, 2000), 942, https://play.google.com/books/reader?id=WGaVZ6fEjjsC.

44. Charles Dickens, *A Christmas Carol* (London: Puffin Books, 2017 [1843]), 118–20.

45. Hopley, *History of Christmas Food*, 170.

46. Davidson, *Oxford Companion to Food*, 813.

47. "Turkey for the Holidays," University of Illinois Extension, accessed 7 February 2018, http://extension.illinois.edu/turkey/turkey_facts.cfm; Jon Kelly, "The Christmas Turkey Naysayers," *BBC News Magazine*, 24 December 2014, http://www.bbc.com/news/magazine-30420477.

48. A. W., *A Book of Cookrye* (London: Edward Allde, 1591 [1584]).

49. Smith, *Turkey: An American Story*, 52.

50. Thomas Dawson, *The Good Huswifes Jewell*, transcribed by Daniel Myers (n.p.: n.p., 2008 [1596]), 13–14, http://www.medievalcookery.com/notes/ghj1596.txt.

51. Smith, *Turkey: An American Story*, 60.

52. Smith, *Turkey: An American Story*, 53–54.

53. Gervase Markham, *Country Contentments; or, The English Huswife* (London: R. Jackson, 1623 [1615]), 89–90.

54. Francois Pierre La Varenne, *The French Cook* (Lewes, East Sussex, UK: Southover, 2001), 41.

55. Judith Flanders, *Christmas: A Biography* (n.p.: Picador, 2017), 7–8.

56. Hannah Glasse, *The Art of Cookery Made Plain and Easy* (London: Strahan, 1747), 139–40.

57. Dickens, *A Christmas Carol*, 68–70.

58. Beeton, *Mrs. Beeton's Household Management*, 486.

59. May, *Accomplisht Cook*, no page number.

60. Hopley, *History of Christmas Food*, 170.

61. Dickens, *A Christmas Carol*, 71.

62. Hopley, *History of Christmas Food*, 11.

63. Eliza Acton, *Modern Cookery in All Its Branches: Reduced to a System of Easy Practice for the Use of Private Families*, 2nd ed. (London: Longman, Brown, Green and Longmans, 1845), 397–98.

64. Smith, *Turkey: An American Story*, 89.

65. Smith, *Turkey: An American Story*, 21.

66. Eliza Leslie, *The Lady's Receipt-Book: A Useful Companion for Large and Small Families* (Philadelphia: Carey & Hart, 1847), 377.

67. Leslie, *Lady's Receipt-Book*, 382, 388; for a discussion of Leslie's menus, see Cathy Kaufman, "The Ideal Christmas Dinner," *Gastronomica* 4, no. 4 (2004): 21.

68. Smith, *Turkey: An American Story*, 88.

69. Kaufman, "Ideal Christmas Dinner," 24.

70. Smith, *Turkey: An American Story*, 91.

71. Pía Spry-Marqués, *Pig/Pork: Archaeology, Zoology and Edibility* (n.p.: Bloomsbury Sigma, 2017), 102, https://play.google.com/books/reader?id=YM8vDgAAQBAJ&pg=GBS.PP1.

72. Miles, *Christmas Customs and Traditions*, 286.

73. James E. Spears, "The 'Boar's' Head Carol and Folk Tradition," *Folklore* 85, no. 3 (1974): 195.

74. Spears, "'Boar's' Head Carol," 196; W. B. Hannon, "Christmas and Its Folklore," *Irish Monthly* 52, no. 607 (1924): 20.

75. Spears, "'Boar's' Head Carol," 195; R. M. Liuzza, trans., *Beowulf* (Toronto: Broadview Literary Texts, 2000), 62, 93, 97–98.

76. Spears, "'Boar's' Head Carol," 196.

77. William E. Studwell, *The Christmas Carol Reader* (New York: Routledge, 2011), 140; Erik Routley, *The English Carol* (New York: Oxford University Press, 1959), 39–40.

78. Brears, *Cooking and Dining in Tudor and Early Stuart England*, 199.

79. Bowler, *World Encyclopedia of Christmas*, 783.

80. Brears, *Cooking and Dining in Medieval England* (Totnes, Devon, UK: Prospect Books, 2012), 165–66.

81. Brears, *Cooking and Dining in Medieval England*, 166.

82. Spears, "'Boar's' Head Carol," 194–98.

83. Hopley, *History of Christmas Food*, 19.

84. Brears, *Cooking and Dining in Tudor and Early Stuart England*, 199–200.

85. William King, *The Art of Cookery: In Imitation of Horace's Art of Poetry* (London: Printed for Bernard Lintott, 1708), 75.

86. Beeton, *Mrs. Beeton's Household Management*, 360–61.

87. Charles Elmé Francatelli, *The Royal English and Foreign Confectionery Book* (London: Chapman and Hall, 1862), 292–94.

88. Spears, "'Boar's' Head Carol," 197.

89. Spears, "'Boar's' Head Carol," 197.

90. Hopley, *History of Christmas Food*, 189.

91. Hopley, *History of Christmas Food*, 189.

92. "Christmas Hams," *Sydney Morning Herald*, 23 December 1843, 3.

93. https://trove.nla.gov.au/newspaper/article/12419594?searchTerm=Christmas%20Ham&searchLimits=l-state=New+South+Wales||||l-title=35|||sort by=dateAsc; Michael Symons, *One Continuous Picnic: A Gastronomic History of Australia* (Melbourne, Australia: Melbourne University Press, 2017), 27; Barbara Santich, *Bold Palates: Australia's Gastronomic Heritage* (Kent Town, South Australia: Wakefield, 2012), 43.

94. Kaufman, "Christmas," 144.

95. May, *Accomplisht Cook*, no page number.

96. Ivan Day, "Roasting the Christmas Beef," *Food History Jottings* (blog), 7 December 2011, http://foodhistorjottings.blogspot.com.au/2011/12/roasting-christmas-beef.html.

97. Anthony Trollope, *Orley Farm* (New York: Harper, 1862), 96.

98. Cited in Davidson, *Oxford Companion to Food*, 744.

99. Beeton, *Mrs. Beeton's Household Management*, 292.

100. Máirtín Mac Con Iomaire and Pádraic Óg Gallagher, "Corned Beef: An Enigmatic Irish Dish," in *Smoked, Cured and Fermented: Proceedings from the 2010 Oxford Symposium on Food and Cookery*, ed. Helen Saberi (Devon, UK: Prospect Books, 2011).

101. Mac Con Iomaire and Óg Gallagher, "Corned Beef."

102. James Joyce, "The Dead," in *The Dubliners* (Adelaide, Australia: University of Adelaide Library, 2014 [1914]), ch. 15, https://ebooks.adelaide.edu.au/j/joyce/james/j8d/complete.html#c1hapter15.

103. Miles, *Christmas Customs and Traditions*, 287.

104. Neilson, *Sir Gawain and the Green Knight*, 19.

105. Hannah Woolley, *The Queen-like Closet or Rich Cabinet*, 2nd ed. (London: BiblioBazaar, 2006 [1672]), 166.

106. Katherine Cahill, *Mrs. Delany's Menus, Medicines and Manners* (Dublin: New Island, 2005), 92.

107. Janet Clarkson, *Pie: A Global History* (London: Reaktion Books, 2009), 60–61, https://play.google.com/books/reader?id=FZoJAgAAQBAJ&pg=GBS.PT1.

108. Hopley, *History of Christmas Food*, 177.

109. Hopley, *History of Christmas Food*, 198.

110. Hopley, *History of Christmas Food*, 36–37.

111. Erica Janik, "Scandinavians' Strange Holiday Lutefisk Tradition," *Smithsonian Magazine*, 8 December 2011, https://www.smithsonianmag.com/travel/scandinavians-strange-holiday-lutefisk-tradition-2218218/#BI0Qzo8Idw1K5Yk1.99.

112. Bowler, *World Encyclopedia of Christmas*, 566–69.

113. Charmaine O'Brien, *The Colonial Kitchen: Australia 1788–1901* (Lanham, MD: Rowman & Littlefield, 2016), 35.

114. Colin Bannerman, *The Upside-Down Pudding* (Canberra: National Library of Australia, 1999), 46.

115. David Spicer, "Christmas Eve Seafood: 100,000 Shoppers Rush to Sydney Fish Market," ABC News, 24 December 2017, http://www.abc.net.au/news/2017-12-24/shoppers-rush-sydney-fish-market-christmas-eve/9284776.

CHAPTER 3

1. For an extensive discussion of pottages, see Peter Brears, *Cooking and Dining in Medieval England* (Totnes, Devon, UK: Prospect Books, 2012), 215–302.

2. Alan Davidson, *The Oxford Companion to Food*, 2nd ed., ed. Tom Jaine (Oxford: Oxford University Press, 2006), 185.

3. C. Anne Wilson's research in this area is discussed on the University of Leeds's Library website: https://library.leeds.ac.uk/special-collections/view/811/stewet_beef_to_potage. The recipe in question appears in *A Collection of Ordinances and Regulations for the Government of the Royal Household, made in Divers Reigns. From King Edward III, to King Willi'm and Queen Mary. Also receipts in Ancient Cookery* (London: Society of Antiquaries, 1790), 432.

4. Claire Hopley, *History of Christmas Food and Feasts* (Barnsley, South Yorkshire, UK: Remember When, 2009), 82.

5. Samuel Pepys, "The Diary of Samuel Pepys," entry from 25 December 1662, https://www.pepysdiary.com/diary/1662/12/.

6. Madame Van Muyden, trans. and ed., *A Foreign View of England in the Reigns of George I and George II: The Letters of Monsieur Césare de Saussure to His Family* (London: John Murray, 1902), 297.

7. Clerk of the Kitchens entry for Christmas Day 1736, cited in "Now Bring Us Some Figgy Pudding," *Historic Royal Palaces* (blog), 16 December 2016, http://blog.hrp.org.uk/curators/historic-royal-georgian-christmas/.

8. Hannah Glasse, *The Art of Cookery Made Plain and Easy* (London: Strahan, 1747), 122.

9. Margaret Dods, *The Cook and Housewife's Manual: Containing the Most Approved Modern Receipts* (Edinburgh: Margaret Dods, 1826), 58.

10. Jeri Quinzio, *Pudding: A Global History* (London: Reaktion Books, 2012), 19–20, 58–59, https://play.google.com/books/reader?id=6xHMDOME0ZwC&printsec=frontcover&pg=GBS.PA17.

11. Colonel Norwood, "A Voyage to Virginia," in *A Collection of voyages and travels: Some now first printed from original manuscripts, others now first published in English: In six volumes with a general preface giving an account of the progress of navigation from its first beginning*, ed. and comp. Awnsham Churchill and John Churchill (London: Churchill, 1732), 153; for a discussion of this source, see Ivan Day, "One Family and Empire Christmas Pudding," *Food History Jottings* (blog), 30 August 2012, http://foodhistorjottings.blogspot.com.au/2012/08/one-family-and-empire-christmas-pudding.html.

12. Henry Teonge, *The Diary of Henry Teonge, Chaplain on Board His Majesty's Ships Assistance, Bristol, and Royal Oak, Anno 1675 to 1679* (London: Charles Knight, 1825), 127–28. For a discussion of this source, see Day, "One Family."

13. Mary Kettilby, *A Collection of Above Three Hundred Receipts in Cookery, Physick and Surgery* (London: Richard Wilkin, 1714), 89.

14. John Nott, *The Cook's and Confectioner's Dictionary; or, The Accomplish'd Housewife's Companion* (London: C. Rivington, 1723), recipe no. 243.

15. Cathy Kaufman, "Christmas," in *Entertaining from Ancient Rome to the Superbowl: An Encyclopedia, vol. 1*, ed. Melitta Weiss Adamson and Francine Segan (Westport, CT: Greenwood, 2008), 144–49.

16. John Mollard, *The Art of Cookery Made Easy and Refined* (London: John Mollard, 1802), 221.

17. Charles Dickens, *A Christmas Carol* (London: Puffin Books, 2017 [1843]), 72.

18. Eliza Acton, *Modern Cookery in All Its Branches*, 2nd ed. (London: Longman, Brown Green and Longmans, 1845), 380.

19. Isabella Beeton, *Mrs. Beeton's Household Management* (Ware, Hertfordshire, UK: Wordsworth, 2006 [1861]), 227–28.

20. Kaori O'Connor, "The King's Christmas Pudding: Globalization, Recipes, and the Commodities of Empire," *Journal of Global History* 4, no. 1 (2009): 134.

21. "On the Kitchen Front: This Weeks Food Facts," *Whitby Gazette*, Ministry of Food, London, December 1940.

22. "The Twenty-Fifth Sunday after Trinity: The Collect," in *An Explanation of the Collects, by Way of Questions and Answers, with Practical Addresses* (London: J. G. and F. Rivington, 1835), 91.

23. O'Connor, "King's Christmas Pudding," 130.

24. Gerry Bowler, *The World Encyclopedia of Christmas* (Toronto: McClelland & Stewart, 2000), 113, https://play.google.com/books/reader?id=WGaVZ6fEjjsC; George Morley Story, W. J. Kirwan, and J. D. A. Widdowson, *Dictionary of Newfoundland English*, 2nd ed. (Toronto: University of Toronto Press, 1990), 50.

25. Gerry Bowler, "Shooting in Christmas," *Gerry Bowler: The Past Isn't Dead, It Isn't Even Past* (blog), 29 September 2017, http://gerrybowler.com/shooting-in-christmas/.

26. Hopley, *History of Christmas Food*, 97.

27. Cissely Plum-porridge [pseud.], *The arraignment, conviction, and imprisoning, of Christmas: On St. Thomas day last* (London: Printed by Simon Minc'd Pye, for Cissely Plum-porridge, 1645).

28. John Taylor, *The Vindication of Christmas: His Twelve Years Observations upon the Times, concerning the lamentable Game called Sweep-stake; Acted by General Plunder and Major General Tax* (London: G. Horton, 1652).

29. Margaret, Duchess of Newcastle, *The Life of William Cavendish, Duke of Newcastle, to Which Is Added the True Relation of My Birth, Breeding and Life* (London: George Routledge, 1890), xxiv.

30. Thomas Hervey, *The Book of Christmas* (London: William Spooner, 1836), 277.

31. Hervey, *Book of Christmas*, 107.

32. "John Bull Showing the Foreign Powers How to Make a Constitutional Plum-Pudding," *Punch*, 23 December 1848, 267; for a discussion of this source, see Tara Moore, "National Identity and Victorian Christmas Foods," in *Consuming Culture in the Long Nineteenth Century: Narratives of Consumption, 1700–1900*, edited by Tamara S. Wagner and Narin Hassan (Lanham, MD: Lexington Books, 2010), 147.

33. Anonymous [Charles Knight], "A Christmas Pudding," *Household Words: A Weekly Journal Conducted by Charles Dickens*, 14 December 1850, 300–304. For a detailed discussion of this source, see O'Connor, "King's Christmas Pudding," 127–55.

34. Anonymous [Charles Knight], "A Christmas Pudding," 301.

35. Anonymous [Charles Knight], "A Christmas Pudding," 303.

36. O'Connor, "King's Christmas Pudding," 140.

37. O'Connor, "King's Christmas Pudding," 141.

38. O'Connor, "King's Christmas Pudding," 144.

39. Day, "One Family."

40. O'Connor, "King's Christmas Pudding," 147–48.

41. O'Connor, "King's Christmas Pudding," 127.

42. O'Connor, "King's Christmas Pudding," 128.

43. Cathy Kaufman, "The Ideal Christmas Dinner," *Gastronomica* 4, no. 4 (2004): 21.

44. Eliza Leslie, *Directions for Cookery: Being a System of the Art in Its Various Branches* (Philadelphia: Carey & Hart, 1837), 303–5.

45. Eliza Leslie, *Miss Leslie's New Cookery Book* (Philadelphia: T. B. Peterson, 1857), 487.

46. Sarah Josepha Hale, *The Good Housekeeper; or, The Way to Live Well and Be Well While We Live, Containing Directions for Choosing and Preparing Food, in Regard to Health, Economy and Taste* (Boston: Weeks, Jordan, 1839), 67.

47. Quinzio, *Pudding: A Global History*, 69–71.

48. Andrew F. Smith, *Food and Drink in American History: A "Full Course" Encyclopedia* (Santa Barbara, CA: ABC-CLIO, 2013), 2:996.

49. Estelle Woods Wilcox, *Buckeye Cookery and Practical Housekeeping* (Marysville, OH: Buckeye, 1877), 204.

50. Kaufman, "Ideal Christmas Dinner," 24.

51. "Sydney," *Sydney Gazette and New South Wales Advertiser*, 2 January 1819, 2.

52. "Police Incidents," *Sydney Herald*, 2 January 1832, 2.

53. Charmaine O'Brien, *The Colonial Kitchen: Australia 1788–1901* (Lanham, MD: Rowman & Littlefield, 2016), 127.

54. "Tasmanian News," *Sydney Gazette and New South Wales Advertiser*, 14 July 1829, 2.

55. Marcus Clarke, *Australasian*, 26 December 1868, cited in Barbara Santich, *In the Land of the Magic Pudding: A Gastronomic Miscellany* (Kent Town, South Australia: Wakefield, 2000), 25–26.

56. John Hunter Kerr, *Glimpses of Life in Victoria: By a Resident* (Edinburgh: Edmonston & Douglas, 1872), 395.

57. Kenneth Stanley Inglis, *The Australian Colonists: An Exploration of Social History, 1788–1870* (Carlton, Victoria, Australia: Melbourne University Press, 1974), 109.

58. Henry Lawson, "The Ghosts of Many Christmases," in *The Romance of the Swag* (Sydney, Australia: University of Sydney Library, 2001 [1907]), 80, http://setis.library.usyd.edu.au/ozlit/pdf/p00104.pdf.

59. Henry Lawson, "That Pretty Girl in the Army," in *Send round the Hat* (Project Gutenberg Australia, 2006 [1907]), http://gutenberg.net.au/ebooks06/0607411h.html#s2.

60. Cited in O'Brien, *Colonial Kitchen*, 126.

61. Rhiannon Donaldson, "Revisiting a 'Well-Worn Theme': The Duality of the Australian Christmas Pudding 1850–1950," *Eras Journal* 6 (2004): 3.

62. Recipe book cited by Donaldson, "'Well-Worn Theme,'" 4.

63. O'Brien, *Colonial Kitchen*, 127.

64. Donaldson, "'Well-Worn Theme,'" 4.

65. For a discussion of the "pavlova wars," see Helen Leach, *The Pavlova Story: A Slice of New Zealand's Culinary History* (Dunedin, New Zealand: Otago University Press, 2008), 11–31.

66. "For the Festive Season," *Advocate*, 10 December 1949, 18.

67. Helen Seagar, "Test and Tell: Christmas under Difficulties," *Argus*, 24 December 1946, 20.

68. "Christmas Eve," *Daily Telegraph*, 25 December 1890, 4.

69. "Mangoes," *Queenslander*, 13 February 1886, 270.

70. "Commercial," *Evening News* (Sydney), 22 December 1910, 7.

71. "Christmas Time: Along the Line," *North Queensland Registrar*, 4 January 1904, 21.

72. "Our First Peacetime Christmas," *Rockhampton Morning Bulletin*, 21 December 1945, 10.

73. Helen Saberi and Alan Davidson, *Trifle* (Totnes, Devon, UK: Prospect Books, 2009), 15–16.

74. Thomas Dawson, *The Good Huswifes Jewell*, transcribed by Daniel Myers (n.p.: n.p., 2008 [1596]), http://www.medievalcookery.com/notes/ghj1596.txt.

75. Glasse, *Art of Cookery*, 285.

76. Saberi and Davidson, *Trifle*, 21–25.

77. Hannah Glasse, *The Compleat Confectioner; or, The Whole Art of Confectionary Made Plain and Easy* (London: J. Cooke, 1765), 83–84. For a discussion of this recipe, see Saberi and Davidson, *Trifle*, 23–24.

78. Beeton, *Mrs. Beeton's Household Management*, 710–11.

79. Eliza Warren, *The Economical Cookery Book* (London: Piper, Stephenson and Spence, 1858), 83, cited by Helen Leach, Mary Browne, and Raelene Inglis, *The Twelve Cakes of Christmas: An Evolutionary History with Recipes* (Dunedin, New Zealand: Otago University Press, 2011), 64.

80. Darina Allen, *Forgotten Skills of Cooking* (London: Kyle Cathie, 2009), 506.

81. Hopley, *History of Christmas Food*, 189.

82. Jeanette Winterson, *12 Stories and 12 Feasts for 12 Days* (London: Jonathan Cape, 2016).

CHAPTER 4

1. Nicola Humble, *Cake: A Global History* (London: Reaktion Books, 2010), 9–10, https://play.google.com/books/reader?id=qclZyk87j_EC&printsec=frontcover&output=reader&hl=en&pg=GBS.PA28.w.0.1.2.

2. Humble, *Cake: A Global History*, 20–25; Peter Brears, *Cooking and Dining in Tudor and Early Stuart England* (London: Prospect Books, 2015), 131.

3. Charles Knight, *London, Volume III* (London: Charles Knight, 1842), 363.

4. Brears, *Cooking and Dining in Tudor and Early Stuart England*, 131.

5. Elizabeth Kent, *A True Gentlewoman's Delight 1653* (London: G. D., 1653), 69, cited in Helen Leach, Mary Browne, and Raelene Inglis, *The Twelve Cakes of Christmas: An Evolutionary History with Recipes* (Dunedin, New Zealand: Otago University Press, 2011), 27.

6. Leach, Browne, and Inglis, *Twelve Cakes of Christmas*, 38–40.

7. Kenelm Digby, *The Closet of Sir Kenelm Digby Opened*, ed. Jane Stevenson and Peter Davidson (Totnes, Devon, UK: Prospect Books, 2010 [1669]), 216–17.

8. Leach, Browne, and Inglis, *Twelve Cakes of Christmas*, 38.

9. Elizabeth Raffald, *The Experienced English Housekeeper* (Lewes, East Sussex, UK: Southover, 1997 [1769]), 134.

10. Humble, *Cake: A Global History*, 24–25.

11. Leach, Browne, and Inglis, *Twelve Cakes of Christmas*, 39.

12. Eliza Smith, *The Compleat Housewife; or, Accomplished Woman's Companion* (London: J. Pemberton, 1729), 137.

13. James Jenks, *The Complete Cook* (Dublin: J. Potts, 1769), 239.

14. John Mollard, *The Art of Cookery Made Easy and Refined* (London: John Mollard, 1802), 286–87.

15. Humble, *Cake: A Global History*, 25.

16. Digby, *Closet of Sir Kenelm Digby*, 220.

17. Digby, *Closet of Sir Kenelm Digby*, 218–19.

18. Bridget Ann Henisch, *Cakes and Characters: An English Christmas Tradition* (London: Prospect Books, 1984), 206.

19. Leach, Browne, and Inglis, *Twelve Cakes of Christmas*, 36.

20. Raffald, *Experienced English Housekeeper*, 134–35.

21. William Hone, *The Everyday Book* (London: William Hone, 1825), 47–49.

22. *Illustrated London News*, 13 January 1849, 21, cited in Henisch, *Cake and Characters*, 148.

23. *Supplement to the Illustrated London News*, Christmas 1850, 485, cited in Henisch, *Cakes and Characters*, 174.

24. Leach, Browne, and Inglis, *Twelve Cakes of Christmas*, 58.

25. "Punch's Sermons to Tradesmen," *Punch*, vol. 20, 1851, 3.

26. Leach, Browne, and Inglis, *Twelve Cakes of Christmas*, 25.

27. Robert Herrick, "Twelfth Night, or King and Queene," in *Cyclopedia of English Literature*, ed. Robert Chambers (Boston: Gould, Kendall and Lincoln, 1847), 141.

28. Claire Hopley, *History of Christmas Food and Feasts* (Barnsley, South Yorkshire, UK: Remember When, 2009), 113.

29. Henry Teonge, *The Diary of Henry Teonge* (London: Charles Knight, 1825), 130–31.

30. Hopley, *History of Christmas Food*, 112.

31. Samuel Pepys, "The Diary of Samuel Pepys," entry from 6 January 1660, https://www.pepysdiary.com/diary/1660/01/.

32. Samuel Pepys, "The Diary of Samuel Pepys," entry from 7 January 1661, https://www.pepysdiary.com/diary/1661/01/.

33. Samuel Pepys, "The Diary of Samuel Pepys," entry from 6 January 1668, https://www.pepysdiary.com/diary/1668/01/.

34. Leach, Browne, and Inglis, *Twelve Cakes of Christmas*, 36.

35. Samuel Pepys, "The Diary of Samuel Pepys," entry from 6 January 1669, https://www.pepysdiary.com/diary/1669/01/.

36. Leach, Browne, and Inglis, *Twelve Cakes of Christmas*, 42.

37. Humble, *Cake: A Global History*, 78–79.

38. Hone, *Everyday Book*, 51–52.

39. Gerry Bowler, *The World Encyclopedia of Christmas* (Toronto: McClelland & Stewart, 2000), 369, https://play.google.com/books/reader?id=WGaVZ6fEjjsC.

40. Humble, *Cake: A Global History*, 76–78.

41. Bowler, *World Encyclopedia of Christmas*, 369.

42. Hopley, *History of Christmas Food*, 117.

43. Leach, Browne, and Inglis, *Twelve Cakes of Christmas*, 58, 61.

44. "Refreshment Rooms! Victoria Confectionary Establishment," *Australian*, 30 December 1841, 3.

45. Leach, Browne, and Inglis, *Twelve Cakes of Christmas*, 60.

46. Elizabeth F. Ellet, *The Practical Housekeeper: A Cyclopaedia of Domestic Economy* (New York: Stringer and Townsend, 1857), 479, http://digital.lib.msu.edu/projects/cookbooks/books/practicalhousekeeper/prho.pdf.

47. Isabella Beeton, *Mrs. Beeton's Household Management* (Ware, Hertfordshire, UK: Wordsworth Editions, 2006 [1861]), 803.

48. Edward Abbott, *The English and Australian Cookery Book* (London: Sampson Low, Son, and Marston, 1864), 154.

49. Leach, Browne, and Inglis, *Twelve Cakes of Christmas*, 76.

50. Margaret Dods, *The Cook and Housewife's Manual: A Practical System of Modern Domestic Cookery and Family Management*, 5th ed. (Edinburgh: Oliver & Boyd, 1833), 375.

51. Margaret Dods, *The Cook and Housewife's Manual: Containing the Most Approved Modern Receipts* (Edinburgh: Margaret Dods, 1826), 317.

52. Hopley, *History of Christmas Food*, 169.

53. Robert Louis Stevenson, *The Incredible Travel Sketches, Essays, Memoirs and Island Works of R. L. Stevenson* (n.p.: Musaicum, 2017), 328–29, https://play.google.com/books/reader?id=9U9ODwAAQBAJ&printsec=frontcover&output=reader&hl=en&pg=GBS.PT327.

54. Alan Davidson, *The Oxford Companion to Food*, 2nd ed., ed. Tom Jaine (Oxford: Oxford University Press, 2006), 82.

55. Humble, *Cake: A Global History*, 79.

56. "News of Food: Christmas Eve Feasts for Europeans Often Include Some Variety of Fish," *New York Times*, 24 December 1945, 12.

57. Humble, *Cake: A Global History*, 119.

58. William Woys Weaver, *The Christmas Cook: Three Centuries of American Yuletide Sweets* (New York: HarperCollins, 1990), 84.

59. Clement A. Miles, *Christmas Customs and Traditions: Their History and Significance* (New York: Dover, 1976 [1912]), 251–60.

CHAPTER 5

1. James W. Parkinson, "Christmas Good Cheer," *Confectioners Journal*, December 1877, cited in William Woys Weaver, *The Christmas Cook: Three Centuries of American Yuletide Sweets* (New York: HarperCollins, 1990), 1.

2. Rebecca Smithers, "7000 Tonnes of Dried Fruit: Inside the World's Largest Mince Pie Factory," *Guardian*, 10 December 2016, https://www.theguardian.com/lifeandstyle/2016/dec/09/inside-worlds-largest-mince-pie-factory-mr-kipling-christmas.

3. Jon Timbs, *Something for Everybody* (London: Lockwood, 1866), 149; for a detailed discussion of the shape of mince pies and evidence that they were modeled after the crib, see Ivan Day, "Shap'd Minc'd Pies Again," *Food History Jottings* (blog), 24 December 2011, http://foodhistorjottings.blogspot.com.au/2011/12/shaped-mincd-pies-again.html.

4. Janet Clarkson, *Pie: A Global History* (London: Reaktion Books, 2009), 43–44, https://play.google.com/books/reader?id=FZoJAgAAQBAJ&pg=GBS.PT1.

5. Alan Davidson, *The Oxford Companion to Food*, 2nd ed., ed. Tom Jaine (Oxford: Oxford University Press, 2006), 509.

6. Thomas Tusser, *Five Hundred Points of Good Husbandry*, ed. William Mavor (London: Lackington, Allen, 1812 [1573]), 73.

7. Robert Herrick, "Ceremonies for Christmas," in *The Book of Elizabethan Verse*, ed. William Stanley Braithwaite (London: Chatto and Windus, 1908), 597.

8. Gervase Markham, *Country Contentments; or, The English Huswife* (London: R. Jackson, 1623 [1615]), 103–4.

9. Peter Brears, *Cooking and Dining in Tudor and Early Stuart England* (London: Prospect Books, 2015), 163.

10. *The Flying Eagle*, 1652, cited in Susan Doran and Christopher Durston, *Princes, Pastors, and People: The Church and Religion in England, 1500–1700* (New York: Routledge, 2003), 106.

11. Thomas Burton, *Diary of Thomas Burton Esq., Member in the Parliaments of Oliver and Richard Cromwell, from 1656 to 1659*, ed. John Towill Rutt (London: Henry Colburn, 1828), 240.

12. R. Fletcher, "Poems and Translations" (1656) in *Observations on Popular Antiquities, Volume 1*, ed. John Brand and Henry Ellis (London: Charles Knight, 1841), 290.

13. Henri Misson, *M. Misson's Memoirs and Observations in his Travels Over England, with some account of Scotland and Ireland* (London: D. Browne, A. Bell, 1719), 34–35.

14. Robert May, *The Accomplisht Cook; or, The Art and Mystery of Cookery* (London: Printed for Obadiah Blagrave, 1660), 213–16.

15. Hannah Bisaker, "Hannah Bisaker: Her Book [of Cookery Receipts] the 12th September. Anno: 1692," The Wellcome Library, 1692, MS 1176.

16. Samuel Pepys, "The Diary of Samuel Pepys," entry from 25 December 1661, https://www.pepysdiary.com/diary/1666/12/25/.

17. Kenelm Digby, *The Closet of Sir Kenelm Digby Opened*, ed. Jane Stevenson and Peter Davidson (Totnes, Devon, UK: Prospect Books, 2010 [1669]), 169.

18. Elizabeth Raffald, *The Experienced English Housekeeper* (Lewes, East Sussex, UK: Southover, 1997 [1769]), 75.

19. Davidson, *Oxford Companion to Food*, 509.

20. Charles Elmé Francatelli, *The Modern Cook: A Practical Guide to the Culinary Art in All Its Branches, Eighth London Edition* (London: Richard Bentley, 1853), 469.

21. Isabella Beeton, *Mrs. Beeton's Household Management* (Ware, Hertfordshire, UK: Wordsworth Editions, 2006 [1861]), 630.

22. Isabella Beeton, *Mrs. Beeton's Book of Household Management: A Guide to Cookery in All Its Branches* (London: Ward, Lock, 1907), 911.

23. Eliza Leslie, *Directions for Cookery: Being a System of the Art in Its Various Branches* (Philadelphia: Carey & Hart, 1837), 282–85.

24. A. B. of Grimsby, *The Frugal Housewife's Manual* (Toronto: Guardian Office, 1840), 15.

25. A. B., *Frugal Housewife's Manual*, 19.

26. Cathy Kaufman, "The Ideal Christmas Dinner," *Gastronomica* 4, no. 4 (2004): 19–20.

27. "Pro Bono Publico," *Australian*, 19 December 1837, 3.

28. Annabella Boswell, *Further Recollections of My Early Days in Australia* (Canberra, Australia: Mulini, 1992), 63.

29. "Christmas Holidays," *Perth Gazette and Independent Journal of Politics and News*, 1 January 1848, 3.

30. Weaver, *Christmas Cook*, 118.

31. Weaver, *Christmas Cook*, 140.

32. Eliza Leslie, *Miss Leslie's New Cookery Book* (Philadelphia: T.B. Peterson, 1857), 605.

33. Cathy Kaufman, "Christmas," in *Entertaining from Ancient Rome to the Superbowl: An Encyclopedia, vol. 1*, ed. Melitta Weiss Adamson and Francine Segan

(Westport, CT: Greenwood, 2008), 151; Davidson, *Oxford Companion to Food*, 339.

34. Sharon Hudgins, "Gingerbread," in *The Oxford Companion to Sugar and Sweets*, ed. Darra Goldstein (Oxford: Oxford University Press, 2015), 304.

35. Amelia Simmons, *American Cookery* (Kansas City, MO: Andrews McMeel, 2012 [1796]), 66.

36. Weaver, *Christmas Cook*, 106.

37. Weaver, *Christmas Cook*, 118–19.

38. Becky Mercuri, "Cookies," in *The Oxford Companion to American Food and Drink*, ed. Andrew F. Smith (Oxford: Oxford University Press, 2007), 183.

39. Weaver, *Christmas Cook*, 114–15.

40. Weaver, *Christmas Cook*, 106–7.

41. Weaver, *Christmas Cook*, 8–10.

42. Lynne Olver, "Christmas Cookies," Food Timeline, accessed 25 August 2016, http://www.foodtimeline.org/christmasfood.html#cookies.

43. Clement A. Miles, *Christmas Customs and Traditions: Their History and Significance* (New York: Dover, 1976 [1912]), 325.

44. Robert Louis Stevenson, *The Incredible Travel Sketches, Essays, Memoirs and Island Works of R. L. Stevenson* (n.p.: Musaicum, 2017), 328–29, https://play.google.com/books/reader?id=9U9ODwAAQBAJ&printsec=frontcover&output=reader&hl=en&pg=GBS.PT327.

45. Davidson, *Oxford Companion to Food*, 78.

46. Davidson, *Oxford Companion to Food*, 720–21.

47. F. Marian McNeill, *The Silver Bough, Vol. III, A Calendar of Scottish National Festivals, Halloween to Yule* (1961), 73–74, https://play.google.com/books/reader?id=fBXYQZuf08C&printsec=frontcover&output=reader&hl=en&pg=GBS.PA73.w.0.0.0.1; James Napier, *Folk Lore; or, Superstitious Beliefs in the West of Scotland within This Century* (Paisley, Scotland: Alex Gardner, 1879), 105; Claire Hopley, *History of Christmas Food and Feasts* (Barnsley, South Yorkshire, UK: Remember When, 2009), 14.

48. McNeill, *Silver Bough*, 76.

49. Boswell, *My Early Days in Australia*, 63.

50. John Healey, "Advertisements," *Otago Witness*, issue 31, 20 December 1851, column 1, page 2, https://paperspast.natlib.govt.nz/newspapers/OW18511220.2.10.1?items_per_page=10&phrase=0&query=shortbread+Christmas&sort_by=byDA.

51. "Christmas Cookery," *Otago Witness*, issue 1881, 9 December 1887.

52. "The Christmas Display: How the Shops Are Dressed," *Evening Star*, issue 8098, 24 December 1889.

53. Weaver, *Christmas Cook*, 183.

54. Penne L. Restad, *Christmas in America: A History* (New York: Oxford University Press, 1995), 59.

55. Weaver, *Christmas Cook*, 184.

56. Laura Mason, *Sugar-Plums and Sherbet: The Prehistory of Sweets* (Totnes, Devon, UK: Prospect Books, 2004), 211.

57. William Hone, *The Everyday Book* (London: William Hone, 1826), 51.

58. Mason, *Sugar-Plums and Sherbet*, 84–85.

59. Davidson, *Oxford Companion to Food*, 210.

60. Ryan Berley, "Candy Canes," in *The Oxford Companion to Sugar and Sweets*, ed. Darra Goldstein (Oxford: Oxford University Press, 2015), 107.

61. Gerry Bowler, *The World Encyclopedia of Christmas* (Toronto: McClelland & Stewart, 2000), 152, https://play.google.com/books/reader?id=WGaVZ6fEjjsC.

62. Andrew F. Smith, *Sugar: A Global History* (London: Reaktion Books, 2015), 73.

63. Andrew F. Smith, *Food and Drink in American History: A "Full Course" Encyclopedia* (Santa Barbara, CA: ABC-CLIO, 2013), 1:182.

64. Eleanor Parkinson, *The Complete Confectioner, Pastry-Cook, and Baker* (Philadelphia: Lea and Blanchard, 1844), 31.

65. Berley, "Candy Canes," 106.

66. Smith, *Sugar: A Global History*, 74.

67. Berley, "Candy Canes," 107.

68. Clement Clarke Moore, "A Visit from Saint Nicholas," 1823.

69. Mason, *Sugar-Plums and Sherbet*, 120; Ivan Day, "Sugar-Plums and Comfits," Historic Food, accessed 20 May 2018, http://www.historicfood.com/Comfits.htm.

70. Jane Levi, "Marzipan," in *The Oxford Companion to Sugar and Sweets*, ed. Darra Goldstein (Oxford: Oxford University Press, 2015), 432.

71. Bishop Lyttleton, ed., "Account of New Year's Gifts, Presented to Queen Elizabeth, 1584–5," *Archaeologia* 1 (1770): 9–11.

72. Peter Kimpton, *Tom Smith's Christmas Crackers: An Illustrated History* (Stroud, Gloucestershire, UK: Tempus, 2004); Bowler, *World Encyclopedia of Christmas*, 218–19.

73. Kimpton, *Tom Smith's Christmas Crackers*, 25–26.

74. Kimpton, *Tom Smith's Christmas Crackers*, 117.

75. Kimpton, *Tom Smith's Christmas Crackers*, 27.

76. Kimpton, *Tom Smith's Christmas Crackers*, 21.

77. Kimpton, *Tom Smith's Christmas Crackers*, 29–32.

78. Kimpton, *Tom Smith's Christmas Crackers*, 33–60.

79. Judith Flanders, *Christmas: A Biography* (n.p.: Picador, 2017), 162–63.

80. See, for example, Sophie D. Coe and Michael D. Coe, *The True History of Chocolate*, 3rd ed. (London: Thames and Hudson, 2013); Sarah Moss and Alexander Badenoch, *Chocolate: A Global History* (London: Reaktion Books, 2009), https://play.google.com/books/reader?id=94Ke9b2aFAC&printsec=frontcover& output=reader&hl=en&pg=GBS.PA1; Mort Rosenblum, *Chocolate: A Bittersweet Saga of Dark and Light* (New York: North Point, 2005).

81. Davidson, *Oxford Companion to Food*, 180; Moss and Badenoch, *Chocolate: A Global History*, 59–61.

82. Davidson, *Oxford Companion to Food*, 180.

83. Smith, *Sugar: A Global History*, 74–76.

84. Smith, *Sugar: A Global History*, 76–77.

85. Ryan Berley, "Chocolates Boxed," in *The Oxford Companion to Sugar and Sweets*, ed. Darra Goldstein (Oxford: Oxford University Press, 2015), 156.

86. Alex Hutchinson, "Selection Boxes," Nestlé, 21 December 2017, https://www.nestle.co.uk/aboutus/history/blog/posts/selection-boxes.

87. "Quality Street Celebrates 75 Years of Revolutionary Confectionery," Nestlé, 2 November 2011, https://www.nestle.co.uk/media/newsfeatures/quality streetcelebrates75yearsofrevolutionaryconfectionery.

88. "1938: Cadbury Roses Are Launched," Cadbury, accessed 21 May 2018, https://www.cadbury.co.uk/our-story?timeline=1938.

89. Berley, "Chocolates Boxed," 156–57.

CHAPTER 6

1. Literature relating to the anthropology and archaeology of alcohol and drinking is extensive. See, for example, Frederick H. Smith, *The Archaeology of Alcohol and Drinking* (Gainesville: University Press of Florida, 2008); Michael Dietler, "Alcohol: Anthropological/Archaeological Perspectives," *Annual Review of Anthropology* 35 (2006): 229–49; Justin Jennings, Kathleen L. Antrobus, Sam J. Atencio, Erin Glavich, Rebecca Johnson, German Loffler, and Christine Luu, "'Drinking Beer in a Blissful Mood': Alcohol Production, Operational Chains, and Feasting in the Ancient World," *Current Anthropology* 46, no. 2 (April 2005): 275–303; Igor de Garine, ed., *Drinking: Anthropological Approaches* (New York: Berghahn Books, 2001).

2. Fanny Dolansky, "Celebrating the Saturnalia: Religious Ritual and Roman Domestic Life," in *A Companion to Families in the Greek and Roman World*, ed. Beryl Rawson (Chichester, West Sussex, UK: Blackwell, 2011), 492, 495.

3. Anglo-Norman carol cited in Reuben Percy and John Timbs, *The Mirror of Literature, Amusement and Instruction, Volume 1* (London: J. Limbird, 1823), 131.

4. Stephen Nissenbaum, *The Battle for Christmas: A Cultural History of America's Most Cherished Holiday* (New York: Vintage, 1997), 3–48.

5. John Pintard, 1827, cited in Nissenbaum, *Battle for Christmas*, 56.

6. Nissenbaum, *Battle for Christmas*, 90–99.

7. Cited in Nissenbaum, *Battle for Christmas*, 93.

8. Cited by Mark Connelly, *Christmas: A History* (London: I. B. Tauris, 2012), 31.

9. Gerry Bowler, "Wassail," in *The World Encyclopedia of Christmas* (Toronto: McClelland & Stewart, 2000), 991, https://play.google.com/books/reader?id=WGaVZ6fEjjsC; Richard Sermon, "Wassail! The Origins of a Drinking Toast," *3rd Stone* 46 (2003): 18.

10. Cited in Sermon, "Wassail!" 16.

11. Alison Sim, *Food & Feast in Tudor England* (Stroud, UK: Sutton, 1997), 115–16; Jacqueline Simpson and Steve Roud, *A Dictionary of English Folklore* (Oxford: Oxford University Press, 2000), 380.

12. Clement A. Miles, *Christmas Customs and Traditions: Their History and Significance* (New York: Dover, 1976 [1912]), 345.

13. Sermon, "Wassail!" 15.

14. Linda Raedisch, *The Old Magic of Christmas: Yuletide Traditions for the Darkest Days of the Year* (Woodbury, MN: Llewellyn, 2013), 228–29.

15. Miles, *Christmas Customs and Traditions*, 345.

16. Miles, *Christmas Customs and Traditions*, 345.

17. Bowler, *World Encyclopedia of Christmas*, 991–93.

18. Bowler, *World Encyclopedia of Christmas*, 991–93.

19. Bowler, *World Encyclopedia of Christmas*, 993–95.

20. William Henry Husk, ed., *Songs of the Nativity: Being Christmas Carols Ancient and Modern* (Cambridge: Cambridge University Press, 2014 [1864]), 150.

21. Ronald Hutton, *The Stations of the Sun: A History of the Ritual Year in Britain* (Oxford: Oxford University Press, 1996), 92–93.

22. Peter Brears, *Cooking and Dining in Tudor and Early Stuart England* (London: Prospect Books, 2015), 425.

23. *A pleasant Countrey new Ditty: Merrily shewing hime To drive the cold Winter away. 1601–1640* (London: H. G.), British Library—Roxburghe, 1.24, 1.25, ebba.english.ucsb.edu/ballad/30024.

24. John Selden, *The Table Talk of John Selden Esq.* (London: William Pickering, 1847), 155.

25. Claire Hopley, *History of Christmas Food and Feasts* (Barnsley, South Yorkshire, UK: Remember When, 2009), 91.

26. Samuel Pepys, "The Diary of Samuel Pepys," entry from 26 December 1661, https://www.pepysdiary.com/diary/1661/12/.

27. Hutton, *Stations of the Sun*, 53–54.

28. Hopley, *History of Christmas Food*, 89; Bowler, *World Encyclopedia of Christmas*, 991.

29. *A Collection of Ordinances and Regulations for the Government of the Royal Household, made in Divers Reigns. From King Edward III, to King Willi'm and Queen Mary. Also Receipts in Ancient Cookery* (London: Society of Antiquaries, 1790), 129.

30. Brears, *Cooking and Dining in Tudor and Early Stuart England*, 425; Hutton, *Stations of the Sun*, 39–40.

31. Bowler, *World Encyclopedia of Christmas*, 993–95; Miles, *Christmas Customs and Traditions*, 286.

32. Ben Jonson, "The Masque of Christmas," in *The Works of Ben Jonson, in Nine Volumes with Notes Critical and Explanatory, and a Bibliographical Memoir*, ed. W. Gifford (London: Nicol, 1816), 275.

33. Hopley, *History of Christmas Food*, 41.

34. Robert Herrick, "Twelfth Night, or King and Queene," in *Cyclopedia of English Literature*, ed. Robert Chambers (Boston: Gould, Kendall and Lincoln, 1847).

35. Dorothy Hartley, *Food in England: A Complete Guide to the Food That Makes Us Who We Are* (London: Little Brown, 1954), 364–65, https://play.google.com/books/reader?id=N-u0AwAAQBAJ&printsec=frontcover&output=reader&hl=en&pg=GBS.PT364.w.6.0.12.

36. Charles Dickens, *The Posthumous Papers of the Pickwick Club, Vol. 1* (Skowhegan, ME: Kellscraft Studio, 2017 [1898]), 298.

37. Hutton, *Stations of the Sun*, 64–65.

38. Thomas Dawson, *The Good Huswifes Jewell*, transcribed by Daniel Myers (n.p.: n.p., 2008), http://www.medievalcookery.com/notes/ghj1596.txt.

39. Elizabeth Gabay, "Mulled Wine," in *The Oxford Companion to Sugar and Sweets*, ed. Darra Goldstein (Oxford: Oxford University Press, 2015), 465; Ivan Day, "Some Christmas Nightcaps," *Food History Jottings* (blog), 18 December 2013, http://foodhistorjottings.blogspot.com.au/2013/12/some-christmas-nightcaps.html.

40. Elizabeth Raffald, *The Experienced English Housekeeper* (Lewes, East Sussex, UK: Southover, 1997 [1769]), 159.

41. Isabella Beeton, *Mrs. Beeton's Household Management* (Ware, Hertford-shire, UK: Wordsworth Editions, 2006 [1861]), 836.

42. Day, "Some Christmas Nightcaps."

43. Jonathan Swift, "Women Who Cry Oranges," in *Miscellanies by Dr. Swift, the Fourteenth Volume, Second Edition* (London: Hitch, Davis, Dodsley and Bower, 1751), 208.

44. Richard Cook, *Night Caps, Being a Collection of Receipts for Making Various Beverages Used in the University* (London: Henry Slatter, 1827), 3.

45. Charles Dickens, *A Christmas Carol* (London: Puffin Books, 2017 [1843]), 125.

46. Day, "Some Christmas Nightcaps."

47. Elizabeth Gabay, "Celebrating Christmas and New Year with Punch," in *Celebration: Proceeding of the Oxford Symposium on Food and Cookery*, ed. Mark McWilliams (Devon, UK: Prospect Books, 2011), 112.

48. Elizabeth Gabay, "Punch," in *The Oxford Companion to Sugar and Sweets*, ed. Darra Goldstein (Oxford: Oxford University Press, 2015), 565.

49. Gabay, "Celebrating Christmas and New Year," 112.

50. Cited in Gabay, "Celebrating Christmas and New Year," 112.

51. Hannah Woolley, *The Queen-like Closet or Rich Cabinet*, 2nd ed. (London: BiblioBazaar, 2006 [1672]), 84.

52. Gabay, "Celebrating Christmas and New Year," 113.

53. John Nott, *The Cook's and Confectioner's Dictionary; or, The Accomplish'd Housewife's Companion* (London: Charles Rivington, 1723), recipe no. 266.

54. Charles Dickens, "To Make Three Pints of Punch," in *The Selected Letters of Charles Dickens*, ed. Jenny Hartley (Oxford: Oxford University Press, 2012), 179.

55. Day, "Some Christmas Nightcaps."

56. Elpis Melena, *Leaves from a Lady's Diary of Her Travels in Barbary, in Two Volumes, Volume 1* (London: Henry Colburn, 1850), 89.

57. Bernard Bigsby, *"That Bowl of Punch!": What It Did and How It Did It; Six Christmas Stories* (Toronto: Hunter, Rose, 1872), 6–7.

58. Gabay, "Celebrating Christmas and New Year," 112.

59. Gabay, "Celebrating Christmas and New Year," 116–18.

60. Alan Davidson, *The Oxford Companion to Food*, 2nd ed., ed. Tom Jaine (Oxford: Oxford University Press, 2006), 627.

61. Kenelm Digby, *The Closet of Sir Kenelm Digby Opened*, ed. Jane Stevenson and Peter Davidson (Totnes, Devon, UK: Prospect Books, 2010 [1669]), 135.

62. Inchiquin Papers, "A Collection of Domestic Recipes and Medical Prescriptions Started by Lady Frances Keightly," Ms 14,786, National Library of Ireland. For a detailed discussion of authorship, dating, and provenance of this manuscript,

see Madeline Shanahan, *Manuscript Recipe Books as Archaeological Objects: Text and Food in the Early Modern World* (Lanham, MD: Lexington Books, 2015), 33.

63. Ivan Day, "Possets," Historic Food, accessed 26 February 2018, http://www.historicfood.com/Posset%20Recipes.htm.

64. *Oxford Dictionaries*, s.v. "Nog," Oxford University Press, 2018, https://en.oxforddictionaries.com/definition/nog#nog-2.

65. *Oxford Dictionaries*, s.v. "Noggin," Oxford University Press, 2018, https://en.oxforddictionaries.com/definition/noggin.

66. Jonathon Boucher, *Boucher's Glossary of Archaic and Provincial Words*, ed. Joseph Hunter (London: Black, Young, and Young, 1833), l.

67. Virginia Scott Jenkins, "Eggnog," in *Oxford Encyclopedia of Food and Drink in America*, vol. 2, 2nd ed., ed. Andrew F. Smith (New York: Oxford University Press, 2013), 671.

68. Cited by Diane Toops, *Eggs: A Global History* (London: Reaktion Books, 2014), 50–51, https://play.google.com/books/reader?id=ZEadAwAAQBAJ&printsec=frontcover&pg=GBS.PT49.w.2.0.5.

69. Mark Edward Lender and James Kirby Martin, *Drinking in America: A History; The Revised and Expanded Edition* (New York: Free Press, 1987), 30–32.

70. Gabay, "Celebrating Christmas and New Year," 114.

71. Gabay, "Celebrating Christmas and New Year," 114–15.

72. Nissenbaum, *Battle for Christmas*, 261.

73. Nissenbaum, *Battle for Christmas*, 263–64.

74. Bowler, *World Encyclopedia of Christmas*, 305.

75. Lettice Bryan, *The Kentucky Housewife* (Cincinnati, OH: Shepard and Stearns, 1839), 408.

76. Jerry Thomas, *The Bar-Tender's Guide: How to Mix Drinks; or, The Bon-Vivant's Companion* (New York: Dick & Fitzgerald, 1862), 40.

77. Jerry Thomas, *The Bar-Tender's Guide: How to Mix All Kinds of Plain and Fancy Drinks . . . An Entirely New and Enlarged Edition* (New York: Dick & Fitzgerald, 1887), 44–45.

78. Lesley Jacobs Solmonson, *Gin: A Global History* (London: Reaktion Books, 2012), 151–52, https://play.google.com/books/reader?id=NBPeHLc5AzcC&printsec=frontcover&pg=GBS.PP1.

79. Darina Allen, *Forgotten Skills of Cooking* (London: Kyle Cathie, 2009), 45; Hopley, *History of Christmas Food*, 214.

80. Ron Wilson, *The Hedgerow Book* (Newton Abbot, Devon, UK: David & Charles, 1979), 17.

81. Solmonson, *Gin: A Global History*, 43–86.

82. Edward Lanzer Joseph, *Warner Arundell: The Adventures of a Creole* (London: Saunders and Oatley, 1838), 65.

83. Ward, *British wonders; or, A poetical description of the several prodigies and most remarkable accidents that have happen'd in Britain since the death of Queen Anne* (London: John Morphew, 1717), 38.

84. Bowler, *World Encyclopedia of Christmas*, 815.

85. Dorothy Duncan, *Canadians at Table, Food, Fellowship and Folklore: A Culinary History of Canada* (Toronto: Dundurn, 2006), 156–57, https://play.google.com/books/reader?id=2YIpttEiV50C&printsec=frontcover&pg=GBS.PP1.

86. F. Marian McNeill, *The Silver Bough, Vol III, A Calendar of Scottish National Festivals, Halloween to Yule* (1961), 115–17.

87. Davidson, *Oxford Companion to Food*, 108.

88. Robert Mudie, *A Historical Account of His Majesty's Visit to Scotland* (Edinburgh: Oliver & Boyd, 1822), 286.

89. A & C Black, *Queen Victoria in Scotland* (Edinburgh, 1842), 46–48.

CONCLUSION

1. Cathy Kaufman, "The Ideal Christmas Dinner," *Gastronomica* 4, no. 4 (2004): 17.

2. Judith Flanders, *Christmas: A Biography* (London: Picador, 2017), 1–2.

3. Kaufman, "Ideal Christmas Dinner," 24.

4. Stephen Nissenbaum, *The Battle for Christmas: A Cultural History of America's Most Cherished Holiday* (New York: Vintage, 1997), xii.

BIBLIOGRAPHY

BOOKS AND JOURNALS

A. B. of Grimsby. *The Frugal Housewife's Manual.* Toronto: Guardian Office, 1840.

A. W. *A Book of Cookrye.* London: Edward Allde, 1591 [1584].

Abbott, Edward. *The English and Australian Cookery Book.* London: Sampson Low, Son, and Marston, 1864.

Acton, Eliza. *Modern Cookery in All Its Branches: Reduced to a System of Easy Practice for the Use of Private Families.* 2nd ed. London: Longman, Brown, Green and Longmans, 1845.

Allen, Darina. *Forgotten Skills of Cooking.* London: Kyle Cathie, 2009.

Andrews, Tamra. *Nectar and Ambrosia: An Encyclopedia of Food in World Mythology.* Santa Barbara, CA: ABC-CLIO, 2000.

Austen, Jane. *Persuasion.* Peterborough, ON: Broadview, 2013 [1817].

Bannerman, Colin. *The Upside-Down Pudding.* Canberra: National Library of Australia, 1999.

Beard, Mary, John North, and Simon Price. *Religions of Rome: Volume 2; A Source Book.* Cambridge: Cambridge University Press, 2003.

Beeton, Isabella. *Mrs. Beeton's Book of Household Management: A Guide to Cookery in All Its Branches.* London: Ward, Lock, 1907.

——. *Mrs. Beeton's Household Management.* Ware, Hertfordshire, UK: Wordsworth Editions, 2006 [1861].

Berley, Ryan. "Candy Canes." In *The Oxford Companion to Sugar and Sweets,* edited by Darra Goldstein. Oxford: Oxford University Press, 2015.

———. "Chocolates Boxed." In *The Oxford Companion to Sugar and Sweets*, edited by Darra Goldstein. Oxford: Oxford University Press, 2015.

Bigham, Shauna, and Robert E. May. "The Time o' All Times? Masters, Slaves, and Christmas in the Old South." *Journal of the Early Republic* 18, no. 2 (1998): 263–88.

Bigsby, Bernard. *"That Bowl of Punch!": What It Did and How It Did It; Six Christmas Stories*. Toronto: Hunter, Rose, 1872.

Bisaker, Hannah. "Hannah Bisaker: Her Book [of Cookery Receipts] the 12th September. Anno: 1692." The Wellcome Library, 1692, MS 1176.

Bishop Lyttleton, ed. "Account of New Year's Gifts, Presented to Queen Elizabeth, 1584–5." *Archaeologia* 1 (1770): 9–11.

Black, A & C. *Queen Victoria in Scotland*. Edinburgh, 1842.

Boswell, Annabella. *Further Recollections of My Early Days in Australia*. Canberra, Australia: Mulini, 1992.

Boucher, Jonathon. *Boucher's Glossary of Archaic and Provincial Words*. Edited by Joseph Hunter. London: Black, Young, and Young, 1833.

Bowler, Gerry. "Shooting in Christmas." *Gerry Bowler: The Past Isn't Dead, It Isn't Even Past* (blog). 29 September 2017. http://gerrybowler.com/shooting-in-christmas/.

———. *The World Encyclopedia of Christmas*. Toronto: McClelland & Stewart, 2000. https://play.google.com/books/reader?id=WGaVZ6fEjjsC.

Brears, Peter. *Cooking and Dining in Medieval England*. Totnes, Devon, UK: Prospect Books, 2012.

———. *Cooking and Dining in Tudor and Early Stuart England*. London: Prospect Books, 2015.

Bryan, Lettice. *The Kentucky Housewife*. Cincinnati, OH: Shepard and Stearns, 1839.

Burton, Thomas. *Diary of Thomas Burton Esq., Member in the Parliaments of Oliver and Richard Cromwell, from 1656 to 1659*. Edited by John Towill Rutt. London: Henry Colburn, 1828.

Cahill, Katherine. *Mrs. Delany's Menus, Medicines and Manners*. Dublin: New Island, 2005.

Capp, Bernard. *England's Culture Wars: Puritan Reformation and Its Enemies in the Interregnum, 1649–1660*. Oxford: Oxford University Press, 2012.

Clarkson, Janet. *Pie: A Global History*. London: Reaktion Books, 2009. https://play.google.com/books/reader?id=FZoJAgAAQBAJ&pg=GBS.PT1.

Coe, Sophie D., and Michael D. Coe. *The True History of Chocolate*. 3rd ed. London: Thames and Hudson, 2013.

A Collection of Ordinances and Regulations for the Government of the Royal Household, made in Divers Reigns. From King Edward III, to King Willi'm and Queen Mary. Also Receipts in Ancient Cookery. London: Society of Antiquaries, 1790.

Colonel Norwood. "A Voyage to Virginia." In *A Collection of voyages and travels: Some now first printed from original manuscripts, others now first published in English: In six volumes with a general preface giving an account of the progress of navigation from its first beginning.* Edited and compiled by Awnsham Churchill and John Churchill. London: Churchill, 1732.

Connelly, Mark. *Christmas: A History.* London: I. B. Taurus, 2012.

Cook, Richard. *Night Caps, Being a Collection of Receipts for Making Various Beverages Used in the University.* London: Henry Slatter, 1827.

Davidson, Alan. *The Oxford Companion to Food.* 2nd ed. Edited by Tom Jaine. Oxford: Oxford University Press, 2006.

Davidson, H. R. Ellis. *Myths and Symbols in Pagan Europe: Early Scandinavian and Celtic Religions.* Syracuse, NY: Syracuse University Press, 1988.

Dawson, Thomas. *The Good Huswifes Jewell.* Transcribed by Daniel Myers. N.p.: n.p., 2008 [1596]. http://www.medievalcookery.com/notes/ghj1596.txt.

Dawson, William Francis. *Christmas: Its Origins and Associations.* London: Elliot Stock, 1902.

De Garine, Igor, ed. *Drinking: Anthropological Approaches.* New York: Berghahn Books, 2001.

Dickens, Charles. *A Christmas Carol.* London: Puffin Books, 2017 [1843].

——. *The Posthumous Papers of the Pickwick Club, Vol. 1.* Skowhegan, ME: Kellscraft Studio, 2017 [1898].

——. "To Make Three Pints of Punch." In *The Selected Letters of Charles Dickens.* Edited by Jenny Hartley. Oxford: Oxford University Press, 2012.

Dietler, Michael. "Alcohol: Anthropological/Archaeological Perspectives." *Annual Review of Anthropology* 35 (2006): 229–49.

Digby, Kenelm. *The Closet of Sir Kenelm Digby Opened.* Edited by Jane Stevenson and Peter Davidson. Totnes, Devon, UK: Prospect Books, 2010 [1669].

Dods, Margaret. *The Cook and Housewife's Manual: A Practical System of Modern Domestic Cookery and Family Management.* 5th ed. Edinburgh: Oliver & Boyd, 1833.

——. *The Cook and Housewife's Manual: Containing the Most Approved Modern Receipts.* Edinburgh: Margaret Dods, 1826.

Dolansky, Fanny. "Celebrating the Saturnalia: Religious Ritual and Roman Domestic Life." In *A Companion to Families in the Greek and Roman World*, edited by Beryl Rawson, 488–503. Chichester, West Sussex, UK: Blackwell, 2011.

Donaldson, Rhiannon. "Revisiting a 'Well-Worn Theme': The Duality of the Australian Christmas Pudding 1850–1950." *Eras Journal* 6 (2004).

Doran, Susan, and Christopher Durston. *Princes, Pastors, and People: The Church and Religion in England, 1500–1700.* New York: Routledge, 2003.

Duncan, Dorothy. *Canadians at Table, Food, Fellowship and Folklore: A Culinary History of Canada.* Toronto: Dundurn, 2006. https://play.google.com/books/reader?id=2YIpttEiV50C&printsec=frontcover&pg=GBS.PP1.

Ellet, Elizabeth F. *The Practical Housekeeper: A Cyclopaedia of Domestic Economy.* New York: Stringer and Townsend, 1857. http://digital.lib.msu.edu/projects/cookbooks/books/practicalhousekeeper/prho.pdf.

An Explanation of the Collects, by Way of Questions and Answers, with Practical Addresses. London: J. G. and F. Rivington, 1835.

Flanders, Judith. *Christmas: A Biography.* London: Picador, 2017.

Flandrin, Jean-Louis. "Introduction: The Early Modern Period." In *Food: A Culinary History*, edited by Jean-Louis Flandrin and Massimo Montanari. New York: Columbia University Press, 1999.

Fletcher, R. "Poems and Translations." In *Observations on Popular Antiquities, Volume 1*, edited by John Brand and Henry Ellis. London: Charles Knight, 1841.

Fothergill, Brooklynne "Tyr." "The Husbandry, Perception and 'Improvement' of Turkeys in Britain, 1500–1900." *Post-medieval Archaeology* 48, no. 1 (2014): 207–28.

Francatelli, Charles Elmé. *The Modern Cook: A Practical Guide to the Culinary Art in All Its Branches, Eighth London Edition.* London: Richard Bentley, 1853.

——. *The Royal English and Foreign Confectionery Book.* London: Chapman and Hall, 1862.

Gabay, Elizabeth. "Celebrating Christmas and New Year with Punch." In *Celebration: Proceeding of the Oxford Symposium on Food and Cookery*, edited by Mark McWilliams, 112–22. Devon, UK: Prospect Books, 2011.

——. "Mulled Wine." In *The Oxford Companion to Sugar and Sweets*, edited by Darra Goldstein, 465–66. Oxford: Oxford University Press, 2015.

——. "Punch." In *The Oxford Companion to Sugar and Sweets*, edited by Darra Goldstein, 565–67. Oxford: Oxford University Press, 2015.

Gay, John. *Fables by the Late Mr. Gay, in One Volume Complete.* London: W. Strahan, 1769.

Glasse, Hannah. *The Art of Cookery Made Plain and Easy.* London: Strahan, 1747.

——. *The Compleat Confectioner; or, The Whole Art of Confectionary Made Plain and Easy.* London: J. Cooke, 1765.

Hale, Sarah Josepha. *The Good Housekeeper; or, The Way to Live Well and Be Well While We Live, Containing Directions for Choosing and Preparing Food, in Regard to Health, Economy and Taste.* Boston: Weeks, Jordan, 1839.

Hall, Edward. *Hall's Chronicle, Containing the History of England.* London: J. Johnson, 1809 [1548].

Hannon, W. B. "Christmas and Its Folklore." *Irish Monthly* 52, no. 607 (1924): 20.

Hansen, William F. *Ariadne's Thread: A Guide to International Tales Found in Folk Literature.* Ithaca, NY: Cornell University Press, 2002.

Hartley, Dorothy. *Food in England: A Complete Guide to the Food That Makes Us Who We Are.* London: Little Brown, 1954. https://play.google.com/books/reader?id=N-u0AwAAQBAJ&printsec=frontcover&output=reader&hl=en&pg=GBS.PT364.w.6.0.12.

Henisch, Bridget Ann. *Cakes and Characters: An English Christmas Tradition.* London: Prospect Books, 1984.

——. *Fast and Feast: Food in Medieval Society.* University Park: Pennsylvania State University Press, 1999.

Herrick, Robert. "Ceremonies for Christmas." In *The Book of Elizabethan Verse,* edited by William Stanley Braithwaite. London: Chatto and Windus, 1908.

——. "Twelfth Night, or King and Queene." In *Cyclopedia of English Literature,* edited by Robert Chambers. Boston: Gould, Kendall and Lincoln, 1847.

Hervey, Thomas. *The Book of Christmas.* London: William Spooner, 1836.

Hijmans, Steven. "Sol Invictus, the Winter Solstice and the Origins of Christmas." *Mouseion,* Series III, vol. 3 (2003): 377–98.

Hone, William. *The Everyday Book.* London: William Hone, 1825.

Hopley, Claire. *History of Christmas Food and Feasts.* Barnsley, South Yorkshire, UK: Remember When, 2009.

Hudgins, Sharon. "Gingerbread." In *The Oxford Companion to Sugar and Sweets,* edited by Darra Goldstein, 302–5. Oxford: Oxford University Press, 2015.

Humble, Nicola. *Cake: A Global History.* London: Reaktion Books, 2010. https://play.google.com/books/reader?id=qclZyk87j_EC&printsec=frontcover&output=reader&hl=en&pg=GBS.PA28.w.0.1.2.

Husk, William Henry, ed. *Songs of the Nativity: Being Christmas Carols Ancient and Modern.* Cambridge: Cambridge University Press, 2014 [1864].

Hutton, Ronald. *The Stations of the Sun: A History of the Ritual Year in Britain.* Oxford: Oxford University Press, 1996.

Inchiquin Papers. "A Collection of Domestic Recipes and Medical Prescriptions Started by Lady Frances Keightly." Ms 14,786, National Library of Ireland.

Inglis, Kenneth Stanley. *The Australian Colonists: An Exploration of Social History, 1788–1870.* Carlton, Victoria, Australia: Melbourne University Press, 1974.

Irving, Washington. *The Sketch Book of Geoffrey Crayon, Gent.* New York: Putnam, 1864. http://www.gutenberg.org/files/2048/2048-h/2048-h.htm#link2H_4_0023.

Jenkins, Virginia Scott. "Eggnog." In *Oxford Encyclopedia of Food and Drink in America*, vol. 2, 2nd ed., edited by Andrew F. Smith, 671. New York: Oxford University Press, 2013.

Jenks, James. *The Complete Cook*. Dublin: J. Potts, 1769.

Jennings, Justin, Kathleen L. Antrobus, Sam J. Atencio, Erin Glavich, Rebecca Johnson, German Loffler, and Christine Luu. "'Drinking Beer in a Blissful Mood': Alcohol Production, Operational Chains, and Feasting in the Ancient World." *Current Anthropology* 46, no. 2 (April 2005): 275–303.

Jonson, Ben. "The Masque of Christmas." In *The Works of Ben Jonson, in Nine Volumes with Notes Critical and Explanatory, and a Bibliographical Memoir*. Edited by W. Gifford. London: Nicol, 1816.

Joseph, Edward Lanzer. *Warner Arundell: The Adventures of a Creole*. London: Saunders and Oatley, 1838.

Joyce, James. "The Dead." In *The Dubliners*. Adelaide, Australia: University of Adelaide Library, 2014 [1914]. https://ebooks.adelaide.edu.au/j/joyce/james/j8d/complete.html#c1hapter15.

Kaufman, Cathy. "Christmas." In *Entertaining from Ancient Rome to the Superbowl: An Encyclopedia, vol. 1*, edited by Melitta Weiss Adamson and Francine Segan. Westport, CT: Greenwood, 2008.

——. "The Ideal Christmas Dinner." *Gastronomica* 4, no. 4 (2004): 17–24.

Kent, Elizabeth. *A True Gentlewoman's Delight*. London: G. D., 1653.

Kerr, John Hunter. *Glimpses of Life in Victoria: By a Resident*. Edinburgh: Edmonston & Douglas, 1872.

Kettilby, Mary. *A Collection of Above Three Hundred Receipts in Cookery, Physick and Surgery*. London: Richard Wilkin, 1714.

Kimpton, Peter. *Tom Smith's Christmas Crackers: An Illustrated History*. Stroud, Gloucestershire, UK: Tempus, 2004.

King, William. *The Art of Cookery: In Imitation of Horace's Art of Poetry*. London: Printed for Bernard Lintott, 1708.

Knight, Charles. *London, Volume III*. London: Charles Knight, 1842.

La Varenne, Francois Pierre. *The French Cook*. Lewes, East Sussex, UK: Southover, 2001.

Lawson, Henry. "The Ghosts of Many Christmases." In *The Romance of the Swag*. Sydney, Australia: University of Sydney Library, 2001 [1907]. http://setis.library.usyd.edu.au/ozlit/pdf/p00104.pdf.

——. "That Pretty Girl in the Army." In *Send round the Hat*. Project Gutenberg Australia, 2006 [1907]. http://gutenberg.net.au/ebooks06/0607411h.html#s2.

Leach, Helen. *The Pavlova Story: A Slice of New Zealand's Culinary History*. Dunedin, New Zealand: Otago University Press, 2008.

Leach, Helen, Mary Browne, and Raelene Inglis. *The Twelve Cakes of Christmas: An Evolutionary History with Recipes*. Dunedin, New Zealand: Otago University Press, 2011.

Lender, Mark Edward, and James Kirby Martin. *Drinking in America: A History; The Revised and Expanded Edition*. New York: Free Press, 1987.

Leslie, Eliza. *Directions for Cookery: Being a System of the Art in Its Various Branches*. Philadelphia: Carey & Hart, 1837.

——. *The Lady's Receipt-Book: A Useful Companion for Large and Small Families*. Philadelphia: Carey & Hart, 1847.

——. *Miss Leslie's New Cookery Book*. Philadelphia: T. B. Peterson, 1857.

Levi, Jane. "Marzipan." In *The Oxford Companion to Sugar and Sweets*, edited by Darra Goldstein, 432–33. Oxford: Oxford University Press, 2015.

Liuzza, R. M., trans. *Beowulf*. Toronto: Broadview Literary Texts, 2000.

London Magazine, July 1746. London: T. Astley, 1746. https://play.google.com/books/reader?id=jvoRAAAAYAAJ&printsec=frontcover&output=reader&hl=en&pg=GBS.PP1.

Mac Con Iomaire, Máirtín, and Pádraic Óg Gallagher. "Corned Beef: An Enigmatic Irish Dish." In *Smoked, Cured and Fermented: Proceedings from the 2010 Oxford Symposium on Food and Cookery*, edited by Helen Saberi, 189–99. Devon, UK: Prospect Books, 2011.

Margaret, Duchess of Newcastle. *The Life of William Cavendish, Duke of Newcastle, to Which Is Added the True Relation of My Birth, Breeding and Life*. London: George Routledge, 1890.

Markham, Gervase. *Country Contentments; or, The English Huswife*. London: R. Jackson, 1623 [1615].

Mason, Laura. *Sugar-Plums and Sherbet: The Prehistory of Sweets*. Totnes, Devon, UK: Prospect Books, 2004.

May, Robert. *The Accomplisht Cook; or, The Art and Mystery of Cookery*. London: Printed for Obadiah Blagrave, 1660.

McNeill, F. Marian. *The Silver Bough, Vol III, A Calendar of Scottish National Festivals, Halloween to Yule*. 1961. https://play.google.com/books/reader?id=fBXYQZuf08C&printsec=frontcover&output=reader&hl=en&pg=GBS.PA73.w.0.0.0.1.

Melena, Elpis. *Leaves from a Lady's Diary of Her Travels in Barbary, in Two Volumes, Volume 1*. London: Henry Colburn, 1850.

Mercuri, Becky. "Cookies." In *The Oxford Companion to American Food and Drink*, edited by Andrew F. Smith. Oxford: Oxford University Press, 2007.

Miles, Clement A. *Christmas Customs and Traditions: Their History and Significance*. New York: Dover, 1976 [1912].

Miller, John F. "Festivals, Roman." In *The Oxford Encyclopedia of Ancient Greece and Rome, vol. 1*, edited by Michael Gagarin, 171–73. Oxford: Oxford University Press, 2010.

Misson, Henri. *M. Misson's Memoirs and Observations in his Travels Over England, with some account of Scotland and Ireland*. London: D. Browne, A. Bell, 1719.

Mollard, John. *The Art of Cookery Made Easy and Refined*. London: John Mollard, 1802.

Moore, Clement Clarke. "A Visit from Saint Nicholas." 1823.

Moore, Tara. "National Identity and Victorian Christmas Foods." In *Consuming Culture in the Long Nineteenth Century: Narratives of Consumption, 1700–1900*, edited by Tamara S. Wagner and Narin Hassan, 141–54. Lanham, MD: Lexington Books, 2010.

———. "Starvation in Victorian Christmas Fiction." *Victorian Literature and Culture* 36, no. 2 (2008): 489–505.

Moss, Sarah, and Alexander Badenoch. *Chocolate: A Global History*. London: Reaktion Books, 2009. https://play.google.com/books/reader?id=94Ke9b2aFAC&printsec=frontcover&output=reader&hl=en&pg=GBS.PA1.

Mudie, Robert. *A Historical Account of His Majesty's Visit to Scotland*. Edinburgh: Oliver & Boyd, 1822.

Mueller, Hans Friedrich. "Saturn." In *The Oxford Encyclopedia of Ancient Greece and Rome, vol. 1*, edited by Michael Gagarin, 221–22. Oxford: Oxford University Press, 2010.

Napier, James. *Folk Lore; or, Superstitious Beliefs in the West of Scotland within This Century*. Paisley, Scotland: Alex Gardner, 1879.

Neilson, W. A., trans. *Sir Gawain and the Green Knight*. Cambridge, ON: In Parentheses Publications Middle English Series, 1999. www.yorku.ca/inpar/sggk_neilson.pdf.

Nissenbaum, Stephen. *The Battle for Christmas: A Cultural History of America's Most Cherished Holiday*. New York: Vintage, 1997.

Nott, John. *The Cook's and Confectioner's Dictionary; or, The Accomplish'd Housewife's Companion*. London: C. Rivington, 1723.

O'Brien, Charmaine. *The Colonial Kitchen: Australia 1788–1901*. Lanham, MD: Rowman & Littlefield, 2016.

O'Connor, Kaori. "The King's Christmas Pudding: Globalization, Recipes, and the Commodities of Empire." *Journal of Global History* 4, no. 1 (2009): 127–55.

Oxford Dictionaries. S.v. "Nog." Oxford University Press, 2018. https://en.oxforddictionaries.com/definition/nog#nog-2.

———. S.v. "Noggin." Oxford University Press, 2018. https://en.oxforddictionaries.com/definition/noggin.

Parkinson, Eleanor. *The Complete Confectioner, Pastry-Cook, and Baker*. Philadelphia: Lea and Blanchard, 1844.

Peacock, Nicholas. *The Diary of Nicholas Peacock, 1740–1751: The Worlds of a County Limerick Farmer and Agent*. Edited by Marie Louise Legg. Dublin: Four Courts, 2005.

Pennant, Thomas. *The Antiquities of London: Comprising Views and Historical Descriptions of Its Principal Buildings; Also Anecdotes of Eminent Persons Connected Therewith*. London: Coxhead, 1818.

Percy, Reuben, and John Timbs. *The Mirror of Literature, Amusement and Instruction, Volume 1*. London: J. Limbird, 1823.

A pleasant Countrey new Ditty: Merrily shewing hime To drive the cold Winter away. 1601–1640. London: H. G., British Library—Roxburghe, 1.24, 1.25. ebba. english.ucsb.edu/ballad/30024.

Plum-porridge, Cissely [pseud.]. *The arraignment, conviction, and imprisoning, of Christmas: On St. Thomas day last*. London: Printed by Simon Minc'd Pye, for Cissely Plum-porridge, 1645.

Quinzio, Jeri. *Pudding: A Global History*. London: Reaktion Books, 2012. https://play.google.com/books/reader?id=6xHMDOME0ZwC&printsec=frontcover&pg=GBS.PA17.

Raedisch, Linda. *The Old Magic of Christmas: Yuletide Traditions for the Darkest Days of the Year*. Woodbury, MN: Llewellyn, 2013.

Raffald, Elizabeth. *The Experienced English Housekeeper*. Lewes, East Sussex, UK: Southover, 1997 [1769].

Restad, Penne L. *Christmas in America: A History*. New York: Oxford University Press, 1995.

Rosenblum, Mort. *Chocolate: A Bittersweet Saga of Dark and Light*. New York: North Point, 2005.

Routley, Erik. *The English Carol*. New York: Oxford University Press, 1959.

Saberi, Helen, and Alan Davidson. *Trifle*. Totnes, Devon, UK: Prospect Books, 2009.

Santich, Barbara. *Bold Palates: Australia's Gastronomic Heritage*. Kent Town, South Australia: Wakefield, 2012.

———. *In the Land of the Magic Pudding: A Gastronomic Miscellany*. Kent Town, South Australia: Wakefield, 2000.

Selden, John. *The Table Talk of John Selden Esq*. London: William Pickering, 1847.

Sermon, Richard. "Wassail! The Origins of a Drinking Toast." *3rd Stone* 46 (2003): 15–19.

Shanahan, Madeline. *Manuscript Recipe Books as Archaeological Objects: Text and Food in the Early Modern World*. Lanham, MD: Lexington Books, 2015.

Sim, Alison. *Food & Feast in Tudor England*. Stroud, UK: Sutton, 1997.

Simmons, Amelia. *American Cookery*. Kansas City, MO: Andrews McMeel, 2012 [1796].

Simpson, Jacqueline, and Steve Roud. *A Dictionary of English Folklore*. Oxford: Oxford University Press, 2000.

Smith, Andrew F. *Food and Drink in American History: A "Full Course" Encyclopedia*. Vols. 1 & 2. Santa Barbara, CA: ABC-CLIO, 2013.

——. *Sugar: A Global History*. London: Reaktion Books, 2015.

——. *The Turkey: An American Story*. Chicago: University of Illinois Press, 2006.

Smith, Eliza. *The Compleat Housewife; or, Accomplished Woman's Companion*. London: J. Pemberton, 1729.

Smith, Frederick H. *The Archaeology of Alcohol and Drinking*. Gainesville: University Press of Florida, 2008.

Solmonson, Lesley Jacobs. *Gin: A Global History*. London: Reaktion Books, 2012. https://play.google.com/books/reader?id=NBPeHLc5AzcC&printsec=frontcover&pg=GBS.PP1.

Spears, James E. "The 'Boar's' Head Carol and Folk Tradition." *Folklore* 85, no. 3 (1974): 194–98.

Spry-Marqués, Pía. *Pig/Pork: Archaeology, Zoology and Edibility*. N.p.: Bloomsbury Sigma, 2017. https://play.google.com/books/reader?id=YM8vDgAAQBAJ&pg=GBS.PP1.

Stevenson, Robert Louis. *The Incredible Travel Sketches, Essays, Memoirs and Island Works of R. L. Stevenson*. N.p.: Musaicum, 2017. https://play.google.com/books/reader?id=9U9ODwAAQBAJ&printsec=frontcover&output=reader&hl=en&pg=GBS.PT327.

Story, George Morley, W. J. Kirwan, and J. D. A. Widdowson. *Dictionary of Newfoundland English*. 2nd ed. Toronto: University of Toronto Press, 1990.

Stowe, John. *The Annals of England to 1603*. N.p., 1603.

Stubbes, Philip. *Philip Stubbes's Anatomy of the Abuses in England in Shakespeare's Youth, AD 1583, Part I*. Edited by Frederick J. Furnivall. London: N. Trübner, 1877–1879.

Studwell, William E. *The Christmas Carol Reader*. New York: Routledge, 2011.

Swift, Jonathan. "Women Who Cry Oranges." In *Miscellanies by Dr. Swift, the Fourteenth Volume, Second Edition*. London: Hitch, Davis, Dodsley and Bower, 1751.

Symons, Michael. *One Continuous Picnic: A Gastronomic History of Australia*. Melbourne, Australia: Melbourne University Press, 2017.

Taylor, John. *The Vindication of Christmas: His Twelve Years Observations upon the Times, concerning the lamentable Game called Sweep-stake; Acted by General Plunder and Major General Tax*. London: G. Horton, 1652.

Teonge, Henry. *The Diary of Henry Teonge, Chaplain on Board His Majesty's Ships Assistance, Bristol, and Royal Oak, Anno 1675 to 1679*. London: Charles Knight, 1825.

Thomas, Jerry. *The Bar-Tender's Guide: How to Mix All Kinds of Plain and Fancy Drinks . . . An Entirely New and Enlarged Edition*. New York: Dick & Fitzgerald, 1887.

——. *The Bar-Tender's Guide: How to Mix Drinks; or, The Bon-Vivant's Companion*. New York: Dick & Fitzgerald, 1862.

Timbs, Jon. *Something for Everybody*. London: Lockwood, 1866.

Toops, Diane. *Eggs: A Global History*. London: Reaktion Books, 2014. https://play.google.com/books/reader?id=ZEadAwAAQBAJ&printsec=frontcover&pg=GBS.PT49.w.2.0.5.

Toussaint-Samat, Maguelonne. *A History of Food*. Chichester, UK: Wiley-Blackwell, 2009.

Trollope, Anthony. *Orley Farm*. New York: Harper, 1862.

Tusser, Thomas. *Five Hundred Points of Good Husbandry*. Edited by William Mavor. London: Lackington, Allen, 1812 [1573].

Van Muyden, Madame, trans. and ed. *A Foreign View of England in the Reigns of George I and George II: The Letters of Monsieur Césare de Saussure to His Family*. London: John Murray, 1902.

Versnel, H. S. *Inconsistencies in Greek & Roman Religion: Transition & Reversal in Myth & Ritual*. Leiden, Netherlands: E. J. Brill, 1994.

Ward. *British wonders; or, A poetical description of the several prodigies and most remarkable accidents that have happen'd in Britain since the death of Queen Anne*. London: John Morphew, 1717.

Warren, Eliza. *The Economical Cookery Book*. London: Piper, Stephenson and Spence, 1858.

Weaver, William Woys. *The Christmas Cook: Three Centuries of American Yuletide Sweets*. New York: HarperCollins, 1990.

Weir, Alison. *Henry VIII, King and Court*. London: Vintage, 2008.

Wilcox, Estelle Woods. *Buckeye Cookery and Practical Housekeeping*. Marysville, OH: Buckeye, 1877.

Wilson, C. Anne. *Food & Drink in Britain: From the Stone Age to the 19th Century*. Chicago: Academy Chicago, 1991.

Wilson, Ron. *The Hedgerow Book*. Newton Abbot, Devon, UK: David & Charles, 1979.

Winterson, Jeanette. *12 Stories and 12 Feasts for 12 Days*. London: Jonathan Cape, 2016.

Woolley, Hannah. *The Queen-like Closet or Rich Cabinet*. 2nd ed. London: BiblioBazaar, 2006 [1672].

Woodward, Hezekiah. *Christmas Day. The old heathens feasting day in honour to Saturn their idol god, the papists massing day, the prophane mans ranting day, the superstitious mans idol day, the multitudes idle day whereon because they cannot do nothing they do worse than nothing, satans, that adversaries working day, the true christian mans fasting day. Taking to heart the heathenish customes, popish superstitions, ranting fashions, fearful provocations, humble abhominations committed against the Lord and his Christ oh that day and days following.* London: Henry Cripps, 1656.

NEWSPAPERS AND MAGAZINES

Advocate. "For the Festive Season." 10 December 1949, 18.
Anonymous [Charles Knight]. "A Christmas Pudding." *Household Words: A Weekly Journal Conducted by Charles Dickens*, December 14, 1850, 300–304.
Australian. "Pro Bono Publico." 19 December 1837, 3.
——. "Refreshment Rooms! Victoria Confectionary Establishment." 30 December 1841, 3.
Daily Telegraph. "Christmas Eve." 25 December 1890, 4.
Evening News (Sydney). "Commercial." 22 December 1910, 7.
Evening Star. "The Christmas Display: How the Shops Are Dressed." Issue 8098, 24 December 1889.
Garlick, Hattie. "Is Christmas Still Christmas If You Eat Out?" *Financial Times*, 24 November 2017. https://www.ft.com/content/b0602ce2-cf0e-11e7-b781-794ce08b24dc.
Healey, John. "Advertisements." *Otago Witness*, issue 31, 20 December 1851, column 1, page 2. https://paperspast.natlib.govt.nz/newspapers/OW185 11220.2.10.1?items_per_page=10&phrase=0&query=shortbread+Christmas& sort_by=byDA.
Janik, Erica. "Scandinavians' Strange Holiday Lutefisk Tradition." *Smithsonian Magazine*, 8 December 2011. https://www.smithsonianmag.com/travel/scandi navians-strange-holiday-lutefisk-tradition-2218218/#BI0Qzo8Idw1K5Yk1.99.
"John Bull Showing the Foreign Powers How to Make a Constitutional Plum-Pudding." *Punch*, 23 December 1848, 267.
Kelly, Jon. "The Christmas Turkey Naysayers." *BBC News Magazine*, 24 December 2014. http://www.bbc.com/news/magazine-30420477.
New York Times. "News of Food: Christmas Eve Feasts for Europeans Often Include Some Variety of Fish." 24 December 1945.

North Queensland Registrar. "Christmas Time: Along the Line." 4 January 1904, 21.

Otago Witness. "Christmas Cookery." Issue 1881, 9 December 1887.

Perth Gazette and Independent Journal of Politics and News. "Christmas Holidays." 1 January 1848, 3.

"Punch's Sermons to Tradesmen." *Punch,* vol. 20, 1851, 3.

Queenslander. "Mangoes." 13 February 1886, 270.

Rockhampton Morning Bulletin. "Our First Peacetime Christmas." 21 December 1945, 10.

Seagar, Helen. "Test and Tell: Christmas Under Difficulties." *Argus,* 24 December 1946.

Smithers, Rebecca. "7000 Tonnes of Dried Fruit: Inside the World's Largest Mince Pie Factory." *Guardian,* 10 December 2016. https://www.theguardian.com/lifeandstyle/2016/dec/09/inside-worlds-largest-mince-pie-factory-mr-kipling-christmas.

Sydney Gazette and New South Wales Advertiser. "Sydney." 2 January 1819, 2.

———. "Tasmanian News." 14 July 1829, 2.

Sydney Herald. "Police Incidents." 2 January 1832, 2.

Sydney Morning Herald. "Christmas Hams." 23 December 1843. https://trove.nla.gov.au/newspaper/article/12419594?searchTerm=Christmas%20Ham&searchLimits=l-state=New+South+Wales|||l-title=35|||sortby=dateAsc.

Whitby Gazette. "On the Kitchen Front: This Weeks Food facts." Ministry of Food. London, December 1940.

WEBSITES AND BLOGS

"1938: Cadbury Roses Are Launched." Cadbury. Accessed 21 May 2018. https://www.cadbury.co.uk/our-story?timeline=1938.

"Christmas Stats and Traditions." British Turkey. Accessed 7 February 2018. http://www.britishturkey.co.uk/facts-and-figures/christmas-stats-and-traditions.html.

Day, Ivan. "One Family and Empire Christmas Pudding." *Food History Jottings* (blog), 30 August 2012. http://foodhistorjottings.blogspot.com.au/2012/08/one-family-and-empire-christmas-pudding.html.

———. "Possets." Historic Food. Accessed 26 February 2018. http://www.historic-food.com/Posset%20Recipes.htm.

——. "Roasting the Christmas Beef." *Food History Jottings* (blog), 7 December 2011. http://foodhistorjottings.blogspot.com.au/2011/12/roasting-christmas-beef.html.

——. "Shap'd Minc'd Pies Again." *Food History Jottings* (blog), 24 December 2011. http://foodhistorjottings.blogspot.com.au/2011/12/shaped-mincd-pies-again.html.

——. "Some Christmas Nightcaps." *Food History Jottings* (blog), 18 December 2013. http://foodhistorjottings.blogspot.com.au/2013/12/some-christmas-nightcaps.html.

——. "Sugar-Plums and Comfits." Historic Food. Accessed 20 May 2018. http://www.historicfood.com/Comfits.htm.

Hutchinson, Alex. "Selection Boxes." Nestlé, 21 December 2017. https://www.nestle.co.uk/aboutus/history/blog/posts/selection-boxes.

"Now Bring Us Some Figgy Pudding." *Historic Royal Palaces* (blog), 16 December 2016. http://blog.hrp.org.uk/curators/historic-royal-georgian-christmas/.

Olver, Lynne. "Christmas Cookies." Food Timeline. Accessed 25 August 2016. http://www.foodtimeline.org/christmasfood.html#cookies.

Pepys, Samuel. The Diary of Samuel Pepys (website). https://www.pepysdiary.com/.

"Quality Street Celebrates 75 Years of Revolutionary Confectionery." Nestlé, 2 November 2011. https://www.nestle.co.uk/media/newsfeatures/qualitystreetcelebrates75yearsofrevolutionaryconfectionery.

Spicer, David. "Christmas Eve Seafood: 100,000 Shoppers Rush to Sydney Fish Market." ABC News, 24 December 2017. http://www.abc.net.au/news/2017-12-24/shoppers-rush-sydney-fish-market-christmas-eve/9284776.

"Stewet Beef to Potage." University of Leeds Library. Accessed 28 June 2018. https://library.leeds.ac.uk/special-collections/view/811/stewet_beef_to_potage.

"Turkey Facts." University of Illinois Extension. Accessed 7 May 2018. http://extension.illinois.edu/turkey/turkey_facts.cfm.

"Turkey for the Holidays." University of Illinois Extension. Accessed 7 February 2018. http://extension.illinois.edu/turkey/turkey_facts.cfm.

INDEX

Abbott, Edward, 112
Aboriginal Australians, 83
Acton, Eliza, 50, 72–73
Adams, Robert, 157
Advent, 60–61
advertising: and cakes, 110; and
    mince pies, 127; and pavlova,
    87; and plum pudding, 80–81;
    and shortbread, 133. *See also*
    commercialization
Albert, prince consort of Great Britain,
    24, 103
alcoholic beverages. *See* drinking
ale, 151
Alfred the Great, 14
Allen, Darina, 92–93
All Saints' Day, 12
All Souls' Day, 12
almonds: in Dundee cake, 113; in
    fruitcake, 98, 99
amounts of food: giant cakes, 97;
    seafood, in Australia, 65; slaughter
    of animals, 36–37, 38
Andrews, Tamra, 41

Anglo-Saxons, 14, 25–26
animal crackers, 129
apples, 89, 147; sauce, 49
archbishop, smoking, 154
Arnold, Joseph, 85
assortments of chocolates, 141
atholl brose, 166–67
Austen, Jane, 39
Australia: and cakes, 110–11; and fruit,
    88–90; and ham, 56–57; and menu,
    64–65, 84–88, 173–74; and mince
    pies, 126–27; and plum pudding,
    80–81, 83–87, 86*f*; and shortbread,
    133

baby cakes, 131
baked goods, 120–33
baking powder, 100
Bannerman, Colin, 65
bannocks, Yule, 132
barbecue, 65, 173
baron of beef, 57, 58*f*
Bawcock, Tom, 61
beadle, smoking, 154

beans, 56, 95, 105–6

Bede. *See* Venerable Bede

beef, 57–60

Beeton, Isabella: on beef, 59; on boar's head, 54–55; on Christmas cake, 111–12; on mincemeat, 125–26; on mulled wine, 153–54; on plum pudding, 73; on trifle, 91–92; on turkey, 44, 48

Bevilacqua, Mary, 131

Bible, on Christmas, 2

bicarbonate of soda, 100

Bigham, Shauna, 21

Big Sister (brand), 87

Bisaker, Hannah, 124

biscuits. *See* cookies; shortbread

bishop, smoking, 154–56, 155*f*

bishops: boy, 15; bread, 116

black bun, 112–13

black-eyed peas, 56

blackthorn, 165

boar, 52–57

boar's head, 52–55, 55*f*; cake, 55–56

Bobs Candies, 136

Bonaparte, Napoleon, 78, 79*f*

A Book of Cookrye, 46

Boswell, Annabella, 127, 133

bourbon, 163

Bowler, Gerry, 77

Boxing Day, 13–14, 26–27; sales, 31–32

boy bishops, 15

brandy: for fruitcake, 99; for mince pies, 121; for plum pudding, 75; sauce, 73

brawn, 53

Brears, Peter, 38

British Women's Patriotic League, 80

broken cake, 116

Browne, Mary, 97, 110

brünies, Yule, 132

brussels sprouts, 50

Bryan, Lettice, 164

Bûche de Noël, 116

Bunte brothers, 136

Cadbury, 140, 141

cakes, 95–117; boar's head, 55–56; preparation techniques, 99; significance of, 95–96. *See also* cookies

Canadian Christmas practices, 30, 62, 126, 159–60, 174

candy, 133–41

candy canes, 135–36

Capp, Bernard, 18

cardinal, smoking, 154

Caroline, queen of Great Britain, 69

caroling, 152

carols: on boar's head, 53–54; on drinking, 144; on pudding, 67; on wassailing, 143, 147–49

Carson, Johnny, 114

carving turkey, 48–49

Catherine de Medici, 41

Catullus, 11

caudle, 153, 161

Cédard, André, 81

characters, for Twelfth Night, 107, 108*f*, 110

Charles II, 78

chewette, 121

Childermas, 14

chocolate, 140–41

Christmas: costs of, 14–15; date of, 2–3, 11; definition of, 2; history of, 2–3, 9–33; survival of, 175

A Christmas Carol (Dickens), 27, 28*f*;
    on Christmas pudding, 72; on
    foods, 9, 29, 40; on goose, 35, 48,
    49; on punch, 158; on smoking
    bishop, 155*f*, 155–56; on turkey,
    44–45
Christmas crackers, 138–39, 170
Christmas Eve, 60
Christmas pudding, 67–85; in
    Australia, 80–81, 83–87, 86*f*;
    evolution of, 68–75; and politics,
    77–81, 78*f*; preparation and
    traditions, 75–77, 76*f*; term, 72;
    versus Twelfth cake, 105
church, and Christmas, 11–13
church warden (drink), 154
cider, 147, 151
Circumcision of Christ, 14
Clarke, Marcus, 84
class, social: and cake versus pudding,
    105; and drink, 166; festivals and,
    10; and poultry, 51; Tudor, 16;
    Victorian, 26
clubs: chocolate, 141; goose, 29, 45;
    pig, 56
coins, in pudding, 77
Colley, Thomas, 157
commercialization, 24; twentieth-
    century, 31–32. *See also* advertising
Commonwealth: and mince pies, 126–
    27; and plum pudding, 83–87, 86*f*;
    and punch, 160
communal feasting, 15, 16, 159, 170
confectionery, 133–41
Connelly, Mark, 4, 26, 29, 30, 145
contemporary Christmas practices,
    30–33
Cook, Richard, 154
cookie exchange (swap), 131

cookies, 127–31; term, 127. *See also*
    shortbread
cornucopias, 134
Cornwall, 61–62, 147
cranberry sauce, 47, 50
currants: in fruitcake, 97; in pudding, 68

dates, 97–98, 138
David, Elizabeth, 59
Davidson, Alan, 90, 114
Davis, Jefferson, 163
Dawson, Thomas, 46, 90, 152–53
Dawson, William Francis, 25–26
Day, Ivan, 57, 70, 156
decorations: for cakes, 100–103, 112;
    candy as, 134, 135–36; for cookies,
    129, 130*f*, 131; marzipan as, 138;
    for table, 170; Tudor, 16
deer, 38
desserts, 67–93, 95–117
Dickens, Charles, 22, 172; on cake, 95;
    on punch, 158; on wassail, 152. *See
    also A Christmas Carol*
Digby, Kenelm, 98, 101, 124, 161
dinner, Christmas: meats and mains,
    35–65; preparation of, 169–70;
    significance of, 4–5; Victorian, 27,
    29; work involved in, 1–2. *See also*
    desserts; menu for Christmas dinner
Dods, Margaret, 70, 113
domestic Christmas practices, 26, 114,
    150–51
Donaldson, Rhiannon, 85–86
dried fruit, 31; in Continental cakes,
    116; in mince pies, 121, 125, 126;
    in pudding, 68, 71, 75, 81, 83
drinc hail, term, 146, 150
drinking, 2, 143–67, 171–72; Anglo-
    Saxons and, 25; and fruitcake,

98; pagan festivals and, 10; and plum pudding, 82, 83; regional specialties, 165–67; St. John's Day and, 14
Dundee cake, 112–13
Dutch Christmas practices, 127–28
Dutching process (for chocolate), 140

Eastern Church, 11
eels, 61
egg flip, 166
eggnog, 160–65, 166; term, 162
eggs: in cake, 99; in mulled wine, 153; in punch, 157
Elf (movie), 119, 133–34
Elizabeth I, 138
Elizabeth II, 113
Ellet, Elizabeth, 111
Empire: and pudding, 77–81; and punch, 156–57, 160; and sloe gin, 165–66; and traditions, 3–4, 173–74; Victorian, 29–30
employer gifts: Boxing Day, 13; turkeys, 43
engastration, 46
English-speaking world, 3–4, 173–74; and plum pudding, 82–90. *See also* Commonwealth
Epiphany, 12, 14, 60. *See also* Twelfth Night
Erntedankfest, 40
Ethelred, king of England, 14
evergreens, 11, 20, 23–24
excess, 2, 29; and drinking, 143–46, 172; importance of, 175; and meats, 37–38; Puritans and, 17–19

Father Christmas, 23. *See also* Santa Claus

feasting, 1–7, 169–76; communal, 15, 16, 159, 170
Feast of the Seven Fishes, 64
Ferrell, Will, 119, 133–34
fertility rituals: and Christmas trees, 23; and meats, 36; and pork, 52; and wassailing, 146–47, 171–72
films, Christmas, 32
fire: and wassailing, 147; and Yule log, 116–17
fireworks, 77
first footing, 113–14, 131–32, 166
fish, 60–65
Flanders, Judith, 47, 173
Fletcher, R., 122–23
Follen, Charles, 134
foods of Christmas, 1–7, 169–76; Dickens on, 9, 29, 40; Puritans and, 18; of Southern Hemisphere, 30
fool, 90
fortune telling, 77, 114, 131–32
Francatelli, Charles Elmé, 55, 125
Fraser, Mrs., 113
French Christmas practices, 107–9, 116
Freyja, 52
Freyr, 52
fruit: apples, 89, 147; apple sauce, 49; in Australia, 88–90; cherries, 56; in fruitcake, 97–98; with ham, 56; in mince pies, 121; sauce for turkey, 47, 50. *See also* dried fruit
fruitcake, 96–100, 109, 111–14
Fry chocolate, 140

Gabay, Elizabeth, 157, 163
Gabel, Laurel, 131
Galette des Rois, 107–8
game birds, 40–52

Garlick, Hattie, 2
Gateau des Rois, 108
Gay, John, 42–43
Geoffrey of Monmouth, 146
George IV, 167
George V, 81
Georgian Christmas practices, 20–24,
    69–70, 134, 145, 167
Geraldini, Alessandro, 41
German holiday practices: boar, 52;
    cookies, 128; mulled wine, 156;
    New Year, 13, 40; stollen, 116;
    trees, 24
gifts, 170; on Boxing Day, 13;
    chocolate, 141; food, 39; fruit, 88,
    89–90; pagan festivals and, 11;
    shortbread, 133; sloe gin, 165;
    turkey, 43
Gill, M., 110, 127
Gillray, James, 78, 79*f*
gin, sloe, 165–66
gingerbread, 128
Glasse, Hannah, 47–48, 69–70, 90–91,
    126
glögg, 156
"Gloucestershire Wassail," 148–49
glüwein, 156
goose, 12, 35, 40–41, 49; clubs, 29, 45
gravy, 49
greenery, 11, 20, 23–24
grog, 157
gunfire, 77, 147

Haakon, king of Norway, 13
Hale, Sarah Josepha, 82
Halloween, 12, 40
ham, 50, 52, 56–57
Harvest Home, 40
Henisch, Bridget Ann, 15, 27, 101

Henry II, 53
Henry III, 15
Henry VII, 151
Henry VIII, 15, 16
Herrick, Robert, 105–6, 121, 151
Hervey, Thomas, 78
het pint, 166
hippocras, 152–53
Hogmanay, 112–14, 131–32, 166
Holy Family, feast of, 14
Holy Innocents' Day, 14
Hone, William, 102–3, 107, 134
Hopley, Claire, 20, 33, 77, 106
hospitality: first footing and, 132;
    medieval, 14–15; Puritans and, 19;
    Southern, 19, 21; Tudor, 16–17;
    Victorian, 26
Humble, Nicola, 95–97, 109, 114
hunting beef, 59

icing, 101, 112
iconic foods: candy canes as, 135;
    Christmas pudding as, 67–68, 73;
    punch as, 160
identity: Christmas and, 175–76;
    pudding and, 77–81; Victorians
    and, 29–30
Imgard, August, 135–36
Inglis, Ken, 4, 84
Inglis, Raelene, 97, 110
Irish Christmas practices, 59, 60, 75,
    92–93
Irving, Washington, 21–22, 23
Italian American Christmas practices,
    64
Italian Christmas practices, 115–16

jelly, 51, 53, 56, 91, 154
Jenks, James, 100

John, king of England, 37, 61
Jonson, Ben, 151
Joseph, Edward Lanzer, 166
Joyce, James, 60
July, Christmas in, 174

Kalends, 10, 11
Kaufman, Cathy, 51, 82, 126, 128, 172, 174
Keiller Marmalade Company, 113
Keller machine, 136
Kerr, John Hunter, 84
Kettilby, Mary, 71
king, ritual: bean, 15, 105–6; Saturnalia and, 11
King, William, 54
king cake, New Orleans, 109
Knickerbockers, 22–23

Lambert, Lord, 122
lambswool, 151
lamprey eels, 61
La Varenne, P. F., 47
lawn sleeves (drink), 154
Lawson, Henry, 85
Leach, Helen, 97, 110
Leslie, Eliza, 50–51, 82, 126, 127–28
Lord of Misrule, 11, 15, 22, 110
lutefisk, 62–64
Luther, Martin, 24
Lysons, Samuel, 148

Mac Con Iomaire, Máirtín, 60
MacDonald, John, 167
Mackintosh, 141
Macquarie, Lachlan, 83
main dishes, 35–65
mangoes, 88, 89
Mardi Gras, 109

Marguerite, queen of Navarre, 41
marketing, and Christmas practices, 24
Markham, Gervase, 47, 122
Marks, Johnny, 32
Martinmas, 12, 40
Mary, Solemnity of, 14
marzipan, 101–2, 112, 138
masques, 16, 149
Mather, Cotton, 18
May, Robert E., 21, 38, 42, 49, 57, 123, 123f–24f
May, Robert L., 32
McCormack, Robert E., 136
meaning, Christmas and, 175–76
Meath, Lord, 81
meats, 35–65, 170–71; and mince pies, 121–25
medieval Christmas practices, 13–15; and confectionery, 135, 138; and drinking, 144; and gingerbread, 128; and meats, 37; and mince pies, 121
Melena, Elpis, 159
menu for Christmas dinner, 4–5, 44, 172; Restoration, 38–39; Victorian, 29
Michaelmas, 40
Miles, Clement A., 4, 12, 147
milk punch, 157
mince pies, 37, 50, 120–27; shapes of, 123f–24f
Misson, Monsieur, 123
molds, for cookies, 129, 130f
Mollard, John, 71–72, 100
Moore, Clement Clarke, 22, 23
Moore, Tara, 29
Mr. Kipling, 120–21
mulled wine, 152–56
mumming, 16, 149

Napoleon. *See* Bonaparte, Napoleon
National Lampoon's Christmas
    Vacation (movie), 35
Nestlé, 141
Newcastle, Marquis of, 78
New Orleans king cake, 109
New Year's Day, 14, 27; cookies,
    127–28; desserts, 112–14
New-York Historical Society, 22
New Zealand, 86–87, 110–11, 133,
    173
Nissenbaum, Stephen, 11–12, 19, 24,
    26, 145, 175–76
Nollaig na mBan, 60
Normans, 25, 144
Norwood, Henry, 70
nostalgia, 2, 172–73; Georgian, 21–22;
    pagan festivals and, 11; plum
    pudding and, 82; Stuart, 16–17;
    Victorian, 24–26
Nott, John, 71, 157
Nuremberg gingerbread, 128
nuts, 89; almonds, 98, 99, 113

O'Brien, Catherine, 161–62
O'Brien, Charmaine, 83
O'Connor, Kaori, 14, 27, 75, 77, 81
Odin, 13
Óg Gallagher, Pádraic, 60
oranges, 89
oxen, 148
Oxford, 52–53
oysters, 62

pagan festivals, 9–13; and drinking,
    144; and poultry, 40–41; and Yule
    log, 117
panettone, 115–16
panforte, 116

parrot pie, 57
pavlova, 87–88
Pavlova, Anna, 87
peacock, 40
Peacock, Nicholas, 43
pearl ash, 100
peas, 56, 95, 105–6
Peery, Susan Mahnke, 131
pennets, 135
Pepys, Samuel, 42, 69, 106–7, 124,
    150
petticoat tails, 132
picnics, 85–87
pies, 174; game, 57; lamprey, 61;
    parrot, 57; poultry and, 47–48;
    stargazy, 61–62. *See also* mince pies
Pintard, John, 22–23, 145
Pitt, William, 78, 79*f*
plum, term, 68, 137
plum porridge (pottage), 68–70;
    Puritans and, 77–78
plum pudding, 67–87; in Australia,
    80–81, 83–87, 86*f*; evolution of,
    68–75; and roast beef, 57; term,
    71
poison, in cake decorations, 105, 110
pope, smoking, 154
pop music, Christmas, 32–33
pork, 52–57
porridge, 68
possets, 161–62
potatoes, 49–50
pottage, 68. *See also* plum porridge
poultry, 38, 40–52; pie, 47–48
pralines, 140
prawns, 62, 65
Prudhomme, Paul, 46
Pucci, Lorenzo, 41
pudding cloth, 70, 80

puddings. *See* Christmas pudding; plum pudding
puff paste, 125
punch, 156–60; bowl, 158–59
Puritans, 17–19, 20–21, 77–78, 122–23, 145

Quality Street, 141
Queen's College, Oxford, 52–53, 54
Quinzio, Jeri, 82

Raedisch, Linda, 147
Raffald, Elizabeth, 99, 101–2, 125, 153
raffles, turkey, 51
raising agents, for cake, 100
raisins: in fruitcake, 97–98; in mince pies, 123; in pudding, 68
rationing and Christmas practices, 31, 73–74, 93
Restad, Penne, 19
Restoration Christmas practices, 20–24, 78, 123; bill of fare, 38–39
Richard II, 57
rituals, 3; atholl brose, 166; boar's head presentation, 52–55, 55*f*; for cakes, 105–9, 110; Christmas pudding preparation, 75–77, 76*f*; first footing, 113–14, 131–32, 166; and menu, 172–73; punch, 158–59; wassailing, 146–52
roast beef, 57–59
Romans, 10–11
Rosca de Reyes, 109
rosemary, 53
Rowntree, 140–41
royal icing, 101, 112, 128
Rudolph the Red-Nosed Reindeer, 32
rum, 160, 163

Saberi, Helen, 90
sack, 98, 163
sacrifical elements, 10–11; and goose, 41; and meats, 36; and pork, 52
salmon, smoked, 62
Samhain, 40
Santa Claus, 23, 32, 145; foods left for, 114, 131, 170
Saturnalia, 10–11, 96, 106, 109, 144
sauces: apple, 49; cranberry, 47, 50; for pudding, 73, 75
Saussure, Cesar de, 20, 69
Scandinavian Christmas practices, 62–64, 128, 156
Scotch bun, 112–14
Scottish holiday practices, 112–14, 131–32, 166
scrap pictures, 129, 131, 139
seafood, 60–65, 173
Selden, John, 150
Sermon, Richard, 146
sherry trifle, 90–93
shipboard Christmas practices, 70–71, 156–57
shop window displays, 30, 102–3, 132, 133, 134
shortbread, 127, 131–33
shortcakes, 132
shred pies, 121
Simmons, Amelia, 128–29
Sir Gawain and the Green Knight, 37, 61
slaughter of animals, 36–37, 38
sloe gin, 165–66
Smith, Andrew F., 41, 42, 47, 51
Smith, Eliza, 99
Smith, Tom, 139
smoking bishop, 154–56, 155*f*

social functions: of alcohol, 143, 172; of feasting, 170
social order, inversion of, 96, 109; Puritans and, 18; Saturnalia and, 11, 109; Tudor, 15–16; Victorian, 26
Sol Invictus, 10
Solstice festivals, 9–13
Southern (U.S.) Christmas practices, 19, 21, 56, 163, 164
Spanish Christmas practices, 109
spiced beef, 59–60
spiced breads, 97
spices: in gingerbread, 128; in mince pies, 121; in mulled wine, 152–53, 154; in wassail bowl, 151–52
springerle boards, 129
St. Andrew, feast day, 12
St. Catherine, feast day, 12
St. Clement, feast day, 12
St. John, feast day, 14
St. Lucia, feast day, 12
St. Nicholas: feast day of, 12; history of, 23. *See also* Santa Claus
St. Patrick, 62
St. Stephen, feast day, 13–14. *See also* Boxing Day
stained glass cake, 116
stamps, for cookies, 129, 130*f*
standing pie, 47–48
stargazy pie, 61–62
Stevenson, Robert Louis, 114, 132
"Stir-Up Sunday," 75, 114
stollen, 116, 138
Strickland, William, 41–42
Stuart Christmas practices, 15–17
Stubbes, Philip, 17–18
stuffing, 49, 50
subtleties, 138

suet, 125–26
sugar, 99, 133, 135, 171
sugarplums, 137
swan, 40, 44, 64
sweets, 119–41, 171; cakes, 55–56, 95–117; puddings and desserts, 67–93
Swift, Jonathan, 154
syllabub, 161

Tchaikovsky, P. I., 137
television specials, Christmas, 32
temperance movement, 82, 145
tensions, Christmas and, 11–12, 32, 175–76; Dickens and, 27; drinking and, 143–46, 172; Georgian, 22; Puritans and, 17–18, 21
Teonge, Henry, 70–71, 106
Thanksgiving, 51, 174
Thomas, Jerry, 164
Thomas, Mary, 57
Thomas the Apostle, feast day, 12
tokens: in Christmas cake, 110; in king cake, 109; in pudding, 77; in Twelfth cake, 105–7
Tom Bawcock's Eve, 61
traditions: baking, 120, 128; first footing, 113–14, 131–32, 166; importance of, 1–2, 175
trees, Christmas, 23–24; candy decorations for, 134, 135–36; cookie decorations for, 129, 131
trifle, 90–93
Trollope, Anthony, 49, 58
Tudor Christmas practices, 15–17, 26, 53, 149
turducken, 46
turkey, 41–45, 43*f*, 174; in America, 50–52; cookery, 46–48; Dickens on,

35, 44–45; versus roast beef, 57–59; serving, 48–50

turkey shoot, 51

Tusser, Thomas, 16, 37, 42, 121

Twelfth cake, 95, 96–109, 104*f*; decline of, 109, 110

Twelfth Night, 14, 15, 16, 26, 27, 60

Twelve Days of Christmas, 12, 13, 14

twentieth-century Christmas practices, 30–33

United States of America, 3–4, 33, 174–75; and British Christmas, 4, 21, 33; and cake, 114, 116; and candy canes, 135–36; and cookies, 127–28; and eggnog, 160, 162–64; and mince pies, 50, 126; and plum pudding, 82–83; and turkey, 50–52

Van Houten, Coenraad, 140

Venerable Bede, 13

venison, 38

Victoria, queen of Great Britain, 24, 167; Christmas feast, 58*f*–59*f*; Twelfth cake, 103, 104*f*

Victorian Christmas practices, 20, 24–30, 172; beef, 57, 58*f*; boar's head cake, 55–56; cake, 114; Christmas crackers, 138–39; drinking, 145–46, 157–60, 167; mince pies, 125; plum pudding, 78–80; turkey, 43–45, 43*f*

La Vigilia, 64

virgins, wassail, 149–50

"A Visit from St. Nicholas" (Moore), 23

Walkers Shortbread, 133

Warren, Elizabeth, 92

wartime Christmas practices, 31, 73–74, 74*f*, 93

Washington, George, 162

wassail bowls, 150*f*, 151

wassailing, 143, 146–52, 150*f*

Weaver, William Woys, 116, 119–20, 129, 134

Wellesley cookie exchange, 131

Welsh, Charlotte, 83

wenches, wassail, 149–50

West Point, 163

Whitman's Sampler, 141

Wilcox, Estelle Woods, 82

William Tuke and Sons of York, 140–41

Wilson, C. Anne, 40, 68

window displays, 30, 102–3, 132, 133, 134

wine, mulled, 152–56

winter festivals, 9–13

Winterson, Jeanette, 93

wishes, pudding and, 75

Woodward, Hezekiah, 17

Woolley, Hannah, 61, 157

Wright, A. T., 145–46

Wynne, Watkin Williams, 151–52

Yorkshire Christmas pie, 47–48

Yule, 13, 40; bannocks, 132; dollies (doughs), 131; log, 116–17

ABOUT THE AUTHOR

Madeline Shanahan, PhD, has worked as a professional historian and archaeologist in Dublin, Sydney, and Melbourne. She is the author of a range of peer-reviewed publications, including her first book, *Manuscript Recipe Books as Archaeological Objects: Text and Food in the Early Modern World* (2015), and a paper published in *Food in Ireland* (2015), which was awarded a Highly Commended in the 2015 Sophie Coe Prize. Her interests include food history, manuscript recipe books, culinary material culture, infant feeding, and women's history.